# runnin'
# down
# some
# lines

23
len

06/29

# runnin'
# down
# some
# lines

## the language
## and culture of
## black teenagers

## Edith A. Folb

HARVARD UNIVERSITY PRESS
Cambridge, Massachusetts
London, England
1980

**Library of Congress Cataloging in Publication Data**

Folb, Edith A
  Runnin' down some lines.

  Bibliography:  p.
  1.  Black English.   2.   Afro-American youth—Cali-
fornia—Los Angeles.   3.   Sociolinguistics.
I.  Title.
PE3102.N42F6     427'.9794'94      79-26708
ISBN 0-674-78039-6

*To Benny, Harvey, Robb and Jocelyn, Jackie and Bertha, who first ran it down to me. And, with deep affection, to my parents Ruth and Alex Folb.*

# preface

A S I SIT looking back over almost nine years of field work with teenagers from South Central Los Angeles, I am struck by a flood of experiences, images, dialogs, and encounters. For a number of other urban anthropologists, such as Ulf Hannerz and Elliot Liebow, the field experience they recounted had a definite time frame. For me, the field work involved several time frames and periods of data acquisition: (1) the pilot study done in 1967; (2) the specific field work for the doctoral thesis, completed in 1971; and (3) the ongoing data gathering from 1972 through the end of 1976, when I moved to San Francisco to teach. I am still collecting data and probably will for many years to come. The black teenagers I have met—and continue to meet—long ago became a part of my life.

It seems, sometimes, that another book is needed to detail the richness of my field experience and the complex process of my own growth during that time. It was a process that began, at least consciously, in the spring of 1964. At that time I left UCLA, midway through a Ph.D. program that was becoming increasingly unimportant to me. I was restless and dissatisfied with school and sought out other ways to explore my personal and professional needs.

It was in the 1960s that I became involved in community-based activities that brought me, a white woman, in contact with a number of black adults and teenagers living in South Central Los Angeles. Through friends I became engaged for a time with Operation Bootstrap, a grassroots work-training organization that arose in the wake of Watts in 1965. There were other contacts—with the Black Panther Party and its attempt to institute a police review board at the city level and with the Mafundi Institute, a community cultural-arts training center for black youth, housed in the heart of South Central.

At the beginning of 1966, I went to work for the County of Los Angeles in its personnel division, and became involved in the Neighborhood Youth Corps Program—one of the many work-training programs introduced during Lyndon Johnson's War on Poverty. The NYC program brought me in contact with still another large teenage population, since many of the enrollees were from the South Central black community.

These experiences, and others that followed, not only introduced me to a large and varied group of people from the black community, but brought me in contact with the vernacular vocabulary that many used, especially teenagers. By the end of 1966, I decided to return to school. I now felt that I was involved with an important subject area— one that grew out of my personal and professional commitments, one that had real meaning for me and, I hoped, would for others. So, in 1967, I began the systematic study of black teenage vernacular vocabulary.

When I started collecting data, I was lucky enough to meet six very special teenagers who became not only my first "informants," but my friends and colleagues through much of my early work. Later on, as I came into contact with more youths and my "credentials" became more solid, I was invited into the daily worlds of a number of my informants. Indeed, some of the greatest rewards from my field work came not from a particular interview or lexical discovery, but from a teenager's including me in some social activity—a jam session, a church meeting and social, a "capping" contest, a day's adventure of "low-riding" around the local high school or favorite hangout, a baby shower. It was at these times that I felt least like the outsider I was. And I deeply thank those young people who trusted and accepted me enough to allow me to be their companion for a time.

This field work has been a part of my life for so many years that it is hard, sometimes, to know if I have separated out the substantive from the trivial in the retelling. For me, it was all substantive. But, finally, this work is one investigator's point of view: it can be nothing more. At best, it is incomplete, selective, and suggestive. It is my attempt to make some portion of black teenage life in the ghetto more comprehensible, less of a mystery to other white outsiders like myself.

Back in 1967 when I began my field work, I had no idea of the journey I was about to take. That journey has led me into places of many kinds and it has brought me into contact with a wide variety of people, all of whom have contributed to my research. I would like to thank some of them for making the journey, and this book, possible.

I am happily indebted to Victoria Fromkin, my adviser, colleague, and friend. She demanded a lot and always gave more than she asked. It was her enthusiastic support of my work that enabled me to take the first real steps into the field.

I am also especially grateful to William Bright. He too has been there for me from the beginning, literally. We came to UCLA at the same time—he as a neophyte professor, I as an undergraduate. Throughout our long years of friendship, he has consistently supported and encouraged my work and hopes. Nor can I ever repay him for the long editorial hours he has given to the manuscript from the time it was work in progress to the present.

There were other professional friends who, in the early days, encouraged me to pursue my research. I particularly want to thank William Labov, David Maurer, Thomas Kochman, Gershon Legman, and the late Jacob Bronowski for turning their experienced eyes to my work, so that I might see its import from different angles.

When I was first getting my bearings in the field, I encountered a number of people whose friendly criticism and good will made the community more accessible to me, literally and psychologically: Leon Montgomery, Jack Tatum, Barbara Williams, Mike Nicolas, Clarence Shaw, Jim Burkes, Gene Tinney, William Elkins, Lonnie Wilson, Bessie Sales, and Travis Watson.

I am indebted to a number of sources for funding my work over the last several years—the Office of Education, the Ford Foundation, and the American Council of Learned Societies. One of the strongest ongoing sources of support was the Center for Afro-American Studies and the Institute of American Cultures at UCLA. I am particularly grateful to Molefi Asante, past director of the Center for Afro-American Studies, for his assistance in securing funds for my research and his belief in the value of my work. I also want to thank Patricia Kennedy and Dorothy Thomas, who guided me through the administrative maze at UCLA.

I was extremely fortunate to have a number of committed people read and respond to my manuscript. I am especially thankful to Thomas Kochman and John Baugh for their careful and candid review of the final manuscript. They made it possible for me to see both the forest and the trees.

Two women made the finished manuscript possible. Kathleen Aswell, my student and friend, spent many hours decoding an illegible handwritten manuscript and transforming it into legible typed copy. Cecila Ceffalo typed the hefty final manuscript, and did so under a tight deadline. She demonstrated not only good spirits throughout but great skill under pressure.

Particular thanks must go to Lynne Hutchison, who read proofs with me. Her eyes saw some mistakes long ago lost to me, and her good humor saw us through a tedious task.

To my friends Peter Culicover, Jill Landefeld, Judy Chicago, Robert Gordon, John Waggaman, Kathleen Fraser, Jane Gurko,

*Preface*

Sally Gearhart, Jerry Bragstad, Marshall Rogers, and Robin Fine I want to extend heartfelt appreciation for sharing the good times and shoring me up during the hard times. I could not have done it alone.

A special thank you to my special friend, Adrian Akmajian.

But the deepest debt of gratitude and thanks goes to the young people who let me into their lives and left their mark imprinted on my own.

Los Angeles                                                                 E.F.

# contents

# foreword

**Claudia Mitchell-Kernan**

SPEECH IS BOTH the primary focus of *Runnin' Down Some Lines* and a channel into the lives of black teenagers who live in the inner city of South Central Los Angeles. Edith Folb subjects the special vocabulary and idiomatic usage of these youth to such fine-grained sociolinguistic analysis that speech becomes a point of departure for a description of their world of experience and an interpretation of the beliefs, attitudes, and values constructed upon that experience.

Speech differences between black Americans and non-blacks have been recorded and commented upon for several centuries. Unfortunately, they have often been misunderstood and misinterpreted by blacks and non-blacks alike. The nineteen-sixties witnessed a reawakening of scholarly interest in these differences. And one of the more significant questions raised during this period related to the validity of research which examined the behavior, attitudes, and values of black Americans within Euro-American normative frameworks. When steps were taken to shed the Eurocentric bias of previous research, many components of black American behavior, among them speech, which had theretofore been conceived deviant, took on a new light. Speech features formerly considered deficient were discovered to have the properties of a rule-governed system, related to though different from standard English.

In the earliest phases of the development of this area of inquiry, phonology, grammar, and syntax received the preponderance of attention in an effort to contrast grammars of black vernacular and standard speech. By the late sixties, descriptions of the distinctive characteristics of Afro-American vernacular speech had appeared in scholarly journals, accompanied by debate as to their appropriate level of structural representation. In rapid course, the structural approaches to black English vernaculars were followed by more sociological orientations. This work took on an interdisciplinary character and employed a number of related conceptual frameworks. Some studies combined ethnographic approaches to communication with sociology of language. Still other sociolinguistic studies established relationships between linguistic and social facts such as ethnicity, class, reference group, and social affiliation. Then there were diachronic approaches that focused on the probable origin and history of Afro-American vernaculars. Recently, richly eclectic work combining elements of all of these approaches has added an important cultural dimension. The most significant yield of the past decade of research and writing has been the establishment of a new conception of the nature of the language differences between black and white America, and a fuller interpretation of their social meaning.

In sum, black America has had a distinctive language history. Africans coming to America's shores in bondage possessed neither a common culture nor a common tongue. It was the exploitation of slavery and post-emancipation economic peonage and political oppression that welded new ethnic groups in the United States and elsewhere in the plantation New World. Like other groups who have adopted English as a second language, these Africans of varied language background brought in linguistic and sociolinguistic patterns common in West African languages. It has been argued rather convincingly that in the process of contact between Africans and Europeans in the New World, new languages emerged—creole languages—which represent a confluence of linguistic traditions and a departure from their parent sources. Black American vernaculars are likely descendants of such languages. In this perspective, black America is not linguistically deficient, but in possession of a rich and varied language portfolio where speech and social structure and speech and culture are tightly interwoven.

Edith Folb's careful research and insightful interpretation contribute significantly to the interdisciplinary area of Afro-American sociolinguistics. Although she is careful not to generalize her findings beyond the sample of individuals and settings she studied in South Central Los Angeles, aspects of her findings clearly transcend the locality of research and are relevant to understanding the lives of other young American blacks. Of central importance, Folb has dealt systematically with an area of speech—vocabulary and idiom—which has heretofore received only impressionistic treatment.

Folb's approach is ethnographic in that it is both naturalistic and reaches beyond strict lexicography to deal extensively with usage in the milieu of use. Her study of usage, in turn, builds a view of how and in what ways the special idiom of black teenagers characterizes a conceptual system, including beliefs and ways of perceiving and interpreting events, which departs from its mainstream counterparts. The usage frame of reference permits a culturally relevant and meaningful basis for understanding how the youth studied construct and assign meaning to their social and physical worlds.

A number of items in the special vocabulary presented by Folb are used by black youths in many parts of the United States. This is of significance, because it is evidence of lines of cultural transmission between the widely dispersed local Afro-American communities in America. Although aspects of this special vocabularly have spread throughout American society via the jazz world and countercultural groups, which have borrowed heavily from it, it is known primarily by insiders. One of Folb's middle-class informants notes this fact: "Sure, I know a lot of the words, but I'm not livin' down there. It's different. Can't pretend it isn't. Some of those terms just not part of my life." A South Central Los Angeles youth echoes this truth: "The brothers up dere in dem Hollywood Hills, out dere at UCLA and all dem li'l ol' colleges, they okay—hear what I'm sayin'? They hip to some o' d' happ'nin's, they blood. But when dude come down here, better take it slow, 'cause gon' be lot shit he ain' got together. Some blood blow his mind, send 'im on a hombug. Run down some lines he done *never* heard!" In a related vein, a youth from Chicago notes the importance of in-group speech as a key to inclusion: "I had to have a fight in order to get in with the 'in' crowd. I'z from Chicago and they wouldn't accept me because I was someone foreign in my language and my slangs were different."

Coinage of new vocabulary in South Central Los Angeles is an ongoing process ascribed by Folb to a variety of sources. She notes that prominent among these sources are black radio stations and the disc jockeys and musicians heard there. Folb's analysis, in combination with earlier work, suggests that the dynamics of linguistic evolution within black speech communities may have a different motivation from linguistic evolution elsewhere. In mainstream America, for example, the prestige function of language is an important factor in promoting language change: you advance socially if you speak well. This factor is also at work in black communities, but for different reasons: "Speakin' proper English wadn't my thing. Long as I got my point across, I didn't care. Come here [San Francisco State University], I've taken it upon myself to learn to speak the white man's language. You got to—to survive." So it is rather a configuration of social functions built upon a unique history that gives language change in black communities its special character.

Across the United States, through the influence of formal education and the mass media, differences between regional dialects are waning. Differences between social dialects, however, remain quite marked and in fact may reflect the entrenchment of the class system of our society. The presence of social dialects suggests barriers to communication and different vectors of language change within the same local area. Geographic space, which used to be a major arbiter of linguistic uniformity and linguistic evolution, is now paralleled in importance by social space. Upwardly mobile speakers of socially stigmatized varieties of English feel compelled to master standard English. Among black Americans this pressure may produce bi-dialectism rather than language replacement.

A number of other social functions of language are at work in shaping the language portfolio of black communities. In this connection, Folb's analysis is supportive of the view that the identity and unifying functions of language play a central role in the creation and maintenance of language differences between blacks and non-blacks in the United States. Moreover, it is possible to see in effect the poetic function of language as a factor generating linguistic creativity among blacks. There is a general human tendency to play with language and to assign aesthetic value to different speech forms. The particular linguistic representations of this tendency and their widespread presence among peoples of African descent in the New World suggest the continuation of aspects of West African sociolinguistic traditions. Again, the testimony of Folb's informants is highly revealing: "Like I kin walk right out here on the street and run up to a pa'tner of mine, run it down, everythin's cool. Say, 'Le's slide over to d' set and dig on the young ladies, try an' catch.' I's different an' better way. Mo' fun way. Communicate with somebody and dey can understand exactly what you talkin'. And, besides, it don't give you away."

The special vocabulary of black teenagers presented in this work appears to serve the referential function of providing labels for concepts which are culturally specific and for which there are no available terms in standard English. This terminology, in turn, is a component of differentiated taxonomies and contrasts sets that also partition the world of experience in ways particular to the subculture of black youth.

Nowhere is the symbolic importance of language in promoting in-group identity and unity more evident than in the domains of specialization which reflect social distance within the black community and between the black community and other speech communities. "Them siditty niggers they be frontin' off all d' time. Colored dudes actin' like white. Pig brothers, Tom-a-Lees, they jus' black people, tommin' fo' d' white folks. Betray they people. Think they better 'n d' brothers and sisters. All kin'a folks down here." Folb records a variety of terms used to label Uncle Toms and their female counterparts. This contrast set includes terms for police informers and people who, in the perspective of these youths, reject their black heritage and culture. Pejorative labels of this kind, according to Folb, may also be applied to middle-class blacks who do not acknowledge their ghetto roots and who attempt to distance themselves from old friends and poor relatives. She adds that they may be applied to old-time, or not so old-time, blacks who are obsequious or subservient in the presence of whites, "oreos," and others who use their blackness for economic and social gain.

The pejorative label "lame" is in widespread use to label the socially incompetent or experientially limited individual. Youth who were reared in the South seem to constitute a special category of outsiders: "Seem like we just use different slangs or somethin'. Like this one dude from Florida he act geechie, you know, square. He talk funny, didn't know no slangs. We didn't beat him up or nothin', but he wadn't in on the rest of the clan." There are also neutral labels for other ethnic groups with whom the teenagers come into contact but, according to Folb, the largest body of white pejorative name terms is reserved for the police.

The vocabulary relating to social categories is a salient reflection of the self-perceived separateness of black Americans as a distinct ethnic group. This view is also articulated directly: "See, all the brothers and sisters they *blood*. Can you dig it? The pig, he try to destroy the people—beat 'em up, rip 'em off, but they righteously stick together. 'Cause blood thicker 'n water, dig? Black people *has* to be together, jus' like family, 'cause ain't nobody gon' take care of 'em 'cept theyself. Honky pig gotta learn we ain't jivin', Jack. People ain' gon' lay down fo' no mo' white bullshit. Gon' tell it like 'tis. Like d' Mafia, you know, got to live together and die together—*be* to-geth-er. Go down side by side."

Edith Folb's treatment of the teenage component of the verbal repertoire of black America is not bowdlerized—it has an authentic character. Her work is especially rich in precisely this respect. The words and narratives of the speakers consistently form the central basis for her analysis and interpretation. The variety of empirical data presented both supports her analysis and offers interested scholars an opportunity for reinterpretation.

There is a rawness here that may strike a discordant note in students of the Afro-American experience who may be disturbed by the "image" problems a work of this kind can create. It should be noted that, counterpoint to the widespread use of taboo language among teenagers, among many blacks there is an equally widespread circumspection and even "prudishness" about such language. Folb has not attempted to characterize all of black America. She scrupulously details the background, social position, age, and sex of the individuals she studied, presenting their different and contradictory points of view. She portrays them as the complex people they are.

Although Folb's treatment is throughout sympathetic, it is not always neutral. Both what she admires about the people she studied and what she regards as unfortunate are presented with equal clarity. I found this quality of her work refreshing and admirable. This kind of honesty inspires a straightforward acknowledgment that many readers are likely to be highly judgmental about some of the attitudes and values held by teenagers in South Central Los Angeles, as well as by some aspects of their behavior. But I would hope that readers will also be stimulated to consider the possible sources of the values and designs for living they may find objectionable.

The youth of South Central Los Angeles speak frankly of the conflicts within their lives and the gap between their aspirations and the reality of their lives. Folb observes, for example, "In the same breath, [teenagers] talk about the tight relationship between their 'play cousin' and themselves, and the next moment tell of a situation in which the would-be friend deserts them during a fight, 'creeps' on their young lady or young man, or 'burns' them for their 'stash'."

Indeed, interpersonal conflict and competition loom large in these lives. Associated with this conflict is an evident concern with manipulation and artifice in human relations. The tensions in male-female relations are depicted in the point of view of one young woman: "Men jus' cain't be trusted. Dey all dogs to me. Don't be tellin' ever'thin' to my ol' man, so ain't no way I'ma tell some off d' wall honky—even a brother—'bout my life. Uh uh! May talk to a sister. Like I consider you like a sister. We got a whole lotta things together." Family turmoil and the alienation it sometimes breeds are poignantly represented in the following narrative of personal experience: "Ain't no brothers livin'. Brothers s'pos' be together wi'chu, go down wi'chu. Don't be tryin' to jam you all d' time. I don't like violence too much. Not now. Had to be violent to survive in d' house. 'Cause those fools [five older brothers] wanted to pounce on me—and *that* hurt! If I got into sumpin' at school, well, I couldn't run on home. My brothers be there. I couldn't say I didn't wanna fight. So I hadda fight. I couldn't just go home, 'cause I *know* I get beat up. Moms go in d' back room and everybody jus' have a field day! Ain't got *no* brothers! Jus' my play brother Henry, he my *one an' only* brother!" One finds, as well, signs of disconcerting cynicism among some individuals: "The brothers—and d' sisters too—they be tryin' to keep on top, get over any way dey kin. Dey do you in a minute!—love wise, fightin' wise—or else jus' blow on you hard and heavy, fuck wi'chu mind. Like the Golden Rule say, 'Do onto others like they do you,' else 'Do onto others *before* they do you'—da's my own version."

There is much evidence in this book of rejection of middle-class values and the elevation of alternative virtues such as street smarts, courage, physical strength, self-possession, and clarity of mind: "Whole lotta dudes ain't got no education. They self-educated, got they learnin' in d' streets. Ain't no organization, but they heavy-weights." This alternative value complex, however, cannot be understood apart from the sources that propel its assertion. Folb is very insightful in this respect. She identifies the targets of their rebellion and the means by which they construct a refuge from a status they regard as imposed from outside, thereby preventing intrusion upon the personal and social space they carve out for themselves.

Evidence presented by Folb of individual attempts to validate vernacular speech in settings where it is seldom tolerated, such as schools, suggests a conscious struggle on the part of some youth against cultural subordination: "I think I lost 'bout 1000 points for talkin' shit [vernacular]. I walk off by her and say, 'Ain't that somethin'!' She [his English teacher] say, 'Good mornin', Jerry.' I say, 'What it is!' She say, 'Tha's no way to answer me.' I say, 'Why not?' Well, da's 100 points right dere. I said, 'What it is' and two 'ain'ts.' My teacher, she taught me all dem fundamentals, don't want to hear no slang. She don't *know* no slang. An' everybody be runnin' it down every day. But not dere."

There is much in Folb's book that invites commentary on continuities within the Afro-American cultural repetoire which reach back to the ante-bellum period. Nowhere is this more marked than in the preoccupation of the teenagers with *survival*. The survival values of food, sex, and prestige which characterized much Afro-American folklore in the pre-emancipation period are altered only in the replacement of food by money. The "bad-man" type of folk hero that emerged after the Civil War continues to find representation in teenage culture. These comparisons are not intended to evoke a view that the values displayed are a legacy of slavery. It can be argued more convincingly that the continued subordination of many segments of black America constitutes a structural impetus for the perpetuation of such values.

Equally striking are parallels between the survival strategies employed in the every day lives of these young people and those employed by their forebears—in particular, art and artifice. To these they add one that was not so prominent in the past—violence, bucking the system. Their tongue-in-cheek cynicism toward the powers-that-be finds the proverbial *Miss Ann* replaced by *Miss Lillian* and *Amy*. Similarly their deep concern with trust in human relations and self-possession and presence of mind as valuable personal attributes invites comparison to the concerns and values of ancestors held in bondage. Their concern with insight into real rather than ideal workings of the social world and the way in which they elevate the importance of understanding human character are reminiscent of the sources of success of the ante-bellum trickster, Brer Rabbit. He consistently triumphed over adversaries through his understanding of their vanities and character. Callousness and injustice are as much a part of their personal narratives as they are of ante-bellum folk narratives. Their environment is still apparently perceived as a hostile and threatening one.

Yet there is very little evidence in this book that the young people studied are in conscious touch with their history. There is even less to suggest that they have a grasp of the means which ensure their cultural subordination today and which will sentence many of them to a life of economic and political irrelevance. The continued ambivalence of some of these teenagers toward their blackness and their people seems guaranteed by the circumstances of their lives. For an unambiguous positive sense of identity to emerge in the face of day-to-day facts of victimization and exploitation would seem to require Herculean efforts in consciousness raising. One condition for productive channeling of their indignation and rebellion might be the development in them of a conception of their people as a historical force and the agents of a three-century-old struggle to become masters of their fate, not dependents appealing to the beneficence of others.

Whatever warp is evident in the way the youth of South Central Los Angeles construct reality must be seen against a background of (1) the continued minstrelization of African and Afro-American culture in the media; (2) history as taught in American schools, which up until recently tended to be far more sympathetic to the demise of a romanticized plantation society than to the victimization and savagery wreaked upon those who furnished the labor upon which this social order was erected; and (3) the continued propagation of the myth that the plight of black Americans springs from their innate character.

For me, a black American and student of Afro-American life and culture, Folb's excellent book has evoked a sense of hope as well as dismay. The hope was compelled by many of the dreams and aspirations of the youth studied. The features of heroism and high-risk taking which figure so centrally in their lives struck a responsive chord, as did their widespread self-criticism. There is much evidence as well of their vitality and creativity, their strong will to survive and triumph over adversity. The desire for greater cohesiveness with other segments of black America is dignified: they are apparently unwilling to unite on just any terms. Finally, there is much evidence to support a view of the competition and conflict depicted as having an underlying basis in egalitarianism. These egalitarian values in the long course of history may one day be conceived as another of Afro-America's contributions to this nation.

Like I like to
listen to brother got
somethin' to say. You kin
learn a lot 'bout
wha's happ'nin' from
some dude really talks.
Brother been around,
dealin', hustlin', gettin' over.
Maybe heavy into
Black Power bag.
Dude run down some
heavy lines.

# 1. setting the scene

**T**HERE IS a country here in the United States that few whites know much about and even fewer have ever visited. It is known by a variety of names, euphemistic and otherwise— "the inner city," "the central city," "the slums," "the other side of town." If the residents are primarily black and predominantly poor, it is most often called "the ghetto." Though the label ghetto is one blacks could well afford to do without, it nevertheless still describes a geopolitical, economic, and racial reality in this country. And until we do away with the conditions that perpetuate it, the ghetto won't go away. Whether we like it or not, the term ghetto tells us not just about a "part of town," but a segregated community of residents who share a complex set of interlocking experiences that grow out of the conditions of enforced ghetto living.

Yet the ghetto is not a homogeneous community. As Ulf Hannerz (1969) has observed, "it consists of a web of intertwining but different individual and group life styles" (p. 12). This book is about one particular group of ghetto residents—black teenagers between the ages of fifteen and twenty who live primarily in the South Central Los Angeles black community and its immediate environs. It is a book about a kind of talk used in this other country, talk that is an integral and characteristic part of the daily lives and conversations of the teenagers who use it. For most whites, it is as foreign as the urban landscape that gives rise to it. Witness the following three conversations overheard in Watts, an enclave within South Central Los Angeles:

*Scene I*
A: Hey, baby, what it is?
B: What it was, brother, what it was.
A: What's it gonna be?
B. Say man, let's trip on down to L.I.Q. and get us some pluck.
*Scene II*
A: What's happenin', man? You steppin' . . .
B: Irvine done vamped on me and my partner. Whupped 'im upside the

head 'fore he could put it in the wind. Shit, pig did 'im so bad, he like to off the brother.

*Scene III*

A: Man, that some fine stuff you mackin' on . . .

B: I hear ya, brother. 'Cept punk over there rankin' my play. Sucker runnin' off at the jibs 'bout his new shot and how it be decked out with lifts and some ol' pimp rest and color bar. Chump better cool it, man, 'cause I'm gonna buy his ticket, *for sure!*

A white English paraphrase might read as follows. Scene I: Greetings are being exchanged between two friends. One suggests, "Let's go to the liquor store and get some wine." Scene II: A man flees from the police. He tells another of his escape and of his friend's fate at their hands—a beating he fears has severely hurt his friend. Scene III: One young man watches his friend talk to a particularly attractive young woman and compliments him on his taste. The second acknowledges the compliment but complains about a third male who is muscling in on his advances by trying to impress the young woman with remarks about his supposed new car and all the special accessories it has. Angered by this move, the second male threatens to challenge the "bullshitter."

For most whites, the words and phrases might as well be Greek. But they are largely English words and phrases being redefined, sometimes reconstructed and rearranged, into new and graphic strings— something lovers of literature should recognize and appreciate. For a young black "running the streets" of Watts, the conversations need no translation. They are part and parcel of life. Even for someone "coming up" in the ghettos of New York or Chicago, Philadelphia or Oakland, it would be easy to understand most of what was being said. Whatever isn't could be filled in from experience with scores of similar situations.

Though each black community, even each neighborhood or street-corner clique, may use words and phrases known only to that group,

*3*

though terms pass in and out of use or may be taken over by main-stream America—or borrowed from it—though new expressions are continually being created and used, there is still a large body of ex-pressions that crosses boundaries of both time and distance. Expressions like *pluck* (wine), *blood* (black person), *beast* (white person), *fronts* (suit of clothes), *gunny* (marijuana), *go from the shoulders* (fight), *run off at the jibs* (talk too much), *git-go* (beginning), *poot-butt* (inexperienced person), *mack* (talk smoothly and seductively to one of the opposite sex), and literally hundreds more have been common currency among blacks for some time, especially in the urban United States.

So there is a kind of talk—a vocabulary—that can tell those who would listen what it means to be young and black and live in a ghetto community. As one teenager put it, "The [white] Man he ain't down wid d' happ'nin's [knowledgeable about what is happening]. Gotta break it down [explain it] fo' 'im. Blood [black person] know where you comin' from. The man need some 'help.' Dig [understand]? Gotta school [teach] 'im 'bout what's happenin'. See, d' way d' brothers and sisters be talkin' just everyday things. Da's just d' ghet-to, man. Hear what I'm sayin'?"

To want to understand more about some of the residents in this other country, then, is to begin to fathom and translate the vocabulary used there, to listen to the meanings assigned to the words and phrases in that vocabulary, to be introduced to the conversations and contexts in which terms get used, and to see the life concerns the words and their meanings focus upon.

This focus on vocabulary—or "lexicon," as it is referred to among linguists—as a way of illuminating black teenage social and cultural concerns is long overdue. As J. L. Dillard (1977) has pointed out, "professional linguists very seldom devote their attention to lexi-cography, and even when they do, they are not usually concerned with vocabulary size and function but with etymology [word history] or a similar matter" (p. 17). Certainly scholars like Thomas Kochman (1972, 1974, 1976), Claudia Mitchell Kernan (1971), Roger Abrahams (1963, 1970a, 1976), Grace Holt (1972), Kenneth Johnson (1972, 1973), and William Labov (1968, 1973) have suggested the important rela-tionship between vocabulary and the user's world view in their respec-tive works. But none has examined an extensive body of terms over an extended period of time in an attempt to uncover the various semantic categories that are part of the user's language system or the way in which vocabulary itself is a manifestation of cultural structure. It is my hope that this book will begin to acknowledge the significance of lexicon in understanding a group's concerns, values, and expectations.

A friend of mine once asked me how such a rich and complex vocabulary came about. What functions did it serve? I found that a difficult question to answer. Lexicographers—people who have devoted their lives to the study of words—also find it a difficult question. Like most forms of human behavior, the ways in which a vocabulary functions in the lives of its users is an intricate and elusive phenomenon, one that goes to the heart of the expressive and social needs of a people. For example, does black teenage vocabulary give the users a sense of insider status, a feeling of pride and self-worth through group identification? Does shared knowledge of the vocabulary reaffirm group and racial cohesion and values? Is the vocabulary's rich expressive, lyrical, and poetic content rooted in African culture and ritual? Did the vocabulary evolve as a necessary survival mechanism for a people forcibly wrenched from their homeland and brought to an alien landscape, and did they create a "foreign" language that was intended to be inaccessible to white ears? And if the vocabulary used by black teenagers today is a social and cultural legacy from the past, does it form a kind of composite social history of black America—where it's been, what it's done, what it thinks and feels, and what it has judged important enough specially to acknowledge and name? Does the black vocabulary provide an emotional and critical outlet for group feelings, teenage and adult, about what it means to be black in white America?

## DEFINITION OF TERMS

In the past, black teenage talk (and adult usage as well) has been referred to by a variety of names: Afro-American slang, black argot, ethnic slang, black ghetto English, spoken soul, black idiom, hip talk, jive talk, bop, and the like. The range of terms undoubtedly results from the difficulty of finding one suitable or all-inclusive label for such a diverse vocabulary. Essentially, each student of black vocabulary has selected a comfortable label. I am no exception. I am using the phrase "black English vernacular vocabulary" to characterize what follows. Though it is a mouthful, it is the label that for me is the most descriptive. Unlike the most popular term "slang," which tends to be too narrow in its application, vernacular vocabulary implies the scope of the terminology being discussed in this book. Many streams have fed into the pool of black vernacular expressions. The lexicon, therefore, is a mixture of general slang, private and sometimes secret argot, specialized jargon, Africanisms, and culture-bound idioms—a far-reaching vocabulary that calls for a broad label. Also, unlike the term slang, which often gets associated with superficial or self-conscious display in talk, vernacular vocabulary suggests the important lack of affectation surrounding black teenage use and the essential and natural part the vocabulary plays in teenage cognitive and expressive behavior.

In addition, the label black English vernacular vocabulary is consistent with other labels that are being used to characterize a parallel dimension of black language. For example, Labov uses the designation black English vernacular to refer to "the uniform grammar [syntax, phonology, and lexicon] used by speakers from eight to twenty in the inner cities and in most areas of the South" (personal correspondence, 1972). I too am focusing on one dimension of black English—black English vernacular—and within that domain, on one aspect of vernacular usage: the vocabulary.

So, like those before me, I have selected a label that most comfortably describes my data. And I am defining black English vernacular vocabulary as that subset of the black English lexicon that includes nonstandard, unconventional, and socially proscribed words and phrases. For purposes of brevity and form, I have shortened the designation to black English vernacular, black vernacular, vernacular, or simply vocabulary. However, in all cases I am referring to one discrete aspect of language and not generalizing to other linguistic dimensions or other aspects of black folk culture, such as music, dance, or religious ritual.

The themes addressed in the following pages in no way exhaust the full range of the black teenager's cognitive domain or the interests and concerns that flesh out that domain. What is represented are the dimensions of teenage life that came up in the course of conversation around the vernacular vocabulary that was volunteered or elicited.

Also, certain areas of interest and concern did not generate much vernacular vocabulary, even when they did arise in conversation. For example, discussion of a teenager's family, especially the mother, often found its way into dialog. But the number of vernacular terms for "the moms" or "the pops" were negligible—an interesting fact in itself. Or what some might see as important historical events of the day, such as the Black Power movement or Viet Nam or Watergate, also generated little in the way of special terms. Again, it wasn't that these events were not noted or discussed, but rather that they produced few vernacular expressions per se.[1]

Though periodic reference will be made to areas of teenage interest that generated little vernacular, the primary focus in this book is on the dimensions of teenage life that produced the most dialog and the greatest body of vernacular expressions.

## THE FIELD-WORK EXPERIENCE

Field work is, I believe, a very special kind of research. Unlike library or laboratory work, it potentially brings the researcher into intimate and ongoing contact with people on their own "turf." It demands that the investigator be more than an observer of human behavior. The field researcher must become a participant in the context and content of the world she or he views. This was particularly true for me, given the subject matter of this book. Entering into a unique language community with its own special brand of talk is akin to being a visitor in a foreign country. And like the foreign visitor, one does not (cannot) learn the language in a few days or a few months, or even in a few years. It takes time, involvement, and sustained contact with the residents of that country.

The field work for this book extended over a period of eight and a half years. It was conducted primarily with youthful residents of South Central Los Angeles—a community that encompasses a 56-mile radius within Greater Los Angeles. Geographically, it is one of the largest urban ghettos in the United States. In the course of those years, I interviewed over three hundred black teenagers (and just plain talked with countless others). They came from all parts of the community. In the pages that follow, I have attempted to provide the reader with a general picture of my experiences: my informant contacts (how and where I met them), my relationship to this population, and my data elicitation and validation procedures.

### INFORMANT CONTACTS

During the 1960s, I was involved with a variety of social-service activities and community-based projects. I actually began the systematic collection of my data on black teenage vernacular soon after I went to work for the County of Los Angeles in its Manpower Training Programs in 1966—specifically, the Neighborhood Youth Corps Program (NYC).

The NYC Program was established by the Economic Opportunities Act of 1965 as one of several so-called antipoverty programs initiated during the Johnson administration. The stated purpose of the county program was "to give eligible youth a start in breaking out of poverty by providing them with suitable work-training experiences and services." The program provided work training for both youth in school and those who had dropped out. One of the major target areas from which youths were recruited was the South Central Los Angeles black community. It was through working with these teenagers, as a job counselor and group leader, that I became actively involved in the collection of vernacular vocabulary.

When the program was still young, the operation was small and intimate. We worked closely with those who came in. I met many black teenagers and came to be friendly with a number of them.

7

Through the county grapevine, other teenagers heard about my work and would call me or drop by my office to check out what I was doing. Many became informants and, again, introduced me to other youths they knew. So an informal contact network was established which continued even after I left the job in 1971. I also met and interviewed teenagers who were part of my weekly discussion groups, those in other counselors' groups, some at job sites I visited or in community-based projects. Still others were met through my personal contacts in the community.

A substantial number of contacts were also made through Teen Post Incorporated. Teen Posts were a network of community recreation centers that arose in the wake of the Watts uprising of 1965. Funded by the Office of Education and directed by local groups, these recreation facilities were concentrated primarily in low-income areas of South Central Los Angeles and East Los Angeles (a large Chicano community). They became gathering places for low-income teenagers who could not afford or find outdoor sports facilities, indoor games, dances, or movies. They also became places where a teenager could just "fall by." Though few street people actually joined the Teen Post in their neighborhood, they nevertheless made use of the game facilities there—pool, ping-pong, cards, dominoes, and record players. Again, through contacts in the community, I was able to go to several of these centers, talk with the staff and the youngsters, join in games, and interview those who were interested or curious. As in the case of the NYC teenagers, I made further contacts through this group.

Another kind of informant contact developed when I returned to university teaching in 1971 and became codirector, instructor, and counselor in the English Composition for Educational Opportunities Program students at the University of California at San Diego. A number of the black EOP students came from South Central Los Angeles and maintained close ties with friends and relatives, even though the campus was a hundred miles from home. Many black students at San Diego felt alienated from the campus and the immediate environment and would head homeward whenever the chance arose. Through these students, I met others from the South Central community who volunteered to be interviewed.

Later the same process of informant contact that occurred at UCSD took place when I taught at the University of California at Irvine in 1974 and 1975. UCI also had a substantial number of black students who came from South Central Los Angeles, some forty miles north. And like their San Diego peers, many of these students felt alienated and sought to remain connected with friends back home. So, again, I was brought into contact with black teenagers from South Central through my involvement with the students at UCI.

PLACES OF CONTACT

There was no single or uniform interview environment. Contexts ranged from some anteroom at a county work facility; to an alcove in a Teen Post center, punctuated by yells from a basketball game or the music from a radio or the high hum of conversation; to someone's porch or kitchen; to a curbside or reclining wall adjacent to a housing project; to a dorm room; to a basketball court.

The contexts were both planned and improvised. In a sense, I always carried my interview information with me. Early on, I committed my interview questions to memory. And the lexical entries to be reviewed literally became part of my person, as if they were my clothes. So, if opportunity and informant came together, that became the context for an interview.

Although approximately half of the three hundred interviews were taped, the other half were transcribed from field notes or questionnaires as soon as possible after an interview. Needless to say, not all contexts allowed for the use of a tape recorder—and at least half of the informants not taped would not have taken favorably to the presence of a tape recorder. What is surprising is that such a large percentage of those I met not only allowed me to tape their talk, but asked to hear their voices and words played back. Few of the teenagers I met had a tape recorder of their own, so it was a novelty and one that drew a lot of attention. On more than a few occasions I was asked to tape the talents of an aspiring horn player or singer or emerging vocal group.

The most "hospitable" physical and psychological environments for interviewing were those farthest away from the white establishment—school, work, probation and parole offices—and closest to a teenager's "turf," preferably on it. However, even those interviews conducted in such inhospitable county surroundings as General Hospital or the Hall of Administration became open and energetic, once we got to talking about topics of mutual interest, happenings in a teenager's life or the vocabulary itself.

MY RELATIONSHIP TO INFORMANTS

One of the most vital and sensitive aspects of my field work—and its potential for success or failure—was the quality of my rapport with informants. This was especially true whenever I was in South Central Los Angeles, where I was very much in the minority. I needed to confront and overcome, as much as possible, the instinctive and understandable distrust and potential hostility automatically directed at me, the "outsider." I was white, I was female, and I was asking personal questions of residents in the community. That description fits any number of white "intruders," including social workers, parole officers, teachers, or the police. Though I had personal and professional friends living in the South Central area, that did not count for much in the early stages of my work. It was the teenagers' trust I needed. Liebow (1967) says that all whites are always outsiders. And I never fooled myself that I was anything else—even though I formed some deep, long-term bonds with a number of the teenagers I met. Unlike Liebow or Hannerz—both of whom had intimate, daily contact with their informants by virtue of their immediate living proximity to the people they met with—I lived outside the South Central Los Angeles community and traveled there for my interviews. Though I spent a good portion of my time in South Central Los Angeles, I was still a visitor to the community.

My intruder status, coupled with the transitory nature of my visits, demanded, I felt, the greatest degree of candor I could manage in telling others who I was, why I was there, and what I was doing. This meant talking to whoever was interested in the personal reasons and experiences that had led me to this field work. What Hannerz (1969) noted in his own work in a black Washington, D.C., neighborhood applied to my own study: "I could not promise that my research would benefit their community much. I could only try to make life in the community more understandable to other outsiders and not . . . cause the neighborhood people any inconvenience by identifying them in writing" (p. 205).

My first field contacts in South Central were through six teenagers I knew from the NYC program and various Teen Post directors and staff members. Some of the directors knew vaguely what my study was about; others had little or no idea what I was doing. So it became particularly important to secure their understanding, and tacit approval. To the extent that it was possible, I discussed my study with the Post director and his or her assistants: my reasons for doing it and their feelings about my doing it. Though some directors were initially wary, they generally became more interested and cooperative as I explained myself and the purpose of my work. In a very important way, the director and the assistants were passing judgment on my person, not on the worth of my research. Therefore, the tacit approval of the staff—allowing me to spend time at the Teen Post, introducing me to potential informants, asking me to participate in volleyball or ping-pong—meant that I was being marked as provisionally "acceptable."

Since few of the Post directors initially informed the teenagers of my visits, I came into contact with a variety of responses when I walked into any given Teen Post. Some kids were openly suspicious; others ignored me; some watched me in silent curiosity. After some time had passed, and I was seen to be talking with the director or a staff member, some of the kids would come by to see what was happening. The younger children, spotting the tape recorder slung conspicuously over my shoulder, demanded to know what it was.[2] It gave me my first real opportunity to let those around me know who I was and why I was there. As Hannerz points out in his own field work, it is important to make the reasons for being there clear as soon as possible.

Often I sat around the Teen Post talking with the staff or a variety of youngsters until sufficient numbers of potential informants had dropped by. Usually this was some time in the evening or on weekend afternoons. In some cases I visited a given Teen Post more than once before interviewing anyone. Though curiosity over my presence at a given Teen Post continued to some degree throughout my time there, the guardedness that initially greeted me usually disappeared as I came to be seen as "okay." Frequently I played dominoes or cards or ping-pong; on the few occasions a table was available, I shot pool—a skill taught to me by my father who, as a young man, made his way in the world by shooting pool for money. It was a skill that, I have been told by some of my male informants, surprised and amused them.

My dress was informal—usually blue jeans, a sweat shirt or sweater, and sandals or tennis shoes. The casualness of my dress was not so much an effort to distinguish myself from those whites who came to the ghetto only "on business," though this was certainly operating, but was a practical response to the contexts in which many of my interviews took place. Taken together, my participation in games and sports, my conversations with Post youths and personnel, and my informality of dress certainly made me feel more comfortable and seemed to relax those around me.

In discussing the impact of being female on field work, particularly in the black community where sex lines are often sharply demarcated, Hannerz notes that "the sex role is an ascribed one, and the field worker may not be able to do much about its effects on his [or her] relationships in the field" (p. 209). It was difficult at the outset, before I knew many teenagers, to gauge in advance what effect my gender would have on informant response. In looking back over those early contacts with Teen Post youths—especially male teenagers—and later on as well, I think that two factors figured prominently in the general geniality surrounding most contacts: I *was* female, and males were therefore all the more curious about me and my study.

The art of "the rap" is a vital ingredient in the daily exchanges between young males and females. It is a practical cultural mechanism "which potentially makes a woman approachable to every Black man." The verbal strategies available to her allow the black woman "to avoid unwanted persistence . . . through the effective utilization of a variety of verbal or non-verbal 'put downs' '' (Kochman, 1971, p. 5) if she so chooses. Many years ago, when I first started conducting group sessions with NYC youths, a young black male spent the better part of the three hour session "running down his line" to me. At the end of the session, I asked him why he had been so persistent if, as it appeared, he had no intention of following through on his "hustle." His reply: "Just practicing." Since that time, I have noticed many other instances of this. As Kochman points out, "Even when he [the black male] is not serious about pursuing a relationship, he will 'rap' to sharpen his line, his wit, or as one informant remarked, to 'deposit his image' '' (ibid., p. 4).

So it was no surprise that a number of the young males I interviewed were particularly cooperative when asked to talk to a "young lady" (a general term applied to any seemingly eligible, youngish female), even though this young lady was thirty years old when she began her field work in 1968. And many young men spent a part of the interview depositing their image.

Not a verbally shy person myself, so I'm told, I honed my own set of verbal strategies to counter the male rap—and to deposit my own image as someone who was interested in taking care of a different kind of business. Mutual verbal play and put-down marked a number of my conversations with young black males. Mostly I experienced it as a natural part of the male-female encounter and felt that it allowed for simultaneous observation and participation in a wide variety of cross-gender speech acts.

A second factor that probably allowed accessibility of contact was curiosity about me and my study. Few of those I interviewed knew what a sociolinguist did or what "vernacular vocabulary" was. That is jargon from another world. I would explain what I was doing by selecting a few of the terms known and used by young blacks and, say, indicate how the same terms were used differently by whites or Chicanos. Or I would run down the latest "dozen" (ritual insult) I had heard and ask if it were known to the informant. Or I would share vocabulary I had picked up from Chicago or San Francisco and ask how the definitions compared with usage in Los Angeles.

My expressed interest in the vernacular seemed to promote involvement and moved teenagers to "high sign" (show off) their knowledge of and facility with the vernacular. This focus on the vernacular prompted not only verbal display, but a sense of pride in the user. Too many young blacks were burdened with a negative and self-deprecating image of their speech. Here was a situation in which their vocabulary use was being positively valued. Even relatively quiet or detached young men would warm up to the subject matter as we would get into the review of terms. Many expressed their enjoyment of the interview and volunteered their friends for future interviews. One teenager in the NYC Program got so enthusiastic at the whole project that he would call me at least once a day to report the latest word happenings from the streets.

Though I don't fool myself into believing I was either "one of the boys" or beyond being conned, I do feel that being female and studying something that most teenage males in particular could "get behind" came together to generate precisely the kinds of dialogs and discussions that yield some of the richest narrative and descriptive data in this book. As time passed, I began to form my own expanding network of informant contacts, and these people became the ones who made me "provisionally acceptable" to their friends, relatives, and acquaintances.

In the case of female informants, I was even more keenly aware of my outsider status. As Beth Day points out in her own work with black females (1972), "many black women simply don't like white women, and cannot relate to them. They believe that they are spoiled, weak, selfish, deceitful, and not to be trusted" (p. 286). From the beginning of my field work, I was acutely aware of this image of white women. For that reason I seldom interviewed or even approached young black women I didn't know without the benefit of a female contact. My intermediary would introduce me to a friend, relative, or acquaintance and, essentially, speak for me. In many instances, the young women who introduced me to others were present at the conversations that followed. I rarely asked a young woman to interview with me until we had come to know something about each other and both of us felt comfortable with such an interview.

Though I was always a white woman in the company of black women, I was also a woman engaging with other women. To the degree that a sense of trust was established between us, we could then talk about our common bonds as women: matters of child bearing, childrearing, love and marriage, desirable and undesirable men folk, and the like. Though I don't pretend our common "womanhood" transcended the facts of life surrounding our racial and socioeconomic differences, I do believe that commonality, once a feeling of trust was established, allowed us to talk with an increased level of candor.

### DATA ELICITATION AND VALIDATION

At the outset of my research in 1967, I collected lexical items from a variety of sources, regional and local. Glossaries from New York, Chicago, Detroit, Philadelphia, as well as San Diego and San Francisco, were tapped. These were in addition to the scores of words and phrases that were used in spontaneous conversation by those black teenagers I daily encountered through the NYC Program. As my informant contacts became more far-reaching, I acquired an even larger body of local vernacular words and phrases—many of which were noted in glossaries I had received from other parts of the United States. Though I stopped the active acquisition of new terminology at the end of 1976, I have informally continued to collect items and now have on record approximately 2500 vernacular words and phrases.[3]

With such a large and ongoing body of data to validate, I decided on two criteria for inclusion of an item in my lexicon. The first criterion was borrowed from David Maurer. In his study of criminal argot in the United States, Maurer judged an item to be known and used by the informant population if "it occurred spontaneously at least three or four times on the tapes or in the interviews." A second criterion that I applied was the ability of at least three informants to provide a similar definition or set of definitions for a given word or phrase that I introduced in the interview, as I reviewed new or questionable entries.

In most instances, the definitions provided for terms that I directly presented to informants were extensional in nature. That is, a person would seldom provide merely a dictionary type of definition for a word or phrase, but would explain its meaning and function by placing it in a context in which it would be used or by presenting a real or hypothetical situation in which the expression would occur as part of the conversation. In this way I was not only able to check out the currency and knowledge of a term, but to see how it functioned in the cognitive domain of the user in spontaneous speech contexts. All of the expressions discussed in this work have been reviewed in one or both of the above ways. If I had any doubt about the currency of a term, after it had been in my accumulated lexicon for a period of time and I hadn't heard it in spontaneous conversation for a while, I would take it back into the field for review.

Although it is often important to distinguish between knowledge and use of a given term, this distinction is not crucial here. With few exceptions, the terms discussed in the text were actively known and used by informants in their spontaneous speech. If this was not so, I have noted it in my discussion. Even those items that were known but not consistently used in daily conversation are valid for inclusion. They tell the reader what is present in the vast vernacular pool and what, then, is available to the user when and if the appropriate context arises. Like many of us, black teenagers actively employ only a portion of the vernacular vocabulary available to them—though they have a more extensive repository of terms at their disposal. What is significant here is the vast numbers of terms that *are* actively brought into play in any given conversation. Those who would bemoan the meager vocabularies of ghetto youths should look again. The data suggest quite the contrary, certainly when it comes to facility with vernacular vocabulary.

### THE VOICES

The voices heard in the chapters that follow are representative of the young blacks I encountered over my years in the field. With few exceptions, the individual narratives and dialogs are the words of different speakers who represent what others have said on the same subject. When names are used to identify or sort out one speaker from another, they are fictional. The voices are primarily from the ghetto (though occasionally middle-class black youths are heard from) and predominantly male (only 50 of the over 300 interviewed were young women). They are the voices of gang members, churchgoers, street hustlers, political activists, young mothers, welfare recipients, and some "well-off." They are "low-riders," with and without police records, drug users and nonusers, school dropouts and scholastic achievers, athletes and musicians, "homeboys," "gang-bangers," "stone foxes," "chickenheads." They are voices that use black English vernacular vocabulary to punctuate and pepper their conversations about youthful concerns and experiences: identification of self and other, forms of manipulation, male-female relations, drug and alcohol use, and the dynamics of language.

Finally, they are voices recorded and transcribed so as to approximate the black English vernacular dialect spoken by many ghetto teenagers. Though no transcription can ever do justice to the intricate orchestration of body, language, facial expression, and vocal rhythm that pervades black verbal expression, some limited attempt is made to convey a sense of original "voice"—a voice that tells a vivid story for those who would listen. It is sometimes humorous, often poignant, and always very human.

# 2. if it ain't cuz, it's fuzz

## name terms in the black community

WHEN WE THINK of name terms or identity labels, we often think of first or last names imposed on us at birth. These names serve as practical labels that give us a legal and social identity in an anonymous world. Just as important, our names give us a sense of psychological reality. They tell us that we exist in the world, that we are unique human beings with an individual history that connects name to person. One of the most frightening aspects of amnesia is your inability to remember your name. Loss of name is akin to loss of a place in the human family.

Another of the unique properties of names is that they are usually lifelong labels—particularly for men. Though women who marry in this culture generally relinquish their maiden name for their husband's surname, and thereby signal an altered social status, they are still identified with a marriage-long, if not a lifelong, name. First names are even more indelibly marked on us. They are given to us at birth and we usually take them to the grave. They are not of our own choosing and, for many of us, not to our particular liking.

Names carry with them little implicit affect. That is, if someone says "Robert Green" or "Bessie Roberts," no one is likely to be stopped in their tracks or struck mute with terror at their mention. Of course, there are exceptions. Names that have become prominent in the public's consciousness—Angela Davis, Gloria Steinem, Cesar Chavez—may very well strike an emotional chord in us. Even in a smaller social arena, one's name may have become associated with strong feelings in the minds of others. The cliché "I never want to hear that name again" suggests such a possibility. But for the most part, our names are not used as vehicles for censure or praise. They have limited descriptive and expressive impact. They label the goods, so to speak.

There is another class of names or identification labels that does carry with it varying degrees of emotional content and descriptive force. These name terms or identity markers are used to characterize a person's perceived behavior, appearance, or relationship to the speaker. Because they are not permanent labels and because they are intimately tied up with personal perceptions, they tell us a great deal about the attitudes, expectations, and values of those who use them. One such set of these name terms are pejoratives, those expressions that negatively characterize others racially (*chink*, *nigger*, *spic*), sexually (*cunt*, *piece*, *cow*, *broad*), or ethnically (*polack*, *kike*, *bohunk*). Though vernacular name terms are not necessarily derogatory, the overall nature of vernacular vocabulary tends towards labels that degrade rather than elevate. Whatever the expressive impact, these descriptive labels are rich mines of cultural information and warrant close attention. As we will see, they are a particularly fertile and far reaching source of information about youthful black culture and behavior.

> Hey, looky here, momma! Lemme run it down to you. Let the "Watts Wonder" tell it like 'tis. Dere all kin'a names fo' d' brothers and sisters. Like you got yo' hope-to-die partner—yo' ace coon, yo' main man, yo' tight—blood and you cain't *git* no closer. He like family—yo' play brother. Some jive ass niggers, hard heads get funny, you go down wid 'im—*side by side*. You got yo' li'l ol' pootbutt, yo' square brain, he don't know wha's happ'nin'. Don' git high—nothin'. He just dedicated to d' home front, do what he momma tell 'im. Them siditty niggers they be frontin' off all d' time. Colored dudes actin' like white. Pig brothers, Tom-a-Lees they jus' black people, tommin' fo' d' white folks. Betray they people. Think they better 'n d' brothers and sisters. All kin'a folks down here.

What the "Watts Wonder" is running down in his own special way is just a fraction of the elaborate set of vernacular name terms found in the lexicon. Taken together, these expressions paint a vivid and intimate picture of teenage interpersonal relationships and the world view that informs it. There are a number of interpersonal themes that stand out in youthful conversation. Though these themes

19

are intricately bound up with each other, they deserve separate space and discussion so that they can be clearly seen and fully appreciated within the larger framework.

## THE FAMILY

"Like you got your righteous kin—*for real* brothers and sisters . . . and den you got your play brothers and sisters. Like yo' partner, yo' *first* partner, yo' *best* partner, he be like a brother to you. Like he in d' family. You be sayin', 'What it is, cuz.' "

What Daniel's statement suggests and what is apparent from looking at black vernacular usage is that there is an extensive set of words and phrases that identifies pseudo-kinship or familylike relations. Expressions like *cuz, brother, sister, soul brother, soul sister, play brother, play sister, play cousin, play mother, bro'* (for brother), *brother man, momma, old lady, old man, dad, daddy* are used to identify and characterize persons who are not family in the literal sense but are connected to the speaker through the bonds of friendship, sexuality, or racial identity. There are two important ways in which the concept of family has directly or indirectly influenced the proliferation of pseudo-kinship vernacular. One has to do with the very nature of family life; the other relates to the deeply felt "family of blackness" that crosses literal lines of kinship.

### THE EXTENDED FAMILY

In the last two decades much has been said about the nature of black culture in the United States. The 1960s saw the patently ethnocentric viewpoint of the white liberal being expressed in a flood of literature depicting black life. In the wake of the civil rights protests of the 50s and 60s, with the onslaught of federal legislation and the war on poverty, these voices cried out for equality and integration. What integration too often meant was the obliteration of black culture itself rather than an end to the shameful conditions under which many black Americans were forced to live. White liberals, in their fervent, even well-intentioned, efforts to "integrate" blacks fully into American society, sought to throw out the baby with the bath—in effect, to make the black over in the image of the white middle-class liberal.

One of the focal points for liberal attack was the lower-class black family structure. And one of the strongest voices decrying the limitations of black family life was Daniel Moynihan's in 1965.[1] What Moynihan and others like him essentially saw as the great failing of the black family was that it wasn't like the white middle-class family: it wasn't patterned after the so-called nuclear family model which relies on an in-depth, parent-to-child closed system of upbringing. The black family has historically relied on and taken strength from an extended family model—one familiar to many cultures of the world and to an earlier time in white American history. "While the white middle class seeks to keep its children off the streets and in the homes, playing with a limited number of other children and developing some meaningful and continuing play relationship (which develop into the early dating and 'going steady' pattern), black mothers teach their children to get out of the home and onto the streets. There they learn to develop relationships of a conventional nature with a potentially large number of their peers" (Abrahams, 1963, p. 18).

Furthermore, many people look out for younger black children. Though much has been made of the "absentee father" in black culture, over half of the low-income teenagers I interviewed had a father, stepfather, or other adult male living in their household.[2] Also, there was no lack of older male companions—big brothers, older cousins, uncles, male friends of the family and streetcorner men—to provide male society for young boys. Again and again young black males talked about being "schooled" by older male figures outside the home. As one young man of fifteen put it, "You got all kinda 'daddies'—dig? They be runnin' down the happ'nin's to you. Tellin' you 'bout dis and dat—you know, how to get over, 'bout them olden days —all kinda thangs. I's a trip!"

Both young girls and young boys look out for children inside and outside the home. As Lewis (1975) points out, it is often the firstborn male or female who "becomes nurse-child to those younger and takes on major responsibility for their care. He or she is in charge of the children's gang, a child-tending group." It is not uncommon to find a household filled with brothers, sisters, half brothers and sisters, nieces and nephews, cousins, and the like—all of whom may provide "mothering" for the very young child, a "characteristic which is deliberately fostered in black children" (pp. 231-232).

Much of the responsibility for bringing up children, then, is shared among youthful members of the household. Unlike the highly possessive middle-class family life, with the mother still primarily and unendingly responsible for upbringing, the low-income black family structure allows for a practical satellite system of child care and attention.

Though many would claim that black women have been sorely oppressed by their child-bearing practices, which are seen to saddle them with large families, and that these child-bearing practices are remnants of slave days when black women were valued primarily as breeders, it seems presumptuous to assume that only negative conditioning or motivation is involved. Many of the young women I talked with took pride in their child-rearing as well as their child-bearing abilities. I found that their reasons for having children ran the gamut

*21*

from accidental pregnancy, to satisfaction in being able to bear a child, to less tangible but no less real desires for companionship, being surrounded by children in old age, having sources of love, affection, and playfulness, being able to see a child grow and develop, to see one's own maternal handiwork. And these feelings did not necessarily focus on a natural-born child. One young woman's story is well worth retelling on this account. It is a poignant statement about the complex feelings of need, defiance, and pride that can be bound up in the act of "mothering."

> I done had bad luck *all* my life in d' family way. Like when I got outa Ventura [women's correctional facility] in '72, I got pregnant. Got all excited 'bout havin' my baby. You know, makin' plans and sewin' clothes—all them kinda things. I lost the baby though, when I went to Juvie. Got busted 'cause I lef' home without d' permission of my parole officer. Just got sick in Juvie and lost d' baby—a little girl. And den after I lost dat one, then I got pregnant again with a set o' twins—a boy and a girl. Oooowheee! I felt real good 'bout dat! Seein' both of 'em grow up together, you know. I had them, but they was too small, so they couldn't live. An' now I just came back off maternity leave. But she died too. She was a full nine-month term baby. She died from Hyland membrane disease—fluid in d' lung. It cain't get no worse. It gots to get better, I says to myself.
>
> My little sister [ a year and a half], well my mother gave her to me, after I lost my last baby. She's considered *as my own*. She don' wants me to go nowhere. Everywhere I go, she wants to follow. She don' wanna sleep with my mother, she wants to sleep with *me*. Because when I was pregnant, I takin' care of her mos' d' time. I bring her up like my own, 'cause I buy her different things, I do for her. She's my own little girl. No play sister, like dat. She fo' real!

So black family life is not only a complex structure of interlocking relationships grounded in an extended family model, but it is one that encourages and supports shared and multileveled child care and upbringing. Furthermore, it literally extends the sense of family beyond the confines of the household into the streets, the hangouts, and the meeting places where young blacks gather. Because many people both inside and beyond the home act like family (watch the children, educate them to street life, pass on personal experiences), it is not surprising that a collection of pseudo-kinship name terms should evolve to characterize more or less close relationships and intimate contacts that are seen to be familylike in nature.

Very often a youth's "set" is made up of both real relatives and "play" relatives, and the distinction between the two is not always clear or well defined. In many cases, it took extended conversation or

repeated encounters with teenagers to find out who was really someone's brother or cousin and who was a pseudo-relative. Often the test
of relationship had more to do with matters of common interest,
mutual activities, and hoped-for reliance and trust than with actual
blood ties. In some cases, the real relatives were literally or figuratively disclaimed—"ain't no brother of mine"—when such relatives
were seen as sources of trouble or bad feeling. One young man started
off a conversation by denying he had any brothers. Later on, he explained that as far as he was concerned his brothers were dead to him.

> Ain't no brothers livin'. Brothers s'pose' be together wi'chu, go down
> wi'chu. Don't be tryin' to jam you all d' time. I don't like violence too
> much. Not now. Had to be violent to survive in d' house. 'Cause those
> fools [five older brothers] wanted to pounce on me—and *that* hurt! If I
> got into sumpin' at school, well, I couldn't run on home. My brothers
> be there. I couldn't say I didn't wanna fight. So I hadda fight. I
> couldn't just go home, 'cause I *know* I get beat up. Moms go in d' back
> room and everybody jus' have a field day! Ain' got *no* brothers! Jus'
> my play brother Henry, he my *one an' only* brother!

Elliot Liebow (1967), in his lucid description of relationships
among the people who hung out at *Talley's Corner*—a streetcorner in
Washington, D.C.--observed that the use of such pseudo-kinship
labels grows out of an attempt to romanticize and upgrade what really
doesn't exist—deep, longlasting, or trusting friendships. Certainly the
conditions of ghetto life do not easily support longstanding friendships. Faced with an unpredictable life situation, where friends may be
there one day and gone the next, where economic survival and self-
interest necessarily undermine trust and allegiance, a person may "attempt to ascribe a past to a relationship that never had one, and to
borrow from the bony structure of kinship . . . to lend structural support to a relationship sorely in need of it. It is as if friendship is an arti-
fact of desire, a wish relationship, a private agreement between two
people to act 'as if,' rather than a real relationship between persons"
(p. 207).

The glorification of tenuous, often transitory relationships also
occurred among the teenagers I talked with. In the same breath they
talk about the tight relationship between their "play cousin" and
themselves, and the next moment tell of a situation in which the
would-be friend deserts them during a fight, "creeps" on their young
lady or young man, or "burns" them for their "stash." Some youths
rejected even the pretense of close friendship in favor of keeping to
themselves. Their reasons were practical, and often moving. One
young man explained it this way:

I usually be by myself. I usually don't be with nobody. I usually travel alone. Whatever I get into, I can make up my own mind before I get into it. It doesn't get lonely. It more or less keeps my mind substantial, because I have a lot to do. See, I know, I'm on parole for number one. I know I can't have no slip-ups. Because jail's not fun. I do maybe more than other people about myself, 'cause if I travel with somebody, he say, "Hey, man, le's do it." He say, "Stay here, I come right back." He may come down with a jar [of pills] in his pocket. And we're walkin' down the street, Irvine swoop. "We makin' a routine check." He got dope on him and I'm busted.

Another youth put it very simply: "I'ma tell you, I'ma *loner!* I'm by myself, so you cain't be tellin' shit on me—'cause I wadn't wi'cha!" Finally, one young man expressed the complex feelings of ambivalence, defensiveness, and pain that were reflected in others' conversations about the nature of friendship: "I don' get too close to nobody. If somethin' happen to 'em, I feel somethin' for 'em. Now, I bump 'em here an' dere. If I don' see 'em, I don' see 'em. I don' really need no close partner. I don' need nobody to watch over my back, 'cause that's what partner's s'pose' be for—to watch yo' back and help you out when you need it. I don' need dat. Las' partner like dat, he got stabbed an' died. Made me feel real bad."

Though Liebow's observation about the often tenuous nature of friendship is reflected in teenage relationships, it is not the whole story. Despite the cynicism of some, deep friendships did exist. Several circumstances, unlike those found by Liebow in Washington, may have contributed to the growth and maintenance of such friendships.

Certainly one of the most important factors was the age difference of the respective groups. Liebow worked with adult males and females rather than with adolescents. As Kochman has pointed out, "Teenagers . . . run together much more than older black men" (personal correspondence). Second, well over half the youths from South Central had either lived in one place all their lives or moved only a limited distance from their early home. Though many were school transfers or dropouts, and others had been incarcerated for periods ranging from several days to years, they invariably hung out in their neighborhoods when circumstances permitted. Many high-school-age youngsters had "running partners" or play brothers and sisters who dated back to grammar-school days, and over the years they had maintained a core peer group made up of relatives and pseudo-relatives. When children did move out of their family's household, they often moved close by, so that actual and play families were still near. Finally, a factor that is peculiar to life in Los Angeles may have also contributed to the maintenance of friendships over distances. Though from low-income backgrounds, some teenagers I met had access to a car—either their own or one borrowed or shared with relatives or friends. As one young man put it, "You gotta have a ride to make it in L.A. Ain' never gon' git over pattin' leather."

Nonetheless, the pattern of friendship and pseudo-friendship among teenagers was often a complex affair of push and pull. Faced with the hard facts of ghetto life, friendships were often sorely tested —some survived, others didn't, some never really existed. At the same time, there were accounts of so-called friends who had "done" you in some way; there were also anecdotes about friends who had been there for you, "just like family." One such story was told me by a young woman who had undergone a particularly harrowing experience, which still was not uncommon in street life.

> My close friends, who are they? I have a lotta *associates* but you really don' know who you friends are until you git into a bind. Den you know who comes to your rescue. Now I got one person, I can really say is my friend. She just like family.
>
> I got cut over my baby's father. I was cut, I thought it was jus' a little thing. Beverley seen my dress covered wi' blood. She say, "Girl, you goin' to d' hospital." "I ain' goin' to no hospital! I ain' cut dat bad!" She say, "Lemme see." So she raised down d' back o' my dress and she looked at it and she say, "Girl, you settin' *wide* open! You gonna go to d' hospital if I gotta drag you!"
>
> I was bleedin' so bad, 'cause every time I close my neck back, it would close it. So, she had d' window up and I could see myself passin' out and she kep' on constantly talkin' to me, so I wouldn't pass out.
>
> When dey got me to the hospital and put me on d' stretcher, she seen me and I was dozin' off. Everytime I *try* to doze off, she come an' wake me, she gimme cigarettes, she did everything to keep me awake— which she did—until they stitch me up. Had fourteen stitches. Now Beverley, she a righteous hope-to-die partner!

On one level it is unimportant whether or not pseudo-kinship terms describe real or fancied familylike bonds. What is important is that such familial name terms serve a psychological need in the lives of those who use the terms, a need that speaks to the ideal, if not always the actualized, desire for closeness and mutual support. Though the word may take the place of the genuine article, it functions as a verbal affirmation, a reminder of what might be. And, perhaps, if you say it long enough it may become real. In some way the persistent use of pseudo-kinship terms is an attempt to establish a new reality. As one black writer puts it, "the revolutionary aspects of Black Language involve the destruction of negative self images . . . To establish your own contexts is to *make* language function in a manner congruent with your level of self-determination" (Porter, in Andrews and Owens, p. 5).

*25*

## THE BLACK SISTERHOOD AND BROTHERHOOD

The history of black people in this country has always been tied up with matters of race. Indeed, skin color has been the primary pretext for persecution and oppression at the hands of many whites who have reflexively and blindly responded to this and nothing else. Racial pejoratives like *boot, spade, coon, speck, spook*, and *sambo* give voice to a level of race hatred that sees blacks as ugly and evil.[3] Though some of these labels are still used in a derogatory sense among blacks—and still attest to vestiges of self-condemnation that long conditioning at the hands of the oppressor has reinforced—more often than not, these expressions are transformed in black usage and have taken on neutral, positive, or playful meaning. As Holt (1972) has noted, "the most 'soulful' terms or referents in black usage today are those which traditionally have been the symbols of oppression" (p. 154).

But these labels of racial identification form only a small part of the lexicon of name terms. There is another set of terms that acknowledge blackness in a consciously positive way. By now, most white Americans are familiar with such black vernacular expressions as *brother, sister, soul brother, soul sister*. These are but a few of the name terms that bind together blacks in terms of another sense of family. The expressions *blood, bleed, folks, members, the people, my people* speak of a kind of kinship that unites black people on the level of race pride and group identity, the figurative "black family." One young man—a member of the Black Panthers—talked about contemporary black consciousness and its relationship to the sense of family in very eloquent terms.

> See, all the brothers and sisters they *blood*. Can you dig it? The pig he try to destroy the people—beat 'em up, rip 'em off, but they righteously stick together. 'Cause blood thicker 'n water, dig? Black people *has* to be together, jus' like family, 'cause ain't nobody gon' take care of 'em 'cept theyself. Honky pig gotta learn we ain't jivin', Jack. People ain' gon' lay down fo' no mo' white bullshit. Gon' tell it like 'tis. Like d' Mafia, you know, got to live together and die together—*be* to-geth-er. Go down side by side.

The sense of family the young Panther spoke about and the terms that describe its members is psychologically different from the pseudo-family relations I talked about in the previous section. There, the establishment of bonds of friendship were seen to be bolstered by identifying the relationship in pseudo-kinship terms—to create a family bond where none perhaps actually existed. Here, the kinship vocabulary acknowledges a deeper, more profound level of bonding—one that cannot easily be taken on or put off, but is an indelible mark of race. It is a sense of relationship that goes beyond any actual or pretended family ties because it is always visible, always with you and therefore always ties you to "your people."

There are two revealing, though often self-deprecating, expressions in the black vernacular which point up the fact that one is always visible and that one's actions are often negatively bound up with race in the eyes of white culture (and black culture too). The expressions are to *act the nigger* and to *show your color*. They generally mean to be foolish or silly, to call attention to yourself. It might be hoped that these expressions, and others like them, would eventually disappear from the lexicon as discarded vestiges of another time, or be transformed in meaning so that showing color is a positive and powerful act. In fact, this transformation has taken place, though these particular expressions have not yet been taken over to express it. In an important sense the concept of "soul"—and its descriptive offspring, *soul brother, soul food, soul music, soul handshake*—is a positive statement about acting the nigger or showing your color. It says that black is not only beautiful but that it demands attention and respect.

Though many writers concerned with black culture have attempted some definition of soul, one of the richest and most expressive definitions I've heard was offered up by a seventeen-year-old, known to his pool-hall associates appropriately as "Mr. Soul."

Lemme hip you to d' happ'nin's, school you on d' soul side. Hip you to all kinda souls—uh-*huh!* Like you fall by dis little ol' party and dey be wall-to-wall-niggas—gettin' down to the *ground!* Fonk-y! Some fiendish dancin' goin' on *dere!* Brothers stylin' some fine vines, beautiful black sisters lookin' *good!*—Afro all blowed out big, takin' pride in they beautiful blackness. You hear James Brown new record? Fonky nigger. He got soul. Git'chu some soul food! Right on! Some o' dat sweet potato pie, chitlins and black-eye peas, corn bread—you fittin' to scoff *heavily!* "Hey brother, what it is! Gimme five on d' soul side. Lay some skin on me, baby!" [Slaps palms with another black.] Niggers bein' niggers, ain't Tommin' fo' no white folks—cain't be doin' that shit no mo'! Do your own thang. Scream some heavy lines down to d' Man. Black Power what it is. All power to d' people—right on! [Shouts of "Right on!" "Teach, brother, teach!" "Amen!" from his entourage.]

The evening Mr. Soul ran down his definition, he was the epitome of soul. In his own words, "I'm ragged down heavy in my soul suit, my nigger fronts, out to catch me a *fine* young lady!" Mr. Soul's fronts were spectacular: black iridescent silk shirt with balloon sleeves, white lamé jump suit, black patent-leather shoes with enormous heels, and a black fedora, "ace-deuced to the side."

"Soul means sass," as Abrahams says. Soul also means connecting up with your roots, rejection of white values, in-group language, music, dress, and ritual. Above all, soul means a sense of racial togetherness, a community of blackness that is reflected in the family-like vernacular found among Los Angeles' young population. Terms like *blood* and *sister* not only serve to raise black consciousness but affirm one's pride in being black and signal to others that all the brothers and sisters are family under the skin because of the skin. It is no accident that the woman's movement has borrowed the expression "sister" to identify their sense of kinship.

Of course terms of racial identity like sister and brother are often used by youths as casual identity markers and do not necessarily carry with them a conscious sense of family. "What it was, blood," or "What's goin' down, bro'?" or "What's happ'nin', sister?" or slapping palms in a soul shake have become ritualized forms of exchange among young blacks. As many have pointed out, a familylike salutation can be a prelude to being "hit up" for something as well as an acknowledgement of blackness: "See somebody, like you walk by, you say, 'Hey, brother, throw me out with a roll' . . . Yeh, 'Hey, cuz, why don't you lemme hold some change?' I *hate* dat bullshit! That's what d' pootbutts use. Like you *know* d' dude, but you don' hardly see 'im and you *want* something. You say, 'Hey cuz, why don't you c'mere.' Jus' tryin' be slick. Tryin' to manipulate." Whether or not these ritual exchanges and the familylike vernacular that accompanies them have become largely unconscious behavior, they still signal a special racial connection across geographical and economic lines that can be consciously reclaimed when the circumstances call for it.

Conscious or unconscious, these terms are also a way of excluding whites. Although the simple form of the soul shake has been taken over by whites who want to identify themselves as non-mainstream or who want to convey some sense of the community implied by the shake to others, one seldom hears white youths using the black expressions brother or sister. What I *have* witnessed between young blacks and whites is the conscious inclusion of certain whites within a circle of blacks by referring to them as brother or sister. It is a mark of affection, trust, and identification that is not lightly given and, at least in my experience, marks an important shift in the depth of a relationship. One young woman associate of mine, who later became a good friend, put it this way: "Mos' of them [whites] they *dead!* Don' got no soul! But you'll find some o' 'em jus' like brothers and sisters. Jus' like you. You jus' like a sister, 'cause you groovy. Got yo' shit together." In fact, the highest compliment a black can pay a white is to call him or her brother or sister, blue-eyed soul brother or blue-eyed soul sister. As Johnson (1972) suggests, such kinship terms "label whites who understand and appreciate black culture, and whose actions toward black people are without the reservation, strangeness, and racism that characterize the actions of many white people'' (p. 145).

There is a final aspect connected with these terms of racial identity that needs to be mentioned because it reveals the effects of continued oppression on black unification and identity, particularly among poor blacks. Like the pseudo-kinship terms, expressions that signal racial identity often voice a level of aspiration, of desire, rather than a real fact of life. Again, the word is not necessarily the thing, though it may be strongly hoped for. The struggle to survive too often intervenes. As one young man put it: "Callin' the dude 'brother' don't make 'im so, don' mean he gonna stand by me. Down here [in Compton, a black community adjacent to Watts] you got to be fo' yo'self first. Got to hustle. Ain' no brother gon' feed yo' face. He takin' care his *own* kinda business. Got to. It's cold, man. White man got his foot on d' brothers' neck, don't give no slack. Got to get d' pig off our back, 'fore we gonna do like brothers and sisters.''

### COLOR CONSCIOUSNESS AND RACIAL IDENTIFICATION

Like race, color has been historically rooted in black consciousness in this country. What's the difference between race and color? A black knows there can be a big difference.[4] During the time of slavery, your color—the shade or hue of your complexion—could destine you for the field or the house (usually the lighter the complexion, the better your position). Your color increasingly came to affect your social and economic position not only in myopic white society but in black culture too, where years of enslavement had managed to systematically ''whitewash'' black consciousness.

During and after slavery, mixed ancestry became a mark of pride and status among blacks, as were other manifestations of whiteness. For example, terms like *mulatto*, *quadroon*, and *octoroon* are reminders of a color-conscious vocabulary that identified the degree of ''white blood'' a black person had.

As E. Franklin Frazier (1957) has suggested, the emerging black bourgeoisie placed a high premium on ''a family heritage which resulted partly from . . . mixed ancestry . . . The members' light skin-color was indicative not only of their white ancestry, but of their descent from the Negroes who were free before the Civil War, or those who had enjoyed the advantages of having served in the houses of their masters'' (pp. 23-24). The oppressive embrace of color-consciousness came full circle from white to black as it systematically filtered into the collective unconscious (and conscious) of a people who were conditioned to see not only their race but the very hue of their skin in normative terms. William Grier and Price Cobbs (1968), in their psychotherapy with blacks, found that one of the deep-seated wells of self-hatred involved the hue of one's skin.

One of the major themes of the Black Power movement was to reclaim color, to embrace the whole spectrum of blackness. Contemporary black rejection of the label Negro for black, as well as the aggressive wresting of the white pejorative nigger from the grip of racism, marks the development not only of a new state of mind but of a different level of color consciousness. As one young activist put it, "Black is beautiful and it comes in all kinda flavors."

Among the young blacks I met, the hue of one's skin was positively, negatively, and neutrally marked in the vernacular. Name terms associated with color consciousness operated on essentially three levels: as a pejorative mark of color, as a playful or affectionate (if sometimes cutting) source of exchange, and as a practical mode of distinguishing one person from another. Each set of terms sheds light on the complex attitudes surrounding color consciousness.

There are a number of color-related name terms that are used in a more or less pejorative sense among black teenagers. Most of these put-downs are directed at those who have a particularly dark complexion. Expressions like *coal bin, black bird, midnight, midnight the cat, blue gum, smokey,* and *smokey the fire bear* are used both playfully and pointedly to characterize extreme blackness. Many experienced being called by such names as they were growing up. One young woman told of the pain and humiliation associated with her blackness from an early age. "In Chicago, they be callin' me 'coal mine' and 'black bird' when I'z comin' up, 'cause I was dark. Mos' d' kinds up there is light. Make me cry. I run home to my momma and tell her how they done did me. She tol' me pay 'em no mind, but they righteously stayed on my case all d' time. Use have fights wi' dem yella broads. Da's when black wasn't knowed as beautiful and I was black like I am now—use bother me. Still do, sometime."

For others, their darkness became the source of longstanding nicknames, such as Smokey or Black Ball. Some of them rebelled and fought their way out from under them; other accepted them stoically or with good humor. "Yeh, dey call me 'Smoke Stack,' you know, 'cause I'm real black. I's alright. Use a get to me when I'z little bitty dude. Now, I just shine it on. Cain't be thumpin' all d' time 'cause of no crazy ol' name. Brother say, 'What it is Smokestack?' 'I's me, brother!' "

In many cases, the nicknames were, and still are, used with much affection and have come to be asserted by the person as a positive mark of distinction. In this sense, the stigma of color laid on blacks by whites has been transcended on a personal level. The Black Power movement has influenced these changes in self-perception. For example, a young woman I knew was early given the nickname Black. Though the name disturbed her when she was younger, it came to take on positive meaning for her. "Mos' d' brothers and sisters call me Black—and my ol' man he call me Black. Even took the name Brother Black when he went in for barbering. All barbers *now* have a name—like Jano, that's a Swahili name. But he took it because his woman was black and like dey say 'Black is beautiful.' They call him Mr. Black and I'm Mrs. Black. I's alright now."

It was interesting to see that whatever responses dark-skinned teenagers had to their nicknames, their older family relatives invariably disliked the names and found them insulting. It appears that these age-graded responses to color are tied to the older generation's continued view that color is linked to status and position. One young woman told the story of how she got her nickname and her great-grandmother's response to it.

> My uncle dat got killed, he named us [she and her sister] Blackie and Whitey. My sister she still have her same name—it's Whitey. My great-grandmother, she couldn't dig that Blackie, so she say, "Uh-uh, I hafta change dat to 'Sissy'." Tha's how come it come about, me gittin' two nicknames. She don' like it. She's very light. Couple friends may come over d' house say, "Hey, Blackie, wha's happ'nin'?" I say, "Ain't nothin' to it." She gits mad. "Don't be callin' dat girl no nigger name!"

Still, the darkness of one's skin is seen as a way of "getting to" someone, of provoking them. For example, *shooting* or *playing the dozens*—a verbal game involving the exchange of ritualized insults primarily directed at your opponent's mother—reflects the potent emotional charge associated with being dark-skinned. William Labov (1968) notes the following examples:

> Your mother's so black she sweats chocolate.
> Your mother's so black she hafta steal to
>    get her clothes.

I've heard the following:

> Your momma's so black she wear tennis shoes so
>    you kin find her in the dark.
> Your momma's so black you can't find her pussy
>    hole in the dark.
> Your momma's so black she wears lights on her
>    titties.

Insults directed at your opponent can also be provocative:

You so black you drink white milk so you kin see yo' pee.
You so black yo' momma can't find you in d' dark.
You so black dey make Bosco from your boogers.

Shooting dozens or "capping" on others can be a very lively and funny verbal contest. On another level, these verbal games expose the points of genuine tension, anger, hostility, and self deprecation—the effects of racism—experienced by young people in this society. When one listens beyond the playful level of verbal exchange, it is difficult not to hear also the level of pain and frustration literally being played out. There is the sense of "joking on the square" involved in many of the ritual insults. And I have seen the joke turn sour and explode into a fight. One young man said he had given up the dozens because "that starts confusion. Dat started a *lotta* confusion, a lotta fightin'." He spoke from experience. A knife scar from his right eye to his mouth was a permanent reminder of a "game" that got out of hand.

There is another set of vernacular terms related to skin color that is generally neutral or positive in meaning. These terms identify blacks who are particularly light-skinned and include such expressions as *yellow*, *high yellow*, *mellow yellow*, *melted butter*, *mulat*, and *geechie*. Though the first four expressions are used to refer to light-skinned persons in general, they are most often used, by both males and females, to identify a woman. Young women are much more often singled out for their light skin, and positively valued for it, particularly by males. When I heard a male say "high yellow" to describe another male, it usually functioned as a pejorative: either it was connected with feelings that the yellow dude thought he was too good for the brothers on the streets, or it implied that he was "funny," a homosexual.

Expressions like *mulat* and *geechie* are used as neutral or negative labels as often as they are used in a positive sense. "Geechie" is particularly interesting because it serves multiple semantic purposes. It is used to identify both very light and very dark people. Also it is used to characterize Asians and blacks who have native American ancestors. One young man explained it in the following way: "That would be mostly towards an Indian—Florida Indian tribe called 'Geechie.' She's [his mother] part Indian, and he'd [father] always tell us when he got mad, 'Your mother's part Geechie!' 'Cause Geechie Indians in Florida have a weird way of talkin'—sorta garbled. My mother she'll drift back into it now and then." As the statement suggests, "geechie" is also associated with people who speak "funny"—particularly those who come from Florida, South Carolina, or Georgia. It is probable that many are responding to certain features of the Gullah dialect (a dialect usually associated with the Sea Islands off the coast of South

Carolina). Though "geechie talk" usually carried a negative connotation, at least one young woman thought it was "pretty cool." "Well he's black [ a young man she had referred to as a geechie], but he got dis outasight language—from Georgia. Call it 'gullah.' It sound like somethin' from another country. I's really pretty, 'cause my play mother—well she's a geechie—but her brother more geechie than she is. What he sound like Latin people speakin' and it's beautiful. I *love* to talk to a man like dat! It sound real sexy."

Then there are some terms that characterize light-skinned people in a derogatory, though often humorous, way. They are much fewer in number than derogatory characterizations of dark-skinned people. One young man explained how these terms could be used to "cap" on someone. "See, you can righteously shoot on someone 'bout they complexion. Get some yella brother think he so bad, real seditty, say, 'Hey Casper, where's yo' sheet, man?' Else rank d' dude in front a young lady—'Hey, wha's goin' down, Buckwheat?' Or like you at a party, see some yellow dude, say kinda loud like, 'Mmmm *hmmm!* Looky dere! Some whole wheat bread in d' flesh!' Be prepared to throw some blows behind dat shit!"

Finally, color consciousness and the vernacular characterizing it operate on a largely descriptive level. "White folks ain't never been wi' black folks. Dey jus' see black, know what I mean? Ain' jus' one black. Kin you dig it?" What this young man is talking about is not only color blindness among whites, but an important dimension of color consciousness among blacks.[5] To say a person is black tells you only the barest facts about racial identity. For most whites, description stops there, and reflects a level of nonperception too often connected to racism and the stereotypic vision it generates: "If you've seen one black, you've seen them all." "They all look alike to me."

But, of course, all black people do not look alike any more than all white people do. Their features, their body build, their hair texture and style, and their skin tones are as varied as those of any racial or ethnic group. Whites readily use a whole range of adjectives and analogies to distinguish one white from another: ruddy, pink, sallow, pale as a ghost. So, too, blacks have a descriptive vocabulary of color to differentiate among people. Whereas color-conscious vernacular can be seen to function in a pejorative, playful, or complimentary way, here some of the same vocabulary becomes basically descriptive, largely functional. Phrases like coffee-colored, dark brown, cream and coffee, cream brown, like chocolate, coal black, honey-colored, yellow, high yellow, or gray indicate the range and variety of skin hues that blacks perceive and whites usually do not. If a characteristic or attribute is important, it will be perceived and, once perceived, it will be labeled. A descriptive vocabulary such as this graphically points to the reality of cultural relativity and differences in world view. What we see and what we don't tells us about our cultural preoccupations.

Though white domination has often forced black people to be aware of color in a negative way, there is also this descriptive level of color awareness that is the natural outgrowth of a culture's need to define and characterize its people in a purely functional way. Because there is so much emotional charge around race in this country, whites and some blacks fail to acknowledge the positive or descriptive aspects of color consciousness. One middle-class black teenager who had both black and white friends and acquaintances recognized the uneasiness experienced by whites in particular when talk about color came up. "See, most white people if you start talkin' about some 'yellow chick' or call some dude 'coal black' they get nervous. Like you're shootin' on the person. They don't understand you just be tellin' it like it is. Get uptight 'cause they don't understand, or else like you're gettin' too close to some of their own prejudice, dig? Black people all the time be talkin' that way. White folks just don't know what's happnin', hear what I'm saying?"

The fact that young blacks may still have negative feelings around being dark-skinned and positive associations with being light suggests that identification with white standards is still operative, and that a positive sense of one's color is still not fully realized. It is extraordinarily difficult for it to be otherwise. Old oppressions die hard especially when the sources of oppression remain alive. Whatever the Establishment lawgivers and soothsayers might like us to believe, racism (and the reinforcement of a negative color consciousness in relation to blacks and other "people of color") is still very much with us.

## SOCIAL TYPES

The extended family, with its multileveled, community system of childrearing, has had a significant influence on the patterns of teenage interaction. Raised in this kind of family context, young blacks have translated the structure into an extended network of peer relationships that takes in a wide sweep of friends, would-be friends, sometime friends, acquaintances, nodding acquaintances, foes and potential foes, lovers and fancied lovers.

As Roger Abrahams (1963) has pointed out in adult contexts, much is made about the number of friends and acquaintances one can claim. This is also true of teenage relations—particularly among young men, whose bonds are more tenuous than young women's. For teenagers who have little money and limited possessions, wealth gets translated into interpersonal terms. How "rich" one is in friendships —real or fancied (even the number of enemies one can claim)—is a mark of social prestige and status. Wealth-related questions, such as who owes you when things get tough and what debts you must settle, are important concerns in teenage black culture. And the range and importance of this peer network is reflected in an intricate hierarchy of name terms that identify and characterize the "social types" within the community.

### LEVELS OF TRUST

As suggested, trust is a sometime thing in the life of ghetto teenagers. Hard times, uncertainty, and tough living conditions sorely test friendships and the degree of mutual support invested in them. In such an ambiguous context, it becomes doubly important to sort out those you can and cannot trust, who is closest to you and who is less than close. "Like you gots to know yo' pa'tner your number-one man your friend in need. Cain't be messin' wid no ol' pootbutt, some rookie. Cain't trust 'em. Like some dudes call theyself yo' friend. Ain' nothin' but hi-an'-goodbye pa'tner—say hi, soon as sumpin' go down —goodbye!"

The continuum of trust is reflected in a vocabulary that subtly differentiates between assumed and real closeness. Though context and circumstance will give positive, negative, or neutral charge to a name term, there are certain labels that stand alone as semantically clear-cut examples of close—or not so close—feeling. One of the closest levels of friendship is reflected in a term like *ace* and its variants *ace coon, ace boon coon, ace coon poon, ace boom boom, a.b.c.* A composite definition of ace gives some sense of the person's potential importance in a teenager's life. "Like if you have a buncha friends, he the baddest. Real tight partner. Righteous, down-to-earth, partner. A partner you kin git *high* with, or you can go down with—back to back! Anything go wrong, you always got on yo' ace! If you cain't count on him, you got a *fool!* He's yo' number one 'spade,' dig?"

There are a variety of other expressions that essentially carry the same sense of friendship and trust as *ace: main man, squeeze, tight, main squeeze, cutty, cutting man.* The sense of personal closeness, of tightness, suggested by such expressions is apparent. In fact, teenage folklore has the terms *tight* and *squeeze* deriving from being in a tight situation—a tight squeeze—and having someone there with you; or, you are squeezed tight together in friendship like peas in a pod.

The term *partner* is perhaps the most commonly used expression connoting friendship, taking its force from the context in which it is used. That is, it can carry either very positive or negative meaning— unlike, say, *main squeeze*, which conveys positive feeling. It is often intensified by prefacing it with such adjectives as hope-to-die, righteous, ace, tight, which serve to enhance the positive feelings attached to the person so labeled. "See, you got yo' partner and you got yo' hope-to-die partner. Dey wi'chu all d' way. Go head up on everthin'."

There is another set of name terms—some of which have made their way into general usage—that are generally neutral or negative designations, such as *dude* and *cat*, *brother* and *sister*, *homeboy* and *homegirl*. Like *partner*, these terms can take on positive reference, depending on the circumstances. One can say, "That dude is a dirty dog," or "The dude fell by my house," or "The cat had on some fine rags"—each implying a different feeling. *Dude*, *cat*, and sometimes *sister* and *brother* carry the same potential meaning as *guy* or *chick* in general slang and are used in similar contexts.

The term *associate* stands somewhere between friend and casual acquaintance. It indicates a level of interpersonal involvement and trust that might be extended to a casual friend—a person you periodically or even regularly hang out with but who is not necessarily a real partner. In some sense, an associate is like a business associate—someone you know through mutual friends and contacts, have dealings with in the course of taking care of business, and who may or may not graduate to the level of a real friend. The expression itself suggests a level of formality, of qualified trust and personal standoffishness: "Your associate, he jus' associates wi'chu, ain' righteously part of d' in-crowd."

Matters of trust depend not only on who will actively "be there" for you, but on who you can count on when you're not around. Young blacks have told stories about friends who got arrested for activities that involved the person as well as his or her friends. In these situations the highest mark of a real partner was that the person didn't *fink*, *cop out*, *tom out*, or *drop a dime* by informing the police of the friend's involvement or whereabouts. To the outsider, this may seem like a romantic, Hollywood-like code of honor. To the teenagers I talked with, it was a very shrewd attitude about appropriate behavior among real friends. In a society where blacks are automatically suspect, where many ghetto teenagers are faced with a marginal standard of subsistence and may resort to illegal ways of getting things they could never have otherwise, the chances of getting arrested are high. It is hoped that friends, acquaintances, and even enemies will not give you away; and peer pressure in support of that stance is great. A term like *fink* and the sense of fink-as-informer conveyed in such expressions as *Tom*, *Tom-a-Lee*, *pig brother*, or *Tom slick* signal a deep level of contempt and resentment associated with this kind of person. "Yeh, pig brother done squealed. He done gave the Man the play. Motherfucker done told everythin' he know." The terms also carry with them an implicit warning about retribution. As one young man put it, "Some cat drop a dime on me, ain' gon' live long iffen I find out . . . 'Cause dey kin shoot me up to Y.A. [Youth Authority] and when I get out gonna be lookin' for dat Tom."

Finally, terms like *nigger* and *motherfucker* and its variants, as well as some of the white pejoratives for blacks already mentioned, run the range from negative to positive, from an expression of intense suspiciousness and distrust to strong feelings of affection, from seriousness to playfulness, from self-denigration to assertion of self-identity. For these terms and others like them, the nuance of meaning and reference is as varied as the speaker's intent and intonation make them.

The term "nigger" has been used by whites to degrade blacks. In black culture the term has broad use and reflects the inversion of meaning a white pejorative can undergo when blacks take it over. As Kenneth Johnson has pointed out (1972), " 'Nigger' can be a derogatory label, a neutral label, or a positive label—a term of endearment—when used by black people. Black comedian Dick Gregory once stated that he resented being called 'nigger' by whites because they 'didn't say it right.' What he meant is that the way whites used the word 'nigger' could not have a neutral or positive meaning as it can when blacks use it" (p. 150).

As for "motherfucker," it too has a life and range all its own in black usage:

> You jus' be sayin' dat any way come to your mind. Like you got some o' dem *sweet* mothafuckas. They righteously together brothers, got they game uptight, they on dey J.O.B.! Right on! Got dem lowlife thugs. They *mean* mothas. Don't be *messin'* wid 'em. Blow you away in a *minute!* Johnny he my ace, now he a *bad* mothafucka. He together. Strong rap to d' young ladies—and he go down wi'chu right now! We tight. Gots dem little ol' punks. Think they together, be talkin' out d' side dey neck! Jive mothafucka don't hold no air! See like da's one o' dem slangs got all differn' kin'a meaning. Don't be callin' young lady dat. Dude use dat talk 'bout other dude.[6]

### LEVELS OF EXPERIENCE

There are a number of ways in which the concept of experience can be understood. Sometimes we say that we've had an unusual or disturbing experience, something out of the ordinary in the course of daily events. At other times we say that *people* are experienced, that they are particularly skilled or proficient at their work or craft. Often we are acknowledging not only the level of expertise they demonstrate but the years of experience that went into refining their particular skill. And sometimes we speak of experience in more personal terms. Here, the experienced person is seen as a man or woman of the world, someone who understands the complexities of life through having lived it—they are social veterans. Very often in mainstream society, experience is tied into your economic position and the status derived from it—he's an experienced businessman, she's an experienced journalist.

In black teenage ghetto culture the focus is invariably otherwise. In mainstream society you are usually asked the question, "What do you do?" The measure of a man (and more recently of a woman) is inevitably evaluated in light of status or occupation in the society. In the black ghetto, where middle-class status, occupation, or office still remain inaccessible and illusory, the mark of a person, especially a male, is what he is, his self and extensions of that self—his personality, the clothes he wears, the possessions he displays, the women he claims as his own, and, not the least, his ability to "rap."

So the question of who you are centers on the person—how you come across, how you "get over." Prestige and status are accorded to those who are socially experienced. This often means being well schooled in street life. Disdain and contempt, playful and not-so-playful barbs, are directed at those who can't take care of business, who aren't social "professionals." And these attitudes toward experience are revealed in a vast vernacular vocabulary that describes the socially inexperienced or incompetent person.

### THE MANY FACES OF THE "LAME"

No single term in teenage vernacular so vividly characterizes the social incompetent as the term *lame*.[7] Used as both noun and adjective, it carries with it the sense of being socially disabled or crippled—experientially limited in one way or another. The composite picture of the lame is far from flattering.

> A lame brand, he don't know how to talk to d' young ladies. He don't know how to talk his bidness . . . Like when you rap to some young lady, he gonna set up and just let you do it—all d' talkin' . . . be eyeballin', don' never *do* nuthin' . . . scared o' girls. Dudes be talkin' to d' young lady, he run aroun', shootin' marbles. Not too situated . . . Dumb sucker *have* no girls, don' know where everything is . . . STONE SUCKER! . . . Sissy boy, hangin' 'round his momma all the time. Dedicated to d' home front.
>
> He don' know what's happ'nin'. He like a school book chump . . . stupid, ignorant, hide in d' books all d' time—like a bookworm. He square to d' wood! . . . Don't get high, don' smoke no weed. Show 'im a reefer, he wouldn't even know what it is! . . . Uncoordinated. He cain't fight or nothin'. Like he followin' you everplace you go . . . wanna be wid everybody, but don't do nothin' . . . They can't catch on to what's happ'nin'. They jus' lame and dey gon' be lame and i's no hope for 'em—no kin'a way, really.

The lame just doesn't know what's happening. And what's happening is talking and "getting over" to women, getting high, being able to fight, being able to dance and play sports, being out of the home—getting street experience, not book learning. Though the picture of the lame takes in a broad sweep of undesirable personal characteristics and, in some sense, is the generic cover term for all kinds of social handicaps, there are many groups of words that paint a more specific picture of social ineptitude and reflect very particular attitudes and values regarding the person so labeled.

Like the term lame, the expression *pootbutt*—and its synonyms *rootiepoot, rumpkin, rookie, wethead, junior flip*—refers to a socially inexperienced person. But where lame refers to inexperience in general terms, pootbutt more specifically connotes someone who is literally young in age or young in the mind—both childish and a child. Where lame often emphasizes a handicap in terms of what you can't or won't do, pootbutt often characterizes your defect in terms of not being ready for people—not being old enough literally or emotionally to take care of business—even though the person may blunder or bully ahead as if he knew what to do or how to act, as the following collection of responses suggests.

> Like a little chump that think he's bad, like to hang around with the in-group . . . Rookie . . . nothin' to 'im, too young, no sense, no nothin' . . . A li'l ol' youngster. Dude jus' got out d' pad. He jus' wet behind d' ears . . . He just *young!* He tryin' be so old, don' know shit! Still wet up under d' lip—damn the ear, 'cause he don' know how to wash his ears . . . Young blood! Momma didn't teach 'im enough. Let 'im out on d' streets too young. Don't nothin' go through his head unless his momma tell 'im so . . . Little guy—little bitty dude, bad little dude, he wanna fight you . . . He always comin' up to you, talk stuff he cain't back it up. Rumpkin . . . he's too young in the mind, don' know what's happ'nin' . . . They thank they cool, but dey ain't. Little kids or a person who acts younger—"Man, I'm bad!" Rumpkin—rumpskin! . . . He still has his childish mind . . . It could be a big guy wid a childish mind—he rank you in a minute.

The pootbutt often can rank someone or something inadvertently—talking out of turn, being silly or childish, disturbing the flow of activity or conversation—or sometimes consciously. For example, one of the most annoying and effective ways of ranking someone (particularly a male) is to interfere with his sexual advances toward a young woman.

> Like a little pootbutt come. Like you tryin' to talk to a young lady. Messes you up, talkin' trash. Yeh, I *hate* people like that! Like you be sittin' up dere rappin' to a young lady. Somebody come over you house.

You be *knowin'* them, but you never invite them over the crib—the first
time they come over there. So, they be sittin' there talkin' to you. They
tryin' to keep yo' mind on them only. Fool sittin' over here makin' dis-
turbances. Cain't concentrate on what she's tryin' tell you. He's tryin'
git you to go in room wif 'im. Nex' thing you know, he's sittin' up
there, talkin' to the chick.

There is an expression in teenage vernacular—"wanna be"—which
aptly sums up the pootbutt. He wants to be something he's not or is
not ready for. Put in another vernacular context, "He holds no
weight."

The concept of weight and what it connotes is an important concern among black teenagers. Weight is associated with social maturity,
with a person who is emotionally and experientially together (not at
loose ends, so to speak). As one young man observed, "Whole lotta
dudes ain't got no education. They self-educated, got they learnin' in
d' streets. Ain't no organization [not a member of an organization like
the Panthers or the Muslims] but they heavyweights. Can rap to you
'bout whole lotta things. But some jus' put some buttons on for a
quarter, say he has [Black] Power." Whatever pretense or posturing
goes on among teenagers who claim life experience, the person with
weight is genuinely respected—not a *lightweight* or *lightfoot*, a *popcorn pimp*, a *nickel-dime nigger*, or a *man with a paper ass*, but a person of substance who carries the weight of real experience and authority.

In sports terms, the lame is seen as a *sack* or a *non*, one who is
*sorry* (lacks athletic ability). He is the physically uncoordinated, slow,
or fearful person. He is seldom asked to play any game and is especially susceptible to "getting his shit slapped away," whatever the
game. "Like he just ain't together. Dude hoppin' around gunnin' or
else shootin' bricks. Just a cripple, man. Ain't ready for d' round ball.
Say, 'Hey, let's do it. Let's play some hoopla.' Fool don' even know
what chu talkin' about!"

Essentially the lame—whether a "wanna be" or a "never was"—
is out of step with his or her peers. And, interestingly, there are a number of name terms that carry over the suggestion of outmoded musical
styles or steps to characterize this socially out-of-step person, such as
*bebopper, bopper, diddybopper, teenybopper, jitterbug.*

A final aspect of the "wanna be" is implied in the vernacular expression "acting the fool." In an attempt to focus attention on himself, a person may act foolishly. He is often seen as young in the head,
someone who acts like a mental defective, whatever the age. This implication of the social fool is aptly embodied in such name terms as
*fool, joker, clown, dunce, duncehead.*

People are not only called to task for the way they act, but for the way they dress. Poverty can be cruel in very many ways. For a young-ster coming up in the ghetto, one of the most visibly demoralizing aspects of being poor is having to wear worn clothes or hand-me-downs. A number of teenagers admitted that one of the many factors that kept them from attending school was shame over their clothes. One young woman told the story of being transferred from a school in Watts to Dorsey High School, located in a low-middle to high-middle-income area of Los Angeles. "Sisters over there be stylin' some nice clothes—levi suits, silk blouse an' all, nice shoes. Like I ain't got nothin' but some raggedy shoes, old dress Fanny [sister] done gave me. I felt righteously down. Didn't even wanna go dere no mo'—so I splits. Didn' go back neither. Shot me to Betsy Ross [girls' school for "difficult" cases]." A young man told of being ashamed to go to Jef-ferson High School in South Central: "I was ditchin' a lot, I wanted to have clothes to go to school on, and everytime I be goin' to school, I be trampy shoes, hole in them and everythin'."

The humiliation associated with dress can cut both ways. Another young woman told about living in Detroit and, as a young girl, experi-encing the jealousy of other girls who had even less than she did.

> We lived in the ghetto, but we was clean-cut kids. My momma she worked hard, but she done kep' my clothes starched, ironed, a ribbon in my hair and white sox and penny loafers, tennis shoes all d' time. Never dingy clothes—and kids get jealous. See Detroit more like a poverty city. They [other kids] come from the South and they have that south-ern way. They jus' couldn't get ready for the big city. They be runnin' round in dem sack dresses. Well, this one particular girl, who parents had about nine or eight kids, she was just a little hobo. She felt she had to beat me up all the time in order to get over. Her and her partners makin' fun o' me, laugh all d' time 'bout how I'z uppity and all dat. I's cold, you know.

So, among young people who place a high premium on the person rather than the position—where how you look relates to who you are, and who you are is often someone who is short on money but long on style—it is not surprising that particular attention (and conflicting feelings) should surround dress.

Some teenagers totally discounted the influence of clothes in their lives—just as others discounted the importance of friends, and for some of the very same reasons: "If you can't have them, then why even bother being concerned about them?" Yet most were clearly con-cerned with clothes and furthermore had very definite opinions about what looked good and what didn't. A great deal of attention was given to style in clothes, and people who dressed in outmoded clothes or clothes that were inappropriate to "what's happening" were consid-ered lame. For example, the expression *funny style* generally has two meanings. In one context, it can refer to anyone who is sexually "different." More often, the noun and adjective refer to someone who dresses in strange or outdated clothes. Another phrase, *don't come half-stepping*, means "Don't do something halfway, do it right." When applied to someone's clothes, it can mean that the person is dressed in a manner inappropriate to the occasion:

> Like this certain person's gonna give this party, and he say, "I'm throwin' this party, man. Don't come like you come to school, don't come like you come to work, don't come half-steppin', come fiendish, righteously dap to a tee, silk to the bone." Like everybody wearin' the *same* thing and they stylin', and some old off-brand dude come up here like wid a pair of tennis shoes on, levis, and a ruffled-up shirt and everybody got they slack suit on and everything. Or like a date. Like you dress yo' self up—some bad-boy bell bottoms, nice shirt. Like you say, "Yeh, we gonna take the young ladies to hear d' Temptations at the Forum. Don't *halfstep!*" In other words, get yo'self together brother.

*Off brand* can refer to inferior or non-brand-name merchandise such as radios or stereos. It can also refer to whatever isn't *your* preference, your brand. "Like say you smoke Winston and dude give you a Kool cigarette. Dat be off brand." The term can also identify a person who is essentially "unknown merchandise," from another part of town, a stranger or just not your brand of person. "Dey off-brand people, dey off brand because dey don' groove with other peoples, ain' wif d' in-crowd. Dey out of it. Else dey wants to be up dere—seditty, high society." *Off brand* can characterize outmoded or inappropriately dressed people. "He's outa style. Like if he's wearin' checkered pants an' everybody else is wearin' flairs, den he be off brand. If you have on some dirty jeans, some jeans that nobody else's wearin'—'Man, tha's some off-brand clothes, don't even match!' "

But most often *off brand* and its vivid synonyms, such as *rainbow, color guard, christmas tree, Santa Claus*, refer specifically to a person who wears too many colors. Questions of style are intimately tied up with color coordination. As one young man observed, "Yeh, we like colorful colors, hear what I'm sayin', but i's either three or fo' colors at the *most!* 'Cept some li'l ol' off brand, don' know wha's happ'nin'." So someone who wears too many or too bizarre colors is a source of amusement and the butt of jokes and put-downs. A sample of the definitions given for *off brand* give some idea of what it means to be too colorful:

> If you's to wear some green shoes or sumpin', black stockin's and red dress and white hat, I say *you* is dressed *off brand!*
> I get a picture when you say that—orange socks, green pants, yellow

shirt and red sweater—I've ran into some people like that. Ain't too
cool.

He's a rainbow!

He wear ol' funny color—have on pink, have red sox on, yellow all dat
stuff.

Awkward cat, weird, dress funny wearin' *loud*-colored shirt, real *loud*
pants, loud shoes—jus' weird!

Nigger psychedelic! He psychedelic to d' *bone!* Call 'im "color guard,"
specially if he got on some bright oranges. Call 'im "caution sign."
Look out! Here he come!

Dress, then, is an important mark of experience. It tells others
how attuned you are to the styles and trends of the day. It lets others
know how socially aware you are, whatever your finances. It marks
you as a hip or a lame person.

Good talk—whether in the form of public performance like
shooting the dozens or running down a *toast* (an epiclike vernacular
poem in narrative form) or in private or semiprivate raps like getting
over to a young lady or capping on some pootbutt—is highly valued
among teenagers. Because talk is such an important and visible mark
of who you are, and therefore can affect your status and prestige,
youths are not only keenly aware of it but early become connoisseurs
of good and bad talk. Though much will be said about talk in the
chapter on manipulative behavior, here I would like to take a look at
the name terms associated with the lame talker.

Lame talk—and the social types connected with it—varies according to circumstances, tone of conversation, and participants.
What may be perfectly acceptable linguistic behavior in one context
becomes inappropriate in another. It's all a matter of knowing when
to talk and what to say, an awareness that seems to elude the lame. In
some cases lame talk refers to *shooting a blank* or a *dud* in playful
banter, as in a *woofing* or *lugging* session (a round of cracking jokes)
or in shooting the dozens. "Like you just woofin' 'bout someone, jus'
settin' up, shootin' jokes on them. 'Momma drink Scope,' shit like
dat. 'Hey man, what's wrong wi'chu shoe? Need shine! Dog done shit
on it!' Haf'a know a comeback. Keep on top so don't get ranked. Say
somethin' back, a dud. You base on the cat, don' nobody laugh. 'No
good!' "

In this case, a lame response is like shooting a blank gun: someone has shot on you and your return volley has no fire power. Another
example of lame talk has to do with *talking trash* or *shit*—talking nonsense or talking just to hear yourself. Name terms like *jive ass, jive
nigger,* or *jive turkey* refer to the talker who bounces the conversa-

tional ball off the wall, from way out in left field, or who demonstrates ignorance about the subject being discussed. Again, there is the sense of someone out of step.

> Someone comin' from left field, talkin' that bop that don't relate to what you sayin', talkin' nonsense—"Moon gonna fall tonight." Just tellin' some jive-ass shit, some off d' wall jokes. Like you settin' dere havin' a good conversation, dude come in talkin' off the wall jive, "I'ma burn your ol' lady, moon gonna fall, sun gonna burn." Crazy ass hole talkin' trash. Or else, if we all talkin' 'bout dope, and the person say somethin' strange 'bout dope, then you know i's untruth, you say, "Man, that's off the wall." It don' go along wi' d' conversation.

Lame talk can refer to the quantity of talk as well as its quality. A *sack mouth* spills out words. They *run off at the jibs:* "Jibbin' too damn much! Cons'anly talkin' 'bout nuthin'. Like a lotta people run off at the jibs when they runnin' offa whites. They cain't control they mouth. Act the fool, won' shut up. Jus' sack mouthin'. Tellin' everythin'." A sack mouth is not only a fool but a potentially dangerous fool. He or she may talk too much around the wrong people and get others in trouble. Though good talk is valued, too much talk is not. Part of the strategy of maintaining one's cool has literally to do with putting the freeze on too much conversation.

Finally, lame talk refers to bad talk, in the sense of provocative or belligerent dialog. Expressions like *smart mouth*, *fat mouth*, *foul mouth*, and *bad mouth* characterize the person whose conversation is *foul* or *cold*—it "stinks" or it "chills" you. "Like you got a foul-mouth woman! Woman say somethin' wrong to you widout even sayin' a bad word to the young lady at all! Da's foul, da's cold. Nasty mouth he's as foul as he can be!"

*Don't let your mouth overload your ass* or *Don't let your mouth write a check your ass can't cash* refers to provocative talk, talk that can often lead to a fight. "You talkin' too much. You gonna fight. Talkin' more than you kin chew. Brother talkin' bad to 'nother brother. Brother git tired o' hearin' 'im talk. Like he say, 'Brother you *leap* and you will receive.' " Although provocative dialog is the meat of many verbal contests, one can quickly cross the fine line between verbal play and physical provocation. Part of what it means to be an experienced talker is to know just where that line is drawn—how far you can or want to provoke another before you get labeled as too *froggy* or *foul* and are forced to do something physical about it.

For many young blacks, provocative or belligerent behavior is a necessity of life. Like many other aspects of ghetto life, physical toughness and aggression are both praised and condemned, held up as a youthful virtue and put down as a dangerous vice. When we look at physical aggression as a form of manipulative behavior, we will see the ambivalence it calls up in many. In the context of lame behavior, it characterizes those who are hard-headed, hot-tempered, and violent. In fact, the vernacular expressions *hardheads* or *heads* identify just such people. Though "head" can refer to any black male, it very often is associated with a physically aggressive male. "Like a dude what's really out fo' nothin', he *looks* hard. Like a hoodlum, a little thug, dude's always gettin' in trouble, don't know how to keep cool, always fightin'—more rougher of the blacks."

The hard head is more than willing to "thump" and often looks for a situation in which he can play out his aggression. The expression to *turn out a set* often refers to what can happen at a party when some hard heads decide to *fall by*.

Synonyms for hardhead, *thug, hood, hoodlum, cutthroat, mad dog, cowboy, varmint, gangster,* not only characterize such teenagers in gangsterlike or frontier terms that connote a sense of lawlessness but suggest that, like a mad dog, such a person is potentially out of control and physically dangerous, someone who can't be talked out of making trouble. Again, the negative view of the hard head is only one side of the coin. The concept of toughness embodied in the image of the gangster and the western bad guy is also much emulated among black males. Of course, it depends on who's being the hardhead—you or the other person.

Finally, there is a sense of lameness that has to do with one's gullibility and naiveté. Because teenage culture values successful manipulative behavior—the ability to outdo or outwit your opponent—people that are easily duped or *tripped out* are seen with varying degrees of contempt or amusement. Though there are endless ways of one-upping your antagonist, one of the favorite tricks is to *send somebody on a hombug*—on a wild goose chase—and great delight is taken in recalling real situations or making up hypothetical ones where someone got taken.

> Some cat'll come down [to Watts]—a wethead. "Yeh, man, can you tell me where Danker Street is?" "Yeh, brother, you go dis way and make a left back dat way an' go 'bout *five miles*. Yeh you'll see it!" "Okay man, tha's cool." Like you tell 'im git some joints somewhere—way over dere. Den dey go way over dere, homeboy ain't dealin'. Send 'im on a long hombug . . .
> You send dem on a big ol' merry-go-round and they end up at d' same place! "Man, it *way* over dere"—'cause you gonna tell 'im a long ways. Like I use to tell people, "It's a party on Vernon and Slauson." Now, Vernon and Slauson they both be runnin' the same way. "Al-right! Al-right!" "I don' know d' address, but you cain't miss it, 'cause music is *loud* an' d' people having' fon!" Send 'em on a stone trip! Righteous lame brain. Fool d' sucker!

*45*

It seems to be no accident that many of the terms used to describe the socially gullible or naive person are the same terms used by the prostitute and her pimp to refer to the potential customer—often seen as sexually inexperienced or easily duped. In both vocabularies, terms like *trick*, *fish*, *sucker*, *chump*, and *square* carry with them a contemptuous and condescending attitude. Since many black males still see the pimp as a folk hero, a person who has wit, guile, and consummate verbal skills, it is very understandable that "pimp talk" would pepper youthful conversation and would be taken over to describe a social dupe.

The terms discussed in this section are often interchangeable labels for the socially inexperienced, inept, or distasteful person—the lame. Yet there is a special connotation, a different qualitative sense, associated with each set of terms. It is the subtlety of the meaning embedded in these groups of name terms that makes them such a rich source of information about teenage interpersonal attitudes and values.

## UNCLE TOM AND AUNT JEMIMA

The major portion of the black population in greater Los Angeles is concentrated within a contiguous geographical area that connects the low-income ghetto of Central and South Central Los Angeles with the more affluent black neighborhoods extending out to the west and northwest. However, there are neighborhoods and residents within the heart of the ghetto that would be considered economically low-middle to middle-class. What this means is that geographical separation between low-income and middle-income teenagers is somewhat diffused.

This is not to suggest that young blacks are not aware of the economic and social differences reflected in different neighborhoods or in different life styles. As their words throughout the book will show, teenagers are much attuned to these differences and have many feelings about them. The point here is that geography is not the only or the prime factor in whatever perceived sense of separation is experienced between groups. Sometimes the split is economic, other times it is not. Often it is as much a psychological point of view as a geographical fact. And many of the attitudes that cleave and the realities that separate are reflected in what might be called black-bourgeoisie name terms.

The expressions "Uncle Tom" and "Aunt Jemima," with their many variants, carry a vast range of pejorative meanings. These name terms are used to identify blacks who are seen to have sold out to the white establishment in one way or another. As already mentioned, they may be police informers ("Like you think you got a real nice partner, and dude—if he get busted—then he'll tom out on every-body.''). They may be people who reject their black heritage and cul-ture in favor of white values, attitudes, and appearances ("Uncle Tom, whitey lover. Dey can't even talk to they own brothers, sisters. They colored and they wanna be white."). They may be middle-class blacks who have forgotten their ghetto roots and have distanced them-selves from old friends and poor relatives ("Dude who betray they people for the benefit of gettin' money. Don' see none o' dey friends no mo'; don' pay no mind to kin dat stay here. Tom done split!"). They may be old-time—or not so old-time—blacks who are obse-quious or subservient in the presence of whites ("People who do fo' other befo' they own people. Jus' don' act right. On his knees fo' whitey—'Hey, Tom, why you lickin' whitey's ass, man?'—motha-fucka ain' no good.''). They may be blacks who put on airs ("Seditty nigger, peoples who act high society."). They may be blacks who use their blackness for economic or social gain but carry a white world view inside them ("You know what 'oreo' mean? Like a sister, brother dey bop 'bout Black Power. All power to d' peoples. Dude don't even 'sociate wi' d' people, stay where whitey stay. Da's cold!"). Finally, they may be black police ("Brother workin' fo' d' pig. Uncle Toms—'Negros' in a police suit.'').

For ghetto teenagers in particular, a Tom is anyone who puts on airs, who acts *hincty*, *seddity*, or *uppity*, no matter whether a middle-class or a ghetto person. Understandably, this attitude is often tied into a complex response of envy, resentment, and desire when another shows off material possessions. One young woman put it in the fol-lowing way:

> Like a boy get a car and then he think he's better than the other one. Then, he begin to think he better than *all* black people, and then—I done seen him—he'll pick up an all-white person before he pick up young lady and take her home. And we *know* him—da's the point. He picked up a white person what he didn't even know. And, then he wouldn't take *us* home. That's the way they git. Then they ratin' people on the way they dress—if they dress better 'n you do. Da's mostly girls dress better 'n you do, den dey don' like you or dey jealous of you.

A young black man, who was transferred from a ghetto school to one in a racially mixed, middle-class neighborhood, described the situ-ation he encountered:

> Now i's alright school, but was some high seditty brothers dere. Every-body high class. Dese *pimps* walkin' 'round, stylin' suits and thangs. I go to Hamilton wid levis an' a sweater an' a pair o' moccasins on. I gits to d' little school, I looks down d' hall, every brother I see either got a

suit on or he stylin' somethin'. I say, "Wait a minute, now. Now, I know dese is niggers, you imagine what dey doin' 'roun' here, fallin' suits out. Ain' in church!"

When I went to class first day, I looked at d' teacher and he ain' mod, he ain' dress' mod, comfortable, nothin'. Dis dude is *tied down!* He gotta little tie pin, tight, he got a suit coat over him. I say, "Wait a minute, how can he teach if ain' even comfortable?" I's cold! I'm mad! I say, "Looky here, y'all gotta get dis together." 'Cause teachers ain' comfortable—how can dey be comfortable in suits? I like a teacher to come to school *mod*. Dat way he comfortable, he kin *blow*. Dis dude here, he be all *choked up* tryin' tell dese subjects.

An' I went to the principal office an' I went in dere and I base. "I'ma lay dead git me a transfer one way or d' other. Now, if you don' wan' me to commence to turnin' dis school out, you git me my transfer!" Say, "Why you wanna transfer? I think Hamilton got d' qualifications to teach you somethin'." "Hamilton got d' qualifications to make me a sissy! Hey, I cain't be comin' to school and feel outa place *neither*. I have pride, you know. I can't be buyin' no suit just to keep up d' style' wi' dese pootbutts you got here!" He got mad! "Wouldn't you rather have me tell you I fittin' to get down an' start some trouble den have me start it an' you hafta come an' git me? 'Cause when you come an' git me, you gotta bring someone dat done *git* me. Don' bring nothin's gonna *talk* to me. 'Cause after I get started, I don' wanna talk to *nobody!*"

Though this story is a funny and sometimes embellished sample of the sedittyness perceived at Hamilton High School, it is also a revealing and touching picture of a young man who felt out of place because of his appearance and manner. Sometimes calling a person seditty or uppity may be as much a strong reaction to one's own sense of poverty as an attack on another's putting on airs.

Feelings of envy and resentment are understandably part of ghetto teenagers' put-down of those who have more than they do. Sadly, those feelings sometimes get played out in violent ways. One young man who had been recently released from the Youth Authority had served time for assaulting another teenager who tried to "cop his leather piece": "Like me, a lotta time I walk down the street, some dudes look at me. They envy me right away, 'cause what I'm wearin'. Dressed in a proper way, maybe gonna look for a job. They'll look at me. Want to take my clothes, 'cause not as fortunate—they jus' don' have it. One night, this dude jacked me up for my leather piece. We got to thumpin', and I pulled out my knife and stabbed him."

In a lighter vein, one South Central teenager told the story of his supposedly affluent cousin who "fronted off" about the quality and price of his clothes:

See Kenneth he live over dere on d' Hill [Baldwin Hills]. Think he so high. Tol' me he know d' Jackson Five, got some bread from 'em. Shit like dat. Tell me how rich he is. If he so rich, he wouldn't hafta put his socks up on d' winda every night to air out. Da's what he did. He buy a ten-dollar pair o' pants—I know dey cost ten-dollar, like levi. He say, "How much do ya' levis cost?" I say, "$10.99." He say, "Man, dat's some cheap levis. Man, I pay $42 for mine!" I look at 'em, I say, "Man how you gonna pay dat?" He say, "Man, dese ain' levis, dis is *stone* alligator!" Now ain' dat somethin'. Like a $10 watch he say cost 'im $57. A Mickey Mouse watch wid d' airplane goin' roun'—$57!

There is, of course, a double bind associated with putting on airs through material display. At the same time that fronting one's car or clothes or other possessions calls up accusations of being seditty, of tomming, material display is an important way of gaining personal prestige and peer acknowledgment, and it figures prominently in teenage forms of manipulation. Material possessions are not only desired but actively pursued—it is the style of pursuit that matters more. As Thomas Kochman has pointed out, "Ghetto blacks don't oppose conspicuous consumption when it functions in terms of *vitality of imagery* (e.g., the pimp); only when it functions in terms of social stratification: as a basis for thinking oneself 'better than the next person' " (personal correspondence). Though matters of circumstance, personal relationships, and momentary attitude will often dictate when someone gets labeled seditty or "outasight," one of the most important factors is whether a person is perceived to be showing off too much— or, as one young woman put it, "Stickin' her ass in d' air like her shit don' smell. She ain't gonna have it long, 'cause somebody gon' whup it fo' her!"

As already mentioned, one of the most negative meanings associated with a Tom is someone who informs on you. In the eyes of many ghetto teenagers, law officers are seen as informers in the sense that they can use their official capacity to send you to jail. Though feelings are mixed when it comes to black police officers—some see them as more understanding because "They're still blood" or easier to get along with—a majority of teenagers I met perceived them as potentially more dangerous and physically aggressive than their white counterparts. "Like they tryin' to show whitey how bad dey are, gon' righteously jam d' brothers. Don' be doin' dat to no *white* folks. Dey harder on dey own kind."

Though some admitted that black officers often had a particularly hard time in the ghetto and were subject to more open hostility and resentment than their white partners, many still felt little sympathy for them; they had sold out their people. One rather extended narrative by a young woman is worth retelling because it is representative of a kind of encounter experienced by black police in the ghetto.

> They [the police] was comin' to pick up a stolen car from d' front o' the door. And she [a woman friend] called 'em a pig. So's dis brother wi' 'em, so he gon' be a black pig. I say, "Yeh, you ain' nothin' but a pepper-kissin' pig's ass and get along wi'chu!" So he called reinforcements, 'cause there was a whole lotta us around.
>
> He kept talkin' 'bout "Yeh, I'm gonna remember you." I say, "Man, lemme tell you somethin'. I don' want you to *forgit* me! I *want* you to remember me." He come grab me. So when he grab me, I just grabbed *him*. Man, it was me an' him dere on my front porch. I was on my own front porch what's so cold!
>
> They takin' me, my father, Sugar Bear and Rocky, they takin' *fo'* of us to jail. When dey takin' me down dere and searched me found out I had 'bout $50 in my pocket. He says, "You work?" "Yeh, you wanna know *where* I work?" Ran it down to the sucker. "Where you git dat $50 from and it ain't yo' payday!" "Do I ask you where you git dat money you got in *yo'* pocket?" "You a smart one, aren't you?" "Nah, I'm not smart. I jus' hate a nigger cop that thank he so-so because he got a badge and a gun on. Sucker, lemme tell you somethin'— You bad, yeh, because you got a gun and a badge. Take it off, take it off and whup me den. I wanna catch you one day when you walkin' down d' street and ain't got it! We'll see who is bad and who is not." He get to talkin' dat trash and I say, "Furthermo' let me *go!*"
>
> They got bunch o' brothers off in dem police bag da's got down dirty and shitty. Den you find some brothers dat *is* off in d' police department dat dey real *nice*. Mostly dey be dirty niggers. Jus' like I told the one dat picked me up.

Significantly, almost none of the middle-class teenagers defined Tom in terms of black police. But then middle-class teenagers had experienced nowhere near the contact and harassment that South Central youths had undergone. Though some had been stopped and questioned by black officers, and a few had undergone some psychological intimidation at their hands, only a handful have ever been taken to the station, let alone jailed. Again, what is important is perceived, labeled, and defined in terms of those attributes that are most significantly associated with the person or things being identified.

Periodically, ghetto teenagers use Tom or Aunt Jemima specifically to identify middle-class blacks who emulate white behavior or reject their black heritage. Often those people are identified with those blacks living on the Hill (in or around the more affluent Baldwin Hills-View Park area of Los Angeles). One example of how blacks might reject their roots was given by a young South Central black who talked about the avoidance of vernacular usage among middle-class people: "Dem peoples dat done come from d' ghettos den got up dere, well dey think dey so-so. An' dey done got seditty, say dey don't have no bidness *usin'* dese kin'a slangs. But they black Americans jus' like we are and they was usin' 'em befo' dey got up dere. Well, why dey quit now?''

Another young woman from South Central told of how her friend had dumped her for a more affluent circle of friends. ''Another girl name Elaine, I used to run with her, but I ain't worried about her no more. Her mind is messed up. She wants money. You wouldn't term them poor, they sorta lower-middle class. She been runnin' wid dese kids from the Hill. She's been influenced by it—she wants money and power, she tol' me.''

There is reason for ghetto teenagers to have negative feelings about their middle-class counterparts. There are middle-class teenagers who are not only condescending toward ghetto blacks but want nothing to do with them. One young man talked about his reason for transferring to Hamilton out of Crenshaw High School (which is in an area serving both ghetto and middle-class teenagers): ''The atmosphere is bad there. Crenshaw is big and it's beautiful and brand new and is jus' in the wrong place. Because the farther South you get in the city, you have the larger accumulation of Negros in the city. That area [near Crenshaw] is becoming predominantly ghetto black and therefore a lotta times the kids go there, different than you. Don't wanna be around them.''

Other middle-class teenagers take offense at the values they find associated with ghetto youths. ''If you go to a party—I hate to mention this—with teenagers who have lower-class values you see all kinda things—taking drugs, lots of fights, an' things, people talkin' real loud. Like, you know, with drugs, the problem [around Los Angeles High School, located in a low-middle to-middle income, largely black neighborhood] was gettin' pretty bad, 'cause they had people writing dirty things on the walls. I don't think if they were in their right mind, they be doin' it. L.A. used to be around middle-class, and now get all kinda minorities.''

But the vast majority of middle-class teenagers are not only sympathetic toward those less fortunate than they are, but deeply angry at the social and economic system in this country that keeps blacks oppressed. In fact, the most politically active and militant young people I met came from the black middle classes. They saw themselves as fortunate in the economic sense, but some at least took little psychological or political sustenance from their economic security. They expressed guilt, self-doubt, and anger at what they saw as their privileged condition. These feelings are not only turned back on themselves but extended outward.

In fact, it was the middle-class black teenager who was hardest on black people—particularly those from the middle classes—for playing the Tom. Many young middle-class blacks were particularly upset with their parents and their parents' friends for their status-conscious and acquisitive behavior. "Like I live in View Park and I really think the people eastside are more real. They don't act like a bunch o' boojie Toms. People that live in my area are so hung up on money—who's got the swimming pool, who got the new car, how many cars your family's got, what your father does. I get the third degree when I go over to a girl's house—where I live, father's occupation, how much he earns, all that shit. It's really cold!"

This self-deprecatory stance on the part of the middle-class teen-ager is reflected in vernacular name terms that specifically disparage the black bourgeoisie, such as *boogie* and its variants, *boochie, buz-hie, bojie, Dr. Thomas, Mr. Thomas, handkerchief head, Negro.* These expressions are common coin among middle-class youths, but, in my experience, are seldom used by young ghetto blacks. Tom and its variations seem to serve the purpose.

The proliferation of self-critical vernacular name terms does not seem especially surprising—particularly in light of black conscious-ness, when middle-class blacks in particular are reassessing what it means to have made it in the white world. Some middle-class teenagers tended to romanticize ghetto life, much as romantics at other times, in other places, have romanticized the "common man." More often, young middle-class blacks realized—or knew from hard experience—that grinding poverty and the conditions surrounding it are hardly romantic. Rather, the sense of connection was with beginnings and heritage and their people's vitality and grit in the face of a long history of oppression. Though some teenagers took over the rhetoric of Black Power without its substance, many more were genuinely commited to making changes to benefit all black people. As one young political activist, involved in developing community work-training programs for unemployed and unskilled blacks, put it: "Everytime I help some of the brothers and sisters, I really help myself. We're all part of the same family, hear what I'm sayin'?"

## THE OUTSIDERS

One of the questions that inevitably came up in conversation with black teenagers was the racial backgrounds of their various friends and acquaintances. Like most people, they hung out with those who shared common interests, activities, and racial identity. Although in-creasing numbers of black teenagers were having contact with whites and other non-blacks in a variety of social settings—in Hollywood, on the Strip, at racially mixed parties, at musical events, at teen clubs, some at school—these encounters were, for the most part, transitory.

Generally, the people claimed as friends were black. This was particularly true for South Central teenagers and reflects a fact of ghetto living, namely, the absence of white residents. As one person put it, "Ain't too many white folks down here you kin be knowin'. Well, put it like this: I don't even think you could find a white kid that go to Jeff [Jefferson High School in the heart of South Central]. You might find one. I don't even think a Mexican go to Jeff. They get beat up and check out and go to other schools. Put it like this, *I* haven't seen one [white] there."

The few white or white-identified teenagers that *do* live in the ghetto are treated with varying degrees of suspicion and distrust and, sometimes, anger is vented on anyone resembling a white. One young man told the following story about another teenager who was from a racially mixed background:

> Jim, he stay cross street from me on 88th. Mother's white an' his father's black. Jim has brother name Dalton. When somebody say somethin', say, "You better be cool, 'cause tha's Jim brother." They wouldn't mess with Jimmy. But *one* time, Jim brother got beat up, so people wadn't as scared o' him as use be.
>
> So one time, me an' Jim went up to Fremont [High School]. Went into bathroom. They's shootin' dice in there and I don't have no money. I say, "C'mon Jim, le's go." So I walks out the bathroom and I thought Jim was right behind me. So I looks back, I don't see 'im. Then one my partners come out the bathroom and tell me, "Hey, Martin, they beatin' up on that white boy." I say, "Oh?" So I walks back in dere. I seen Jim on the ground, got beat up. So I pull d' dudes off o' 'im, tol' 'em to lighten up 'cause I know 'im. My brother beat 'im up—everybody beat 'im up 'cause he half white.

Being accepted in a virtually all-black environment when you are or appear to be white has to do with getting in with a set that can run interference for you. As in most peer groups, acceptance depends on demonstrating behavior and attitudes congruent with the group's. This is particularly true for someone who is perceived to be an enemy until proven otherwise. Another young man told about his friendship with a white who lived in the ghetto.

> Most my friends are black. Rafael, he Chicano dude I runs with sometime. He cool. Simpson—he my partner—white dude live over on Avalon and 80th, he accepted like one of us. The way he got in good, he tried to get wi' d' happenin's. Like he talk like one o' us—slang language. At leas' he caught on quick. He talk to brothers and sisters too. Sisters like him a lot. He got a nice personality. Since fellas see he's with some colored dudes, so he gets in good. So, if he play cool, act like one o' us, he's okay.

Aside from sporadic or limited contact with whites, young blacks have more opportunities for contact with Chicanos and Asians—especially Japanese—who live in or adjacent to the black community. While ghetto teenagers claimed more contact with Chicanos, young middle-class blacks came in touch with more Asians. This reflects a residential and economic fact of life: the majority of non-blacks who live in or adjacent to the South Central ghetto are low-income Chicanos, while in the Baldwin Hills area, a large middle-class black population lives side by side with a sizable middle-class Japanese community.

### NON-WHITES

*Chicanos.* Feeling toward Chicanos was decidedly mixed. Many from the ghetto openly distrusted them, as sneaky, prone to knife you in the back, or drop a dime on you. One black teenager told of an encounter with a Chicano at probation camp that cost him a trip to a Youth Authority facility.

> Got busted behind assault—wid my fist. Dere was dis Mexican dude, real sneaky dude, first time he kick me in the wrong spot and I hadda get 'im for dat. Dis was up at camp—Muntz [probation camp]. I was sittin' on my bed. Dis Mexican kept throwin' the ball over my bed. I say, "You throw it over dere again, I'ma keep it!" So dude pretend like he stop, den he sneak behin' me and push me into my locker. So he went over to his locker, he had a big ol' cross he was gonna hit me with. An' I hit 'im in the eye a couple times. Counselor grab me, sent me down, shoot me to Norwalk.

Others saw Chicanos as stupid or easily duped: "I stoled a dollar from dis Chicano dude when I was in jail. Dude ain't too smart. 'Cause sometime when he want to sneak some cigarettes, he wan' play friendly wid me—'cause I knowed all d' dudes that was buyin' for 'im. So I say, 'Uh huh, I'm goin' home tomorra, goin' fool him.' I said, 'Man, they bring us cigarettes tomorra.' Tomorra morning came, he say, 'You got my dollar, ain' got no cigarettes!' I say, 'Bye, sucker!' "

Still others saw Chicanos as *bato locos* (crazy dudes): they didn't act like blacks and therefore were unpredictable and not to be trusted. Finally, many made no distinction between Chicanos and whites and often characterized them in terms usually identified with white people —*grey, honky, whitey, peckerwood, paddywood.* In fact, the expression *peckerwood* was as often defined in terms of a Chicano as a white. One teenager explained this way, "Mexicans! Shit! We don' never see nobody white at our school! We see Mexicans, so I guess the brother takes it out on Mexicans."

54

A number of pejoratives for Chicanos came up in conversation. Aside from common slang terms like *Mex*, *spic*, and *wetback*, most of the pejoratives characterized Chicanos in terms of the foods associated with them. This list was extensive: *taco, taco bender, bean, beaner, bean choker, chili choker, chili bean, tostado, burrito*. These same pejoratives were often directed at other blacks when they were seen to be acting like Chicanos—or just generally when someone acted in a way the speaker didn't particularly like. "Like you as' somebody for somethin', like, 'Gimme a nickel,' 'I ain' got it.' 'You ain' nothin' but a chili choker!' In other words, you actin' like one dem damn Mexicans. Tha's a cold case! Sumpin' go down wrong, dey call d' brother 'taco'."

As far as my experience went, few pejoratives for Chicanos dealt with such "common" attributes as skin color, physical characteristics, or behavioral mannerisms. One reason Chicanos may not be elaborately stereotyped in pejorative terms is because they are not generally viewed as white—that is, as the "oppressor" or as "other"—but as "brothers under the skin." Therefore, racial differences as well as behavioral mannerisms are literally not seen, except in the very obvious case of food preference.

There was certainly evidence in the vernacular and in teenage narratives to give support to the claim that, despite put-downs, Chicanos are seen more often as same rather than other. For example, about the same number of young blacks had positive or neutral feelings about Chicanos as those who had negative responses. A majority of the teenagers I talked with counted at least one Chicano among their circle of friends and acquaintances. Some considered them as close partners and brothers.

In the vernacular, the expression *ese* (pronounced "essay")—the equivalent of "dude"—was used like *bato* to refer to a Chicano. Often, the term was embellished when one wanted to refer to a Chicano who was like a brother, either in behavior or in the sense of being a good friend. So a person would refer to the Chicano as a *cool ese, okay ese, righteous ese, together ese*. Also, the expressions *ese bato/vato/vacho* were commonly used in connection with a Chicano who was like a brother. One young man provided a profile of the *cool ese* or *ese vacho* that saw him as very much "we" and not "they":

> Tha's what you call an ese's outasight. Hangs around wid d' brothers.
> He kin get down any kinda way tha's necessary. If a brother comes
> down more or less fonky, he can *fight*, jus' like a brother. He kin git
> over jus' like a brother. He kin talk anyway a brother talks and con-
> verse just the way he has to. I's a person that has fine ol' soul!

Finally, there were terms like *Chico*, *Felipe*, and *Cholo* used in a variety of contexts not unlike the contexts in which name terms related to blacks were used. Often these expressions carried with them playful or affectionate overtones; other times they were used in an openly hostile and derisive way. As one young man explained it, "See some cool ese, say, 'Hey Chico, what it is?' But, don' be callin' no ese Cholo or Chico if you don' be knowin' d' dude, 'cause he'll righteously fire on you. Sometime, jus' be sayin' dat name if you woofin' on some ese—could be cappin' on blood too. Tell 'im, 'Hey Felipe, momma shit beans, da's how she got you, man!' "

Though Chicanos are the primary Spanish-speaking culture that blacks in South Central come into contact with—when they come into contact with Hispanic people at all—no distinction is made between, say, Puerto Ricans, Cubans, and Chicanos. Even in those neighborhoods where Cubans are the major Hispanic culture, young blacks still identify them as Chicano. Little differentiation is made between people who, on a general level, are seen as all the same. When pressed, a number of teenagers not only saw no difference between Cubans and Chicanos, but didn't realize there was a difference.

*Asians.* In general, attitudes and feelings toward Asians were less intense than toward Chicanos. In part, this is because most of the vernacular vocabulary in my study came from ghetto teenagers who had infrequent contact with Asians. With the exception of some dozen young people, none of the others from South Central claimed an Asian as a close friend or even good acquaintance. Even among middle-class blacks, the number of Asian friends was limited. At least one explanation was given by a young man who played sports with some Asians at Dorsey High. "Like they stick together—*real tight*. You don't see 'em too much hanging out with the brothers. They stay with their own kind—sorta snobby really." The stereotypic qualities attributed to Asians were smartness, clannishness, quietness, nonmilitancy, and snobbishness. Yet with the popularization of Asian martial arts through movies, magazines, and television, and teenage fascination with it, increasing numbers of black youths began to see another stereotypic trait associated with Asians. The fact that skill at martial arts conflicted with other qualities assigned to Asians is of little importance; stereotyping does not necessarily follow rational patterns. The important point is that at least some were seeing Asians as tough where they had previously seen them as weak. One teenager who had been transferred from school to school because, as he put it, "I was a hardhead," delighted in a story about a supposed encounter with some tough *buddhaheads:*

I went to Uni for three days. Got dere, didn' nobody tell who was all in d' school. An' nothin' what was happenin'. I gets up here, I looks. I say, "Wait a minute!" I don' see *no* brothers. *Now* I figure out why he sent me here! I see all dese big ol' buddhaheads, I see all dese white folks. I say, "Wait a minute, dis man's jivin' me *around*."

First day, I walk down d' hall dere was two buddahead, dey stop me and dey say, "What you doin' here *black boy?*" I say, "Wait a minute buddhaheads, you talkin' crazy, Jack." D' dude didn't know I could fight or somethin' and he jam me against d' locker. I come off d' locker like a catput', teared 'im up. His partner jus' kick back, eyes wi' open. An' when I downed him, he tol' me, "You know what you jus' did? You jus' cause you reputation, Jack, 'cause dat's suppose' be d' baddest dude in d' school." I say, "What! Dis dude ain' holdin' no air! An' he suppose' be bad? Take me to yo' leader, chump!" I'm mad now. "Dude didn' lay a han' on me, d' time he push me. You call him bad? What do he *know?*" He tol' me he suppose' know a little Karate. I say, "Ain' dis cold!"

For the most part, Asians—whether Chinese, Japanese, Thai, or Korean—are undifferentiated in teenage vernacular, as with people of Hispanic background. With the exception of pejoratives like *Chink* for Chinese, *Nip* for Japanese, and *Flip* for Filipino, name terms do not make cultural distinctions. The most common target for pejorative stereotyping is the shape of an Asian person's eyes. This is seen in the use of terms like *tight, tight eyes, slants, slant eyes, slits*. Though food-related pejoratives like *ricer* and *chopstick* are part of vernacular usage, there are no expressions that relate to skin color. At least one explanation is that prejudicial terms associated with Asians, *yellow* or *yellow skin*—terms used by low-income whites—are associated with black racial identification rather than with Asians. As one young man put it when I raised these terms with him, "Don't be callin' no buddhahead dat, call a fine-lookin' sister 'yellow.' "

By far, the most common name term for Asians was *buddhahead*. Like *dude* or *ese*, the term can take on neutral, negative, or even positive meaning depending on the context in which it is used and the attitude of the speaker toward the person being identified. As one young male explained it, "Buddhahead like it be slant. Could be a tight partner even. Depend on d' dude and where he's comin' from."

### THE MAN

Without question, the largest single body of vernacular name terms, with the exception of intraracial labels, are those for whites. Almost none of them are complimentary; most express attitudes and feelings ranging from ironic mockery to outright hatred.

There is unfortunately very little in the ghetto youth's perceived experience of the white establishment that prompts much more than neutral reactions to "the Man." From a teenage perspective, the white is seen as blatantly prejudiced—sometimes carrying that prejudice to a level of insensitivity or brutality that is both physically and psychologically humiliating. One young man I was walking with watched as a group of whites drove through the black ghetto: "Most the time, you know, in dem white cars, they look at you like you got somethin'— like some disease or we animals. I's cold man! Dem honkies righteously prejudice!" Others see whites as rip-off artists who are trying to make a fast buck in the ghetto at the blacks' expense: "Like you go into d' white man store git chu some slacks or somethin', dey be twenty dollar. Go up to Hollywood, see d' *same* thang and it be *ten* dollar, I ain't jivin'! Ain' dat somethin'!" One young woman told of her experience with the local food market: "Like you go in dere, meat ain' no good—it jus' don' *smell* right, vegetables and d' fruit they all rotten, cans all bended outa shape. Think white folks' store like dat?"

Young blacks see discrimination and insensitivity in the way they are treated in the white's institutions: "Like a lotta d' brothers over dere they was tryin' to put deir heart into d' school. Tryin' to outdo what d' white folks up dere says dey cain't do. I think the teachers was righteously tryin' to keep 'em back. 'Cause dey know dey gonna 'chieve dat by keepin' to the book and tryin' to do everythang in they power to outdo them—people in school. The school was righteously prejudice'."

Others remember back to hurtful childhood encounters with openly prejudiced teachers. "When a kid get up in the morning, unless you got somethin' under your belt, some food under your belt, you start off bad in livin'. And they go to school and it's just like teachers tryin' to pile on things in your head and you ain't worried about that, you worried about where you next meal's gonna come from. They worried about they check. Don't care whether you hungry."

Still others have watched the mass exodus of whites from neighborhoods that were "going black" and wondered at the depths of white hostility and fear that a black presence generates. "Couple years before, it was all white—because it was all white area. No 'Negros' allowed out there. And they started moving, going back farther south and going further west, moving their kids out. So, mostly, it's all black now. So, we just come to the conclusion that the whites are gonna keep moving to the Valleys, moving north and keep putting their money into police, keep gettin' the people in gonna enforce the police."

Youthful resentment and anger toward whites can build up and spill over in a variety of retaliatory ways. Sometimes it worked at the level of duping or outsmarting Whitey, playing on his fears and prejudice. One such story was told to me by a young man who sent some whites on a humbug when they came into Watts: "Sometimes, these pink boys they come down to go over dere 'n visit d' Watts Towers. They come to the liquor store and get sodas. Don't know. We send 'em *way* out! 'Cause they don' know where d' hell dey are. Tell 'em anything. They so scare' bein' here, don' know wha's happ'nin' anyway. Serve 'em right.'' Other times retribution is more physical:

One time it was this cab driver, when I'z workin' and it was rainin' one evening. So, it was pay day and three of us decided to catch a cab. So we called and it was about 4:30. Was about 5:30 'fore the cab got there. We kept callin'. So when the man came, we told him. He say, "Well, if you don't shut up, you'll hafta get out.'' We all looked. So we jus' told him where we wanted to go. He said, "Well, gimme some money first.''

By this time Brenda got pretty pissed off. I was too, but I kin'a hold mine for awhile. And so she told the driver, we wouldn't give him any money. So he say, "When I cross Crenshaw, you gonna hafta give me some money.'' We started tellin' him what it is. He just kept drivin'. Then, he stopped on some street and said he wouldn't go any further. And, he called a policeman over to the car. And the policeman said we had to give him some money because he said it was in the taxi cab's rules that if he believes that we gonna walk off from him and not pay him, that we had to pay him something. So the honky said $2. He even *offered* us $2 to get *outa* the cab! He didn't wanna take us! But we were determined to make him take us. And so, we gave him the $2.

So we hadda pick up my baby. He was gonna pull off and leave me. And Brenda told him—she's a little fat thing—"Don't you pull off!'' So he stopped, and I got in the car again. Then, he pulled around the corner and stopped at Crenshaw and Adams and there was another policeman there and we wanted to go to Crenshaw Shopping Center. Policeman told us, "Well, we'll trail you!'' Now, ain't that cold!

We took his cab number and we report him. So we waited for a hearing because it was really *sickening*, but nothing happened. So then, Brenda got her boy friend and some of his friends to call over in Beverly Hills and call for that cab and I don't know what happened. He came up there an' . . . [they beat him up?]. Yeh.

The intensity and scope of young black reaction to whites was reflected in the long list of names that characterized whites. Generally speaking, the lexicon divided whites into three categories—whites in general, Jews, and white police. Each category, when looked at separately, highlighted a different set of attributes, as well as the attitudes and feelings associated with the white man.[8]

*The White Man.* Hannerz has observed:

Just as black people are taught about the meaning of blackness by other blacks, they learn about white people and race relations within the

> ghetto community rather than in face-to-face contacts with whites. White people are being typed by black people . . . just as white people among themselves are typing black people. In both cases the vocabulary becomes a cultural storehouse for hostility, a part of the community's own information about its external affairs which is seldom contradicted by other sources. (1969, pp. 165-166)

Ghetto blacks often have little exposure to whites in their daily dealings and therefore base their responses and their vernacular characterizations on the few whites they do encounter—the police, the shopkeeper, the pawnbroker, the store manager, the social worker, the parole or probation officer. It could be said that one result of this infrequent, transitory, and often negative encounter is that the vernacular characterizing whites, though it carries strong emotional force, is not particularly descriptive of discrete white behavior or mannerisms that could lend themselves to stereotypic labeling. For example, some of the potentially neutral vernacular terms for whites such as *paddy, paddywood, the Man,* or *Charlie* carry little in the way of stereotyped qualities. They derive their impact from the historical and contemporary contexts in which they are used. Even more graphic and derogatory labels, *cracker, peckerwood, pecker, devil, beast, honky beast, pig, swine, swine-eater,* and the *whips,* while characterizing whites as animal-like, brutal, or evil, do not "picture" whites very extensively. The single most descriptive attribute young blacks focus on in their labeling of whites is color—or the lack of it—such as *whitey, gray, gray boy, pinks, pink boys, white eyes, chalk, lily, pale face, rabbit,* and *red neck.* This focus on a single attribute might suggest to some the limited nature of black stereotypes of whites. However, viewed from another perspective, it could also be said that young blacks, particularly ghetto blacks, have very accurately and clearly "seen" whites for what they are perceived to be in the black community. They are evil (*devil, yacoo*), they are bestial (*beast, pig, swine*), they wield oppressive powers (*whips*), and above all they are people of no color, no soul. Or, put another way, they are people whose lack of color is highly suspect and certainly to be noted in any definition of these outsiders. David Heise (1966) has noted that people select words whose connotation are in line with their personal feelings toward the subject or object being described. In so doing, people "avoid dissonance, by using only those words which are congruent with their personal experience" (p. 230). Certainly the experience of young blacks, whether limited or not, is vividly reflected in the vernacular used to describe whites. Though whites may not like the way they are seen by these young people, though they may argue that the picture is incomplete or not descriptive, it is the picture, nonetheless, that the majority of black teenagers most often painted.

It should again be said that stereotypes in general, and pejoratives in particular, characterize people in terms of what most often touches a group's real or imagined fears about others. Though stereotypes are incomplete pictures, they nonetheless illuminate very real psychological reactions. In the case of ghetto experiences and perceptions, the stereotype too often gets reinforced through real events and actions that do little to allay suspicious and hostile responses. As one young woman succinctly put it, "The Man ain't done shit fo' me! Sittin' up dere in his fancy office talkin' shit 'bout helpin' black folks. What he done? Talk ain't got me no job, don't pay no rent. White man school ain't gettin' me no real education. He jus' righteously talkin' out d' side of his neck!"

*Jews and Antisemitism.* If whites in general are seen in unfavorable terms, the Jew is sometimes singled out for special negative attention. In a number of stories told about white people, special note was made of whether or not a person was taken to be Jewish. For example, one young woman in elaborating on what it meant to *shoot a dud* said: "He's sayin' somethin' he ain' got no business sayin'. D' little ol' Jew boy in d' office try to talk so hip and I jus' looks at him—so counterfeit. Yeh, he's phony. I cain't even hold a conversation wid 'im, cause everything I say, he don' even know what I'm talkin' about."

A number of vernacular terms singled out Jews as the white person being identified—none of them were particularly flattering. *Goldberg* and *Goldstein* were more or less neutral labels of identification depending on the context in which they were used. Other labels, *slick-em-plenty*, *fast-talkin' Charlie*, *three balls*, and *Mr. Money*, characterized the Jew—particularly the Jewish merchant—as someone who fast-talked ghetto residents out of their money or their possessions or both (such as the pawnbroker, with the three balls above the shop identifying the business); and who themselves had "long money," with the implication that they had made it from blacks. For example, one teenager defined "fast-talkin' Charlie" as "a slicker, one o' dem ol' fast-talkers. Someone who's slick. Like Jews, you call 'em dat, 'cause dey *are* fast talkin'. When you come in d' store, dey get to talkin', be tryin' to make dat bidness." Furthermore, Jews are associated with certain stereotypic facial features (as they are elsewhere), such as large noses. So there are a number of vernacular terms that characterize apparent Jews as *hook, hookface, hooknose.* I say apparent Jews because whites who display characteristics associated with what is seen as Jewish behavior or looks are often labeled as such. I heard a variety of non-Jewish people, such as Italians, Armenians, and Greeks, being called by these terms because they showed stereotypic Jewish features or they behaved in some manner associated with Jews. On the other hand, if and when it came up in conversation that I was Jewish, young blacks were generally surprised. I didn't fit their stereotype. One young woman summed up the kind of response I often got when she told me, "*You* is a Jew? Ain' you Mexican? You Jew—don't look it, sure don't act it."

Whether someone labeled as Jewish is actually Jewish or not isn't as significant as the fact that Jews, rather than Catholics or Greeks or Italians, are singled out of the seemingly amorphous white mass for some special consideration. In Los Angeles, at least, one explanation has to do directly with patterns of residential movement. Often the white residents that blacks see leaving the neighborhood when they move in (as well as those who stay) are Jews. Having lived in Los Angeles most of my life, I have witnessed and been part of both the leaving and the staying. A friend of mine who was looking into the effects of migration on black linguistic behavior once wryly commented on residential movement patterns in Los Angeles: "Yeh, you [Jews] move out and we [blacks] move in. All these 'for sale' signs come out, you *know* the 'niggas' movin' in!" Many of the black neighborhoods in Los Angeles were once predominantly Jewish. And whether people moved or not, many local Jewish merchants continued to live, work, and own property in or around the neighborhood and newly developing black community. Therefore, many of the whites that blacks continued to have any contact with (particularly in the ghetto) were, in fact, Jewish.

Whether the treatment blacks experienced at the hands of Jewish landlords, merchants, or residents is negative is not the issue in this instance. What seems more at issue is their visibility—they were around, they were identifiable, and they were subject to vernacular labeling as a group apart from other whites. That this characterization could have been anything but uncomplimentary was unlikely, given the resentment that the white's economic pressure and power generate in the ghetto. Whatever the Jewish merchant was, he was white, suspect, and a visible focal point for specific pejorative attack.

It is an interesting side note that virtually none of the vernacular collected over the years for this book is Yiddish or reflects Yiddish influence, with the tenuous exception of the vernacular terms assigned to Jews, even though Yiddish has left a significant mark on general American slang. It could be happenstance; it could be circumstance. However visible Jews as a group might have been or continue to be to young blacks, there is little of the kind of sustained or informal communication that would allow for the exchange of vernacular. It could also reflect the age of the population being addressed. Aside from cursory contacts with Jewish storekeepers, or even more sustained interaction with a variety of employment counselors, social workers, or parole officers—a significant number of whom were Jewish—the young ghetto resident is seldom in earshot of informal Jewish dialog, where Yiddish expressions might be picked up. For example, almost none of those I encountered knew the Yiddish pejorative *shvartzer* (a black person), although a number of older black people I knew who had worked as domestics in Jewish households or had been otherwise employed by Jews knew this term and scores of other Yiddish words.

*The Police.* The largest body of white name terms—particularly pejorative terms—are reserved for the police.[9] And it is not difficult to see why, for the picture was still a grim one at the time I left in the mid-70s. There was a popular expression among ghetto teenagers that gave some hint of the polarized relation between the police and the youthful black community: "If it ain't cuz, it's fuzz" (if it ain't another black, it's the police—and beware). The level of tension that existed between the police and young blacks was intense, highly charged, and ongoing. Like the proverbial iceberg, the periodic clashes between police and youth that made the evening news was only the tip of a massive body of barely submerged grievances, suspicions, fears, accusations, and counteraccusations. The Watts uprising of 1965 gave the world some idea of the explosive force contained under the surface tension between police and young blacks. It was, after all, an altercation between the police and a youth named Marquette Frye that escalated into urban warfare in South Central Los Angeles that summer.

In 1976, over ten years later, the siege still continued despite police relations programs and so-called youth opportunities. Though there were ebbs and flows, the tension was always there and each side periodically pointed accusing fingers at the other. From a teenage point of view, the police epitomized all that was oppressive in white society. The stories they told and the incidents I witnessed were not pretty. But a few are important to relate in order to give some idea of the constant uneasiness experienced by ghetto teenagers who moved in an environment that was always marked by potentially dangerous encounters with the police.

> They stop me an' dis other dude. We walkin' goin' by dis lady house. Dis lady she call the police on some other dude 'cause he was breakin' out her house, her windows in her house. So, dude say, "Police!" We turned around like fools and start walkin' d' other way. Police hop in they car, went around and stopped us. Dis other one, he's short'n I am. Dis fat policeman reached his han' under [his friend's] pants and started squeezin' 'em, made 'im cry an' hit 'im. Made me kin'a nervous. I started shakin', I thought he's gonna do me d' same way for nottin'.
>
> Cain't mess around with 77 [77th precinct in the heart of South Central]. Yeh, wid dat assault wid a deadly weapon, when they took us down, they took us off in the back room. We was mad! We was

> tryin' to talk to 'em on the way down. Say, "Shut up!" When we got down dere, we got the handcuffs on, they come in dere and just get to jumpin' on us. They had all of 'em standin' at the door, watchin' for the sergeant while d' two dat arrested us jump on us. All the rest of 'em standin' at d' door lookin' fo' d' sergeant.

Sometimes, the stories are humorous, even though the realities are not.

> Time I got busted for, I didn't have no part of. Dis is at Fremont [High School]. Everybody goes over to d' cafe. Tha's right nex' to Fremont on d' corner. People go dere, they talk to d' young ladies an' eat over dere. Low riders go over dere, bounce dey lift couple times and dey jus' be standin' roun' talkin'. So d' cats on the side the cafe dey be over dere shootin' dice, tryin' to make some quick bucks. So, police dey stage a raid dere, swoop. An' I had order a hamburger, I got picked up! They took me to 77th. Dey kep' me dere three hours. Den, they cut me loose. I miss out on my hamburger!

At the same time that young people talked about the psychological and physical coercion they experienced at the hands of the police, they also talked of the hostile, very abusive responses that the presence and implied power of the police generated among ghetto residents. Some of this anger was released in the form of cop baiting. I heard the following exchange between two black teenagers who had been stopped by two white police officers for a faulty tail light. Question: "What you have for dinner, bro'?" Answer: "Swine, you know, oink, oink, oink!" The two broke into gales of laughter while an angry officer silently wrote out a ticket.

One young man who had experienced particularly rough treatment at the hands of the police (two patrol officers broke his left arm and fractured two ribs) explained why he felt the police became so violent. "Like people down here dey righteously *hate* d' pigs! Make it hard on 'em, throw rocks an' bottles, call 'em all kin'a name—'pig,' 'swine,' and they turn mean. People call 'em names and make 'em mad, so they gits to callin' name back. Callin' you 'boy' and 'nigger.' Tryin' to make you mad. Dey want you to say somethin', den dey jam you. Den the people git mad, shoot on 'em all ways."

So fear and suspicion breed retaliation and still more oppression —and the vicious circle remains unbroken. The situation is further exacerbated when police vent their feelings of frustration through "overzealous" reactions to what is seen as suspicious behavior. As one officer put it, "When you've worked down here [77th precinct] long enough, everything looks suspicious." Again and again teenagers accused of some illegal activity told stories of being arrested, going to

court, and having the charges dismissed for insufficient or contradictory evidence because the arresting officer had been too eager for a
"collar." One young man who claimed to have been "busted on a
hombug" told the following story:

> I got busted just dis last time for posession. Police puts it on me. On the
> serious! They tried to bust me for some credit cards, but the guy say he
> wadn't gon' press no charges. So he gon' come round and say, "Well, if
> we ain't gon' git you fo' possession of stolen property, we gon' get you
> for possession of marijuana" and showed me this joint.
>
> He had wrote dis report, the arrest report different. When he got
> up on the stand, start blowin', *he* handcuffed me, but his pa'tner hand-
> cuffed me in his report. In the report, he say dat he didn't search me,
> den when he got up dere he say he searched me. An' d' judge asks his
> what did he arrest me fo'? He say he arrest me for possession of stolen
> property. The judge say, "You can't arrest nobody for possession, but
> receivin' stolen property." So the judge just dismissed it.

Another boasted about outwitting the police (a story that points
up the perpetual combativeness that fuels so many police-teenage encounters):

> I'z taken to jail for narcotics, cut loose and had d' case dropped. Look
> in d' trunk, they thought they had a good ol' thang. [How did you beat
> it?] Easy. Ain't no damn police officer s'pose stop me or get to inter-
> coursin' wid me in the *day* time sayin' that I had to have my *lights* on! It
> was durin' the summer time—dat ol' messed up time. I's about six
> o'clock. It ain't hardly dark yet. He put the time down! I looks. Ain't
> he stupid sonavabitch! This is what I call an ignorant *fool*—he went
> through illegal search and seizure. I shot the code to him—"illegal
> search and seizure!" Plus, I don' have no problem, 'cause he stop me at
> *that time of day!* And they looked at that police, and they looked at me
> and they say, "We gotta talk to *you.* Case dismissed!" I said, "Thank
> you!" An' I looked over dere at d' officers, and I clicked my heels
> together and I say, "FOOL!" That was it.

So a battle of wits as well as a test of wills characterize many
youthful encounters with the police. Because of the highly charged
relationship between police and teenagers, battles are not only joined
verbally, but literally. A number of teenagers get arrested for assault
on an officer—with a chain, a bumper jack, fists—after some incident
has rapidly escalated from verbal to physical confrontation. One incident that happened while I was at Will Rogers Park in Watts was a
tragic example of how pent-up anger and hatred, years of mutual distrust and impoverished communication, inflamed a situation and
brought it to the point of open warfare:

Police officer beat up my sister east side—Will Rogers Park. Didn't you hear dem shots? Dat was me doin' d' shootin'—me an' d' police on other side d' park. I shot one in d' leg, the other one in d' shoulder.

'Cause, my sister she *was* loaded, she was asleep on d' park bench. The police come up dere and grabbed her and tried to wake her up. An' I seem 'em. She had jumped up and he fired. Hit her right dere in d' nose and busted it! I say, "What?" I ran over dere and grabbed 'im. He turned around and rrrrrrrrr rrrrrrrrr. When he hit d' dust jus' took his little gun. When I turn around d' police he pull his pump out, when I shot 'im. I say, "You gon' shoot me—god *damn!*"

Dis dude come behind me an' he was runnin' 'cause he seen the police—what you call a "citizen"—he runs by me an' hits me some kin'a way from behind, like bump me. When I spun around, dis police had dropped d' bench on me. I say, "What?" We get rasslin'. I looks up and seen a club. Oh-oh! BOOP! Next thing I know, I was bein' drug off to jail.

Such situations are the tragic stuff that riots and urban warfare are made of. And few whites have a grasp of the complex and potent forces that fuel the encounters. One young man summed it up: "Ain' nothin' happ'nin' down here. Watts riot didn't really change nothin'. All dat poverty money what got spent, never got to d' people. Still cain't get a job, polices ever'time on yo' case. People just don't have no hope. Next time d' riot ain' gon' just stay down here. It's a whole bunch o' white folks gon' know 'bout what's happ'nin' up dere in Hollywood and Beverly Hills." This is the voice of 1976, not 1965, speaking.

Against this backdrop a vast police-related vocabulary has developed and been used. Terms range from the more or less neutral designations like *fuzz* (said to derive from the expression *the man with the fuzzy balls*, the man in power), *the bust, the heat*; through proper names like *Big John, Peter Jay, Charlie Irvine*; to derisive pejoratives like *pig, swine, the hog, gray dog*. The characterization of the police is elaborate and connotes such perceived attributes as brutality (*billy* for billy club, *mallet, whup-a-child*), fascistic exercise of power (*gestaps, gestapos, goon squad*), typocritical morality (*divine right, deputy do-right, do-right, Johnny-be-good*), and corruption (*union wage*).

In addition to their perceived behavior, the police are characterized in terms of the uniforms and the colors that mark them as the legal arm of the establishment (*blue coats, blue boys, little boy blue*) as well as in relation to the vehicles and flashing lights that identify their continuous presence in the lives of blacks (*black and white, salt and pepper, three eyes, three-bullet-Joey*, and *blinker* for helicopter). Characteristic of the police-related lexicon is an ironic, if sometimes grim, humor that is embodied in names like *J. Edgar, Junior Walker and the All Stars, Uncle Nab, nail 'em and jail 'em, Sherlock Holmes,* and other expressions like *pig heaven* (police station) or *Sam and Dave* (partners in a patrol car).

Finally, all police are not seen as the same. Though there are a number of terms that are used to describe cops in general, there is also a "specialty" vocabulary that characterizes police in terms of their assignments as well as in terms of the places they patrol. So you find expressions like *freeway Freddy* for highway patrol; *Watts rat patrol* for local street patrols; *Mr. Hombug* for campus security police; *mod squad* for young undercover officers on the streets or on campuses; *metros* for the metropolitan police; *narcs* for narcotics officers; *Mr. Sin* for vice cops; and *rollers* for detectives.

These, then, are some of the vernacular labels used to describe and characterize whites in general, Jews and police in particular. Most are derogatory, some are neutral, virtually none is complimentary. Vernacular vocabulary seldom elevates, and certainly black teenage vernacular does not elevate or affirm the perceived enemy. One young man provided an apt summary for this whole, far-reaching discussion of name terms when he said: "Ain't but two kinda people in d' world here—dem dat do you and dem dat don't. You call 'em like you see 'em."

# 3. do unto others before they do you

## forms of manipulation

ONE EVENING a young black woman friend and I got together for some wine and conversation. We moved back and forth across a whole range of topics—from sex, to the latest dances, to the people we knew in common, to the qualities of interpersonal relations. We got into a particularly long rap about how people deal with each other. It was a lively, at times heated, discussion. Finally Cynthia said to me,

> Girl, lemme run it down to you. Ain' nothin' happ'nin' 'cept a whole lotta frontin' and gamin' goin' on down here [in South Central]. The brothers—and d' sisters too—they be tryin' to keep on top, get over any way dey kin. Dey do you in a minute!—love wise, fightin' wise—or else jus' blow on you hard and heavy, fuck wi'chu mind. Gots to have your program together else some nigger gon' righteously do you. Like the Golden Rule say, "Do onto others like they do you" else "Do onto others *before* they do you"—da's my own version. Bertha [Cynthia's sister] she got her own self sayin'—"Do onto others, den split!"
> Preacher don' be sayin' non o' *dat* shit in church, but i's for *real* girl!

To some, Cynthia's statement may seem uncompromising and stark, but it voices the sentiment of many of the black teenagers I met —particularly those from the ghetto, namely, that the world can be a cold, indifferent, often unfair place. Life is hard and relationships uncertain. To make it, a person needs to keep on top of the game and that often means doing battle with others in a variety of ways—not all the time, not with all people, sometimes playfully, other times not.

The sense of "doing battle" is an integral part of the world view of many black youths. At odds with a white majority that daily reminds teenagers of their second-class citizenship and their tenth-rate economic opportunities, it is not surprising that there "emerges a view of life in which contest or coercion is expected in any interpersonal encounter" (Abrahams, 1963, p. 16). "Consequently, life is seen as a constant hustle, and the one who does best is the one who manipulates most and is manipulated least'' (p. 19). "Do unto others before they do you'' is the name of the game. And game it is, in many instances. Manipulation or coercive exchange is not by definition or circumstance hostile or antagonistic—though it is that too. Often, like a game, it is a battle of wills and of wits in which the contestants creatively vie for center stage, take space, and often invade the space of others. Indeed, the vernacular expressions to *game someone* or to *run a game on someone*—to outwit, outsmart, or outdo another—convey the sense of contest and the power plays implicit in much teenage behavior.

The vernacular lexicon reflects the extent to which manipulative behavior informs and controls teenage interactions. Fully a fourth of the vernacular expressions transcribed from conversations and interviews with young blacks describe or characterize some form of manipulative or coercive activity. As we will see, the fabric and texture of manipulative behavior are most diverse and reflect the many levels on which personal exchange takes place.

## POWER AND SOCIAL CONTROL

The concept of power is central to the discussion of teenage interpersonal behavior. To understand the forms that manipulative, competitive or aggressive behavior take requires an understanding of the power options open to the young people I met.

The word "power" has many semantic readings; it depends on who is defining it and in what context. In broad terms, it is the ability to do, to act, to produce. In interpersonal terms, it is the ability to assert control or direction over others. On an international level, it often refers to one nation's influence or domination over another. In a capitalistic structure, power is often equated with controlling the how and what of production—and reaping the financial harvest that results from such production. So power is often money and by extension what money can buy. One of the most significant indicators of one's purchasing power in a capitalistic society is the acquisition and control of property.

But one needn't own property to control it—to stake a claim on it. Humans are territorial animals, as Edward Hall (1969), Konrad Lorenz (1966), Robert Ardrey (1966), and others have shown us. We may lay claim to an area and defend it against intruders, whether or not we legally own it. An acquaintance told me that the regulars in his laundromat complained to him about newcomers who came in and were careless about keeping the place clean. A few regulars had even reprimanded the uninitiated. Psychologically, the regulars saw the laundromat as their private space, claimed by virtue of their regular use. They resented trespassers. Gangs, for one, stake out and claim property they don't own. But it is a moot point, because they control and exert power over the territory—not through the right of purchase, but through the force of appropriation and convention.

Power can also be translated into interpersonal terms—one's control over other people, their physical well-being as well as their psychological and emotional states. In its more benign forms, personal power runs the gamut from the parent's power to ease the child's physical or emotional hurt to the government's power to dispense health and welfare assistance. In its darker forms, it means psychological and physical torture, brainwashing, or purposeful deprivation of life-sustaining supports (food, shelter, clothing, tools). In this sense, power is not only what you have or claim, but how you behave. In many cases, personal power is much more potent than the power gained through purchase or appropriation because it can be more immediately meted out and experienced. A "no trespassing" sign is less immediately experienced as a threat (as an assertion of power) than a man with a rifle ordering you off the property. Of course there is often an intimate relation between personal and proprietary power. As the example suggests, one may protect his or her acquisitions through personal coercion or intimidation.

Power can also mean control over oneself. Expressions like will-power, self-control, self-help, pulling yourself up by your bootstraps, all refer to intrapersonal power. Psychotherapy, meditation, and the array of "anonymous" organizations (Alcoholics Anonymous, Eaters Anonymous, Smokers Anonymous) all acknowledge and reinforce the power of the self over the self. In a less obvious way, power over oneself implies control over the body as well as the mind. This not only means psychological self-control and discipline of the body, as reflected in the adage "mind over body," but also the more far-reaching political and social power to control the fate of one's body. Antisterilization laws and the legalization of abortion are legal expressions of oppressed people's presumed rights to the health, welfare, and disposition of their own bodies.

So power can be read in a number of ways—it is having money and what money can buy; it is claiming control over territory, whether owned or appropriated; it is wielding personal control and influence over others; and it is exerting and maintaining control over oneself. Though there are certainly other interpretations of power, the ones I have cited figure importantly in the world view and daily experiences of the young blacks I encountered. And it is the particular and concrete ways in which these forms of power get played out that shed light on teenage interaction.

## TERRITORIAL POWER AND SOCIAL CONTROL

### GEOGRAPHY

In general, black teenagers are very conscious of geographical boundaries. On the broadest territorial level, youths from different parts of the country may challenge one another about which city, state, or region is the "baddest." The following narrative is both funny in itself and indicative of the kind of regional rivalry that gets bandied back and forth. The exchange took place at a Job Corps site.

> Georgia boy they think they *bad*, bad. Ain' shit. Talk funny too, slow.
> Don't be usin' the same words, seems like. Ever'body go to Job Corps,
> they say, who don't get along the most. Georgia boy and L.A. They be
> braggin' just too much. Hear Georgia this and Georgia dat—way cross,
> Georgia. Thought the cat was jokin'. I say, "Where yo' from?" "Way
> cross, Georgia." I say, "You makin' fun o' me, man?" He say, "No,
> man." I say, "What's way across Georgia?" I thought was cross
> Georgia, someway. He say, "No, man, tha's name of the city—Way-
> cross! It's bad!"

On a local level, divisions between parts of town are made. For example, the South Central black community, which extends over 56 square miles, is not perceived as one continuous, undifferentiated area, but is talked about in terms of the east side and the west side. And young people describing the respective parts of town have very definite opinions about how they differ. A sampling of responses to my question about how the east side and the west side differ gives the reader some idea of the diversity of feelings surrounding geography.

> *On Rowdiness:* On d' east side, you have to use a stronger philosophy
> . . . you have to really be in the bag. East side kin'a rowdy. I's rowdy.
> You go on the west side i's quieter, you have a good time. Gonna be a
> clown in there [east side] who wanna start sumpin'. They like cowboys.
> Have shotguns, shootin' each other. Don' like eas' si'—cutthroats. Like
> on east side I had to do some fightin' over dere, i's pretty rough. West

side, a brother try to talk his way out a fight, but on the east side talkin'
ain' *nothin'*. It's not safe to walk late at night, you know, you take a
chance of gettin' jammed anytime. Da's what ruined me—the east side
here. Even on the west side, you know, there are some places, but I feel
more safer over here.

*Rejoinder 1:* West side may have better facilities, but they young
people are *just* as rowdy as on the east side. I was from the east side—
gangs in Watts. Sick of gangs in Watts, and I'ma go west side. Go to the
west side, they fightin', they tearin' up everything, low-ridin', whores.
You know, I thought the environment gonna be different, but no. You
can go on the west side, in the 50s, used to be pretty rough where I used
to live, 'cause Gladiators [a gang] over there. You can't say east side is
all rough 'cause it's not.

*On Environment:* Better houses on west and upkeep better. Houses
without windows, grass taller den you are. East side you get much more
the feeling of the slums. West side, they keep it kinda clean over here.
No trash. Buildings stay kin'a clean and painted. It's slums [east side]—
dirty, it's filthy. The housing on the east side—shit! All dem houses no
good. People live in houses that should've been tore down before my
mother's time! East side, shit! They got liquor sto' jus' about on ever'
other corner. Dudes all over on d' streets 'cause they can't work and
ain't got no place to go, so they jus' stand on d' streets. People round
east side jus' don' have theyselves together.

*Rejoinder 2:* It's all accordin' to what neighborhood you in. I
know people from church got beautiful homes on d' east side. Housin'
not too much different, 'cept some places, west side, have smaller little
spot run down. Back in other side of Main they say is cleaner [on the
east side]. But I still don't see the difference is dey got longer streets and
bigger, better houses. A lot east side people have better than people in
the "Jungles" [west side housing complex].

Though the lower-income east side is generally seen by both east
side and west side residents as less desirable for the reasons mentioned, there is a definite sense of territoriality that divides residents
and asserts itself when "push come to shove"—when people from the
"other side" are seen as intruding upon one's space. As one young
man put it, "East side don't like west side and west side don't like east
side. Dudes come out dis district [to east side] wanna get down wi'
dem. You go out dere in dat district, one word say to dem, everybody
go down—east side against west. People jump each other if dey mess
around too much. Den dey think twice fo' dey come over again."

This sense of claimed territory ("This is my part of town, and you
better act right or suffer the consequences") is most apparent at small
gatherings, dances, record hops, and parties where people know who's
from their part of town and who isn't. Often a seemingly minor clash
can escalate into a fight, such as the incident an acquaintance related
to me when I asked him where he'd been the last few days:

Woman! I was cut by some nigger from J.D. [Jordan Downs Housing project on the east side]. Me an' my partners fell by dis party over dere. Some nice lookin' young ladies. Gits to dancin' wi' dis sister. Dis dude come over start jammin' me 'bout dancin' wid his ol' lady. I tol' 'im, "Well shine it on." Got belligerent, wanted to thump. Talkin' shit 'bout he gon' send me back my own side o' town. So, I jus' fired on 'im. Then, his boys got me—he had all his boys wid 'im. I was tellin' my man to help me. Guess he split. Nex' thang I knew, I got crowned. I got 35 lousy stitches off dat mother!

The sense of territoriality that asserts itself when east-sider meets west-sider is as much a state of mind as a fact of geography. In reality, when I asked teenagers which street or boulevard divided the east side from the west side they responded with a whole array of streets—from Main, to Broadway, to Central, to Vermont, to Western—a distance that covers a mile or so. The fact that one particular thoroughfare was not agreed upon is actually unimportant. What is of real significance is the proprietary feelings expressed by young residents toward recognized or perceived outsiders. In an environment where young people are often wary of others within their own territory, newcomers are definitely suspect—and responses to them are like those expressed by the laudromat habituees. In fact, new faces generally meet with suspicion, if not outright hostility, especially when they are out-of-towners. "When dudes come out here, dey think they know everything. Never make it. They come out callin' theyselves—'jus' call me New York.' Nothin'. People don' dig that shit. Get jacked up behind dat front." The same is true for outsiders from a cross-town black community like Venice (about ten miles away). "I don' stay down in Watts very long. Me an' my partner we ride down d' street, we get some hard looks. Like from a different place—Venice 'specially. Else go to parties, go up to d' door, you say, 'I'm from Venice,' dey jack you up." Territorial feelings about Venice are reciprocated when I talked to young blacks who live there. I asked one young man if his friends from Watts visit him. "No, Venice too rowdy—'Ghost Town' and 'Dodge City.' I had a friend come down here, went to a party. He got jumped on. When firs' move here, it was worse den when I went to jail. I had seven fights in one week."

Implicit in these responses to outsiders is a sense of control and power that comes from being on one's home ground: "I say whether you can enter or you can't, so you better get straight or else." As one person put it, "No punk from someplace else gonna come over here, tell me what's happenin'. Tell *him* what it is! He be in *my* territory now. Run it down to him!"

For young people who have virtually no property rights, territorial power plays are important sources of control and direction over one's immediate environment. There are also many other ways territoriality gets played out in teenage interaction.

GANGS

*The Streets.* If east-west boundary lines are sometimes ambiguous, and the sense of territoriality seems less a matter of strict geography than a state of mind, the same is not true for gangs and their claim on territory. To understand what territory means to gangs is, in large part, to understand what "the streets" mean to the young blacks I met.

For most middle-class whites, streets are passageways: you traverse them to get from one place to another. The fact that mainstreamers seldom talk about streets in a concrete or particularized way —the streets—suggests that they generally are seen as neutral, unclaimed throughways.[1]

For young blacks, especially ghetto youths, the streets have particular importance. In a setting where family life extends beyond the home into the streets,[2] the streets become centers of activity, the place where things happen. Yet the streets are not equated with the household. As one teenager put it, "The streets is any place 'cept home, church or school." What he is suggesting, and what is apparent from firsthand experience, is that the streets are special, a kind of domain that allows a young person a range of activity and movement not directly subject to adult or establishment authority or control.

For many youths the streets are their home (sometimes literally) where the major part of their life is played out, where they seek out comrades, where they prove themselves in personal interaction, where they test the skills and maneuvers necessary to getting on in life. It is the training ground for survival and provides a hard and practical education.

> But when things got tough, only one way to get it [money] and tha's in the streets—hustlin'. [Stealing?] Not my bag. Too much risk for too little. You can rip off a leather piece and get the same time as you can get for rippin' off a car. So, if you gonna hustle, do it right. Mostly, my hustle be women. A lotta girls turn out earlier than boys. She [one of the young prostitutes he had working for him] was out on the corner ever' night by the time she was thirteen, twelve.

More than one teenager defined the vernacular expression to *school someone* in terms of educating one in the ways of the streets. One young man talked about the "course" in psychology a knowledge of the streets had given him.

> Don't need no school, no college education to learn psychology. I learn about people on the streets. Three or fo' categories [of people]—that's

all we ever used: ones who were on top and who could make it; the ones who you made it *by;* and the one who *could* make it and jus' didn't wanna; and the ones who were jus' half-steppin'. Those were the only categories you use to 'valuate people by.

Indeed the expressions homeboy or homegirl, when used in a pejorative sense, often refer to someone who sticks close to home (close to his or her mother) and has little feel for life on the streets—someone who is "unschooled."

> I can't *stand* an educated fool. Where he can tell you *anything* about a book, but when it comes to life and out on the street, he don' know shit! He's dumb to the facts. He sneak in wid d' crowd and den the crowd asks him something, he freeze up. I don' believe in coverin' up fo' no educated fool. Like I know you hafta have education to get over, but if you can't confront with the world outside, you can't say you schooled. Later on fo' it. They really don' know what they are and somebody confront them, blow 'em away.

Because the streets are such a vital and integral part of much teen-age life, they are not seen merely as passageways or neutral spaces. For young blacks, many of whom spend little time in the home, who seek and sometimes get little in the way of ego-gratification or stimulation there, who have minimal possessions of their own, the streets become "real property" in both senses. And claims are made out there—sometimes the predominantly psychological proprietorship reflected in east-west confrontation; sometimes the more literal claims made by organized groups such as gangs.

*Gang Territory and Power.* One young man, T.J., spent some time explaining to me the nature of gangs and the ways they assert control:

> See, there's all kin'a li'l ol' groups on d' streets. Like you have yo' little clique—dey yo' tight partners—dey like d' set you get down with, get high, thump, you be together in d' neighborhood. Gots yo' so-called gangs—jus' make 'em up. Like we call ourselves The Magnificent Seven! Seven people all we had. It was a gang to me. Like a hangout at d' taco stand over near Broadway. Dat be our base. Like our territory around it, nobody mess wid us. They knew we had a hellified thang goin'! Den you got yo' righteous hope-to-die gangs—Parks, Outlaws, Businessmen, a few buildin' up now—Brim Boys. East side got Pueblos. Got they own little territory. You cross d' line, dey jam you!

As the narrative suggests, groups claim actual territory—from claims made on the neighborhood to the taco stand and its surroundings, to the larger geographical hunks appropriated by the more formal gang. The gang level of proprietorship is probably the most visible, and because of its scope it can be the most powerful in influencing and controlling behavior.

Gangs are generally more numerous in Los Angeles than in eastern cities. The sheer space available for appropriation supports numbers. Of course not all gangs are equally powerful in terms of size, organization, or the areas they control. Some, like the Huns, the Barbarians, the Decons, the Greeks, the Fellas, and Fleshtown have, at various times, reigned in some part of Watts. Others, like the old time Gladiators and the Businessmen and the more contemporary Avenues, Parks, Brims, Pirus, and Crips exert their influence over large areas. In the early 70s, the Avenues, for example, were said to control widespread neighborhoods through key members who live in each. One Avenue described the organization. "Like Dawson, he's the head. Then, he's got a lotta partners like Coyote, Tonga, Davey Boy and dey jus' live in different parts of the neighborhood. They kin'a far distant so they can get a bunch o' cats. Control dis part where each other stay so dey kin go a lotta places." Others, like the Crips who have both east side and west side constituents, cover a particularly wide range of territory.

Though various gangs have temporary or longstanding alliances with each other against other gangs (often in terms of east side and west side divisions) there is a strong sense of competition. Jockeying for power asserts itself when gang members meet.

> I jus' stopped goin' [to gang functions]. I jus' wanted to gas someplace else. I cut it loose when I went to jail. I got out, I jus' say, "Wow this ain't my thang!" I's like a competition. I got into a terrible thump. Like we'll go to a party, some dude'll holler out—tha's why I don' like 'em no more—some dude get to dancin', singin' to a record makin' his own words, den holler out—"Blood Alley!" Some dude holler out, "We're Gladiators!" Next thang you know, "We d' bes'!" All o' sudden, "Who say dat?" Nex' thang, they thumpin'.

Both personal and gang tensions and rivalries that are just below the surface of sociability are apt to ignite in compacted or intimate social spaces, say at parties. Then the personal affront gets translated in territorial terms. "Most the time we have a fight, be at a party. One time, this other dude was dancin' and I accidently step on his feet. And, so he say, 'Man, watch it!' I say, '*You* watch it!—punk!' So he say, 'Where you from?' I say, 'I from Watts.' He say, 'I from Slauson'—POP!"

In such surroundings gang members carry their territory with them, asserting territoriality and vying for power, whether within neutral or "occupied" spaces. At other times, the spaces are definitely not neutral, and teenagers are well aware of the potential danger implicit in challenging members on their own turf, however "cold" the provocation—that is, unless you are well represented and can call up reserves. As one young woman pointed out:

> Like I'z at dis party over in Gladiator territory. So dis Gladiator girl—
> they dancin' like dey owned d' floor—so we doin' the cha-cha and I accidently stepped on dis young lady's feet. I mean, the floor's crowded.
> Well, who *knows*. So I say, I'm sorry. She rolled her eyes at me. Den I
> hear later, "Dat bitch over dere stepped on my feet—*dere!* Dat heifer
> do it again, I'ma kick her ass!" So I'm type person don' like be taken
> on a dare. But it don' make no sense for me go up dere, stomp dat
> heifer's feet one mo' time, you know?
>
> I got fo' brothers here—all my brothers is with me, 'cept for d'
> preacher. But I say, "Well, dis is d' Gladiator territory—I hear they
> pretty bad." I say, "My brothers cain't whup all dese niggers in here, so
> I guess I better shine it on." So I didn't say nothin' cold—but if she
> over in *my* territory, I swear to God, I would've went up dere and say,
> "Bitch, you talkin' 'bout me? 'Cause if you is I'ma whup yo' black
> ass!"

As this story points out, physical confrontation is not the only way territorial power is asserted; the intimidation experienced by being on alien ground can be a sufficient psychological control over action.

The territory staked out and claimed by gangs is both public and private space. As already mentioned, certain neighborhoods or whole districts are claimed by a gang as theirs, and the streets that bound these districts act as actual (and psychological) dividing lines between various gang provinces. One's choice of gang allegiance or membership is largely dictated by which side of a boundary line one lives on. "I stayed in d' projects [Pueblo Housing Projects]—didn't belong to no gang, but I consider the Pueblos my people. Parks come over dere, I go down wi' d' Pueblos. Gots to. Live in dey territory."

Young people don't have to be in a gang to identify with one—and with the sense of territoriality that goes along with such a claim.

> No, I don't belong to no gang, but I consider the Pueblos my gang. I
> guess we gotta fight for each other. [Who do you fight against?] Parks,
> Businessmen, Avenues, Baby Parks. Went down against d' Parks.
> 'Cause they came over dere and shot up one our little boys and we went
> over dere, shot up d' park. Did it with a couple o' boys. Don' nobody
> mess with us. We pretty bad. We don' mess wid nobody dat don' mess
> with us.

The psychology and literal force exerted on individuals by gang boundary lines is very real. Sometimes these divisions create particular binds for individuals. For example, what does someone do when he (or she) lives on a street that divides two territories? "I couldn't join the Businessmen 'cause the corner by my house was considered the boundary by the Gladiators; and I couldn't join the Gladiators because the corner on the other side was Businessmen. But I had friends in both. Had to, else I be righteously jacked up every way!''

Gang members are closely watched when they venture into alien territory, and one trespasses at one's own risk. "What really starts gang fights, like Viking come over to Businessmen's territory and gits to messin' with the wrong woman and get jacked up. Then, he come back an' tell them and they go back and jack up some Businessmen. Tha's how they all start.''

So gangs control many of the passageways within a given geographical space. Gang domination of these streets means, in effect, they are no longer neutral throughways but toll ways: "You pay some heavy dues if you mess around, get to actin' funny in some gang territory.''

Gangs not only lay claim to certain streets or whole geographical sections, but also to certain public or private structures within these sections. Parks, playgrounds, housing projects, eating places, even schools (and the grounds surrounding them) become recognized as belonging to or, at the least, associated with a particular gang. As one teenager wryly observed, "Ain' much happ'nin' *in* school, but fall by Fremont an' you know what's happ'nin' *outside*—Avenues happ'nin'!''

Many times a particular building—a hamburger stand or a park recreation hall—becomes the actual hangout for gang members and their associates. And the gang covertly or overtly controls the direction and tenor of events that take place there.

> I knew Dawson before I got in the Parks. Like d' Avenues' leader Dawson. He's big an' like he'll go in a party and he'll put his arm out and jus' start collectin' leather pieces. Den, he'll—they'll—jus' take bumper jacks. Like at Sportsmen record hops. He'll go up dere with him 'an dude name Daniel with bumper jacks. Make dey own kinda party!

Gangs, like real estate developers, often advertise their property claims. Sometimes this is done through "personal advertising.'' That is, gang members advertise membership (and by extension, territorial prerogatives) through gang uniforms or gang hand signs.

> I'z Watts gang. Three finger high sign. Each gang, you know, he dress different. Like Slausons had belts an' straw hats, sandals, levis, white T-shirts—big belts. People still wear the dress in summertime. All a sudden dese dudes start wearing green jackets. They call 'em, Green Marines. Be sayin', "Dis our territory.'' Or now you got Avenues put on leather piece. One those brims—caps use'a wear in Chicago. They walk around frontin', high signin' their gang.

Gangs also advertise on a grander scale. Whereas development companies tell you "This is mine" through a variety of signs, billboards, bus benches, or other outdoor advertising methods, gang members are more resourceful; they have to be. They preempt public spaces—building walls, freeway beams, park and bus benches, the sides and insides of buses—as free advertising spaces on which they let the world know who they are (collectively and individually), how "bad" they are, who they challenge (who challenges them), and where they do or want to claim territory. Graffiti, then, are public-free advertising. In my own neighborhood, for example, the following graffiti were taken off a local park bench.

The Crazy Half Man Brims Venice/C C

Lil Half Man from Brims

SWEET PEE
  GODFATHER CRIP   E/S

Baby CA—RIP
  M.M.
    W/S

CRIPS are COOL

Other advertisements were spray-painted across commercial building walls down the block from where I lived.

    ICE
COLD BLOODED
Gangbanging
GODFATHER
CA—RIPS

AIN'T TRIPPIN HE CUR-RIPIN

FUCK
OUTLAWS
BRIMS
  E/S
    Crips
      BABY
        MONK
          Original
            CRIP

CRIPLETS
  W/S

Baby Goldie

Babyhod

Crip Johnny

G F C

Still other graffiti were emblazoned across freeway beams warning other gangs to stay out.

> You are now entering Black P. Stone territory.
> No Crips, Brims, Outlaws, Vanness Gang,
> Bounty Hunters, Godfathers, or any other gangs
>   allowed.
> The jungle is Black Stone territory.
> Crips is cool but the Stones rule.
> > Kojak of the Black P. Stones

On one level, gang graffiti are very similar to the way animals stake out or claim territory by leaving scent marks. In both instances actual or desired proprietorship is being asserted. Graffiti are not only a way of letting others know of your existence, but a method for territorial expansion as well as control. They challenge others to make counterclaims on the same territory—if they choose to or can. It is a visual-verbal power play and, by its nature, often invites dialog not unlike the face-to-face capping that characterizes some forms of verbal manipulation and control.

Finally, graffiti, by their very existence say "I am," "I exist in the world." They are, therefore, an important psychological affirmation of who you are (individually and collectively) and more basically, *that* you are, that you exist in the first place. It gives a sense of personal power to the writer by laying individual claim to the turf he or she occupies—the individual's logo.

One young Crip, who showed me some of his handiwork on a parking-lot wall, expressed what many feel when they write graffiti: "Dey's my people—and da's *me!* Baby Boy—bad ass CA-RIP! Ain' nobody else!"

Thus territory and territoriality provide a range of ways in which young people can experience power and control. On the broadest level, a teenager who has virtually no legal property rights can exert a real sense of psychological proprietorship that allows a claim to a part of town or—in the case of more specific groups such as gangs—to a bounded geographical area as "mine." By extension, teenagers also gain certain powers over who is welcome in their domain, the circumstances of their visit, what is appropriate and inappropriate behavior when they are there, and some real muscle to back up their claims.

The literal claims on territory made by quasi-organized or organized groups further concretize the sense of possession. At this level, claims are less diffuse and more nearly realized, and have the effect of providing a more or less secured area in which one can move and act. Though groups periodically trespass on each others' territory and disputes arise, there is still a feeling not only that this territory is mine—I have control over it—but I'm known here and can call upon others to come to my support when needed. Though this support may not always be forthcoming, there is a real need to believe that it is available. For teenagers who move in an indifferent, often dangerous world, the feeling that certain areas are safe places because they are "owned by the group" is significant—whether it is a fiction or not.

Territoriality also allows an assertion of self: "I am" by virtue of "where I am." If one feels powerless in the Man's world, then the experiences of controlling other's behavior through assertion of territorial claims is psychologically potent. The other side of the same coin is that one can experience a sense of personal power (as well as collective power) through having an actual voice in the world that carries weight: "Do not tread on me or my territory."

CAR CULTURE AND TERRITORIALITY

In a sprawling city the size of Los Angeles, the car is seen as a necessary evil. Los Angeles rivals any city in the country in terms of sheer numbers of cars on the road or in the garages. On the most basic level, the automobile provides mobility in the urban sprawl of greater Los Angeles (though the sardine-can freeways and clogged surface streets might suggest otherwise). Cars can also be status markers—symbols of affluence for many, statements about a particular life style for others. The person who drives a Lincoln Continental and the person who drives a VW van as his or her primary mode of transportation are telling others different things about the image they wish to project into the world about their life style. Cars have sexual and sensual as well as social overtones for their owners, as Vance Packard suggested years ago in his book, *The Hidden Persuaders*. And next to a home, a car is often the single most important investment many people make, their second most significant piece of property.

For many of the black teenagers I met, the car had particular significance. Unlike Los Angeles mainstream culture, where the automobile is taken for granted as necessary (a chicken in every pot and at least one car in every garage), many youths from low-income backgrounds see the car as a luxury item. Large segments of conversation were given over to the discussion of cars—how to get them, what kind, how to fix them up, who did and didn't have one. Though many young blacks claimed ownership of a car, it turns out that less than half really possessed or had ongoing access to a functioning automobile. Some had minimal access to a family or friend's car; others had wrecked the car they had and couldn't afford to fix it; still others had had their car impounded and didn't have the money to reclaim it; a number had had their car repossessed; many were too young to own a car under their own name.

So there is a great gap between the reality of possessing a car and the fantasy. Yet the interest and preoccupation with cars—particularly among males—were constant. And the dreams aired are both poignant and painful to hear because they give the lie to the so-called American Dream. "I don't have a ride right now. Don't like American-made cars. I always wants a foreign model car—so I can't have d' car I want, I don' want a car. I wanna Jag—Jag 70 XKE, Benz 70. They cost some dough. My money ain' long enough—maybe sometime. So I be takin' the extra car [Rapid Transit District bus]." And it is not surprising that two of the most frequent charges brought against the teenagers I met were grand theft auto and joyriding. As one young man put it, "If you ain't got a ride, you be tryin' to get one—any kinda way."

By far the most popular car among those I met was the Cadillac—variously referred to in the vernacular as the *blade, calf, hog, kitty, cat, kitty cat*, or by special model names, the *B* (Brougham), *El D, Rado, slingshot* (El Dorado), *D.V.* or *coupe* (Coupe d' Ville)—with the Lincoln Continental and the Buick Riviera (*Riv, Rivie, Rivie hog*) and the Buick Electra (*deuce 25, deuce and a quarter*) running somewhat behind. More recently the Mercedes-Benz, the Porsche, and the Jaguar were gaining in popularity. However, popularity and possession were not usually synonymous. Though some teenagers had older-model Cadillacs or Buicks, they were few in number. Mostly the cars I saw were Old-model Chevies, Fords, Mercurys—some even bordering on such classics as Hudsons or Studebakers. Because cars are precious possessions, those who do have them see them in very proprietary terms. Not only do they afford mobility and prestige, but they become total environments unto themselves. They are literally like mobile homes. There is an expression in the vernacular, to *freak off something*, which more than any other characterizes the extent to which a car becomes transformed into a total environment. To freak off something means to fix up lavishly, decorate, or enhance an environment. The two environments most often referred to were one's *crib* (apartment or home) and one's *ride* (car). The experience of riding around in a fiendishly freaked-off car is like no other. An acquaintance of mine had such a car. Though description doesn't do it justice, it gives some idea of the design and care that go into creating such a setting.

The car was a '65 Chevy Impala. The body had a "metal flake" paint job that was black with iridescent metallic green shimmering through. The car had been lifted: hydraulic lifts installed in the chassis which allowed the driver to throw a switch in the car and electrically raise and lower the car's body at will. Translated in vernacular terms, he could *bounce, dribble,* or *drop* his ride as he drove down the streets. The car was equipped with electric doors and windows and could be locked automatically from inside. The windows were smoked so that people couldn't see in, but you could clearly see out. The wheel covers were Cragers—magnesium inner rims, deep-set, with numerous circles punched out for decoration. The wheels themselves had oversized tires that allowed for speed and extra maneuverability.

The interior was voluptuous. The upholstery was black velour-like material fashioned in a "tuck and roll" upholstery pattern. Black high-pile carpeting extended from the floor onto the top of the dash and the area under the back window. The regular steering wheel had been replaced with a "doughnut wheel" about seven inches in diameter. The car was equipped with a stereo tape deck and a "color bar," an electronic color band connected to the car's radio and stereo system that gives off different patterned colors in response to the different frequencies emitted from the sound source. As a final touch, a design pattern had been carefully etched in white paint around the door handles, window cranks, and the various knobs and accessories in the dashboard. As the car's owner described it, "It's black on black [black interior and exterior] an' don't give *no* slack!" It was magnificent. Few of the cars I saw were so elaborately decked out ("long money" or a hustler's resourcefulness are required to get such elaborate accessories together). Yet accessories like lifts, doughnut wheels, elaborated upholstery, and special wheel covers are not uncommon. And young people who are car devotees will spend whatever money they can get to freak off their cars.

Cars, then, become transformed into special environments that are like dwellings. Given the fact that many of these youths spend most of their time on the streets, this attention to creating a mobile home is understandable and important to a street-oriented style of living. More recently, some teenagers have started talking about the environmental potentials of the "recreational" vehicle. "Yeh, I likes a camper. *Ooooh,* so many things I kin do wid a camper! Get wired up! If I don' wanna go home, I kin go in d' back pop a roll, get beautiful in d' *back!* Swoop on some young lady, invite her dere too. Lay some fiendish pipe in dere!"

With the car, you experience many of the same qualities associated with stationary territory, but with the additional asset of being mobile. You can, in a sense, take your territory with you. Furthermore, in a car you are less immediately vulnerable to those who might challenge you on the streets.

It is interesting to note that few young blacks were, as of the end of 1976, "into" motorcycles in the same way they were into cars. Although by 1975 I started to see some freaked-off cycles in South Central, the car still ruled the streets and drive-in hangouts. One explanation is that it is perceived as easier—legally or otherwise—to get a car than a bike: a car is more "available" than a motorcycle. Stealing a motorcycle, for example, is a riskier proposition than stealing a car, since you are more visible to passers-by. Also bike owners often chain or bar their bikes to prevent theft—which makes it a messy business. But more important, a car is enclosed, a bike not. The closed car offers a sense of security and invulnerability that the exposed bike cannot. As one young man explained it, "Gimme a short any day! Cycle's fast, but a bullet is faster. Ain' nothin' between you and some crazy cowboy 'cept air and talk—an' he ain' talkin' if he fittin' to shoot you." As my acquaintance pointed out, "Ain't nobody gon' git in that ride 'cept I say so!" So the car becomes like a fortress—more or less impenetrable to outsiders, entered on the owner's terms.

Finally, the fact that a teenager can make a personal and unique statement to others by the way he freaks off his (or sometimes her) car is akin to the architect's imprint in mainstream culture. Each says: "This is what I've wrought. It is my distinctive work." Car decoration or "costuming" is very similar in intent to personal or verbal costuming.

The teenagers I met were creating unique, personalized environments out of the cars available to them long before the middle-class craze for decorating and furnishing vans and campers came on the scene. Their life style—by choice and otherwise—has been in the streets, and they have found ways creatively to cope with what the streets mete out to them. Like nomadic people, they decorate themselves and their forms of transportation in lieu of leaving their mark on some fixed structure.

## PERFORMANCE, CONTEST, AND SOCIAL CONTROL

### PERSONAL SPACE AND TERRITORIALITY

We have seen that power is sometimes exerted through the control and manipulation of geographical units, territorial claims made on the turf one experiences as one's own. Though proprietary rights almost never mean legal ownership, the space being claimed is very real.

However, there is another kind of territorial claim that young people exert over a different type of space which is less tangible or visible but equally potent in its effect. It is the power over what Edward Hall (1969) has termed social or personal space—the personal space or "invisible bubble" that individuals maintain around themselves when interacting with others. Though the radius of that social-personal space varies from culture to culture, it nonetheless exists and is very real. We have all been aware of having our personal space intruded upon at one time or another, the feeling of uneasiness or crowding that emerges when someone penetrates our intrapersonal bubble. For example, someone sitting down directly next to us at a bus stop bench: if there's room, the instinct is to move away from the person—to reestablish the perimeters of our personal space bubble. In the context of this discussion, I'd like to expand on Hall's concept by observing that others not only can invade our social-personal space by physically moving in too close, but can also intrude on our social space by "taking up" great chunks of space by their very presence, by the sheer force of their being. So power (coercive or manipulative behavior) over others can be exerted by literally invading another's personal territory or by staking claim to a large and intrusive area of one's own space in the presence of others. Those concerned with black culture have noted that whites perceive blacks as taking up a great deal of social space. Psychologically, whites see blacks as loud, boisterous, intrusive, and the like. Though blacks do "take more space" than most mainstream whites, from an intraracial viewpoint this is seen as quite ordinary behavior. What is important here is not to measure blacks against some white yardstick of behavior, but to understand when and how young blacks perceive territorial infringement on their space.

A corollary to invading the social space of others or taking up a large arena of space for oneself is the psychological consequence. When someone's space is intruded on—in whatever way—it necessarily means some infringement on one's psychological environment as well. In the teenage vernacular lexicon there is an expression that clearly speaks to the many levels on which invasion of one's social, personal, and psychological space can occur. The phrase to *jam someone*, among other meanings, refers to a situation in which someone physically or verbally assaults another with words or bodily force with the intent of *messing up their mind*—or, as one teenager put it, "To righteously fuck with d' person mind-wise, fightin'-wise, all ways." The expression itself connotes, for those who use it, the act of literally or psychologically jamming someone into a corner.

*87*

Here, then, power gets played out in a different kind of arena. Control and manipulation over others are effected through territorial claims made on their personal, social, and psychological space.

### THE PERFORMANCE-COMBAT ARENA

There are three recurring images in teenage vernacular vocabulary that seem to put in perspective much of the manipulative or coercive behavior that teenagers play out in their attempts to exert power over another's personal and psychological space. The first is the idea of "the game"; the second, the concept of "the front"; and the third, the notion of "the action."

The game is just that—a contest of wills, wits, physical force, or some combination thereof in which the contestants creatively do battle with each other, often in front of appreciative third parties. As already suggested, the vernacular expressions to *game someone* and to *run a game on someone* convey the sense of contest and jockeying for one-up power which is found in much teenage behavior. The game also implies reaping financial, material, or emotional rewards at the expense of another—whether he or she knows it or not. In this sense gaming on someone is like refining or honing one's hustling skills. Among ghetto teenagers the ultimate game, or (as one young man put it) "the baddest game from the get-go," is still pimping, and the premier player is the pimp. Indeed one of the common vernacular expressions for a would-be or actual pimp is the term *player*. Though more will be said about the pimp when we look at various fronts assumed by young blacks in running their game, it is important to note here that the pimp is seen as a consummate gamesman who has many manipulative strategies in his arsenal, and uses them with finesse and style to get what he wants.

So the heart of the game is combative, a contest-oriented process. Players compete for different kinds of payoffs—money, recognition, prestige and status, women, men. The game is like a sports event with all the associated characteristic power plays—audiences, rewards, winners, and losers. Again, the sense of the game or gaming is seen in the rather elegant vernacular expression that refers to the world of the pimp and his prostitutes—the *sporting life*.

The second image that suffuses teenage interaction is the front. The expression to *front off* means to show off what you are or what you have. That may mean your material possessions (car, clothes, home), your special companion, your verbal abilities, your physical prowess. Your front may change according to the kind of image you want to put out in the world. The concept is very much like the dramaturgical notion of the persona—it is a mask, the personality you wear for the world to see and to react to; it is the role or roles you assume for the duration of the play (*the play* is a vernacular expression that means both the interaction between male and female prior to sex—or whatever is then occurring—the action of the moment). The front is closely aligned with the performancelike quality of the theater. Indeed the front is a creative performance itself, complete with costumes, props (cars, weapons, companions); "lines" (which in the vernacular refers generally to conversation and particularly to smooth conversation, especially directed toward the opposite sex); scenes (a typical definition offered for the expression to *scene on someone* was "frontin' off, showing off in front of somebody, tryin' impress 'em"); staging and movement (to *get your act together* refers to being in control of yourself on stage, so to speak); and sets (a set in vernacular refers to those people you hang out with, or the performance of a set of musical selections). Very often, your friends and associates act as the human backdrop against which you play out your scene. Also implicit in both the game and the front is the attempt to step on people's lines, to upstage others. Put in Edward Hall's spatial terms, it means directly or indirectly to intrude on another's personal space or claim a large hunk of social space for yourself.

Finally, there is the notion of action, which pervades both the game and the front. Because the manipulative behavior and the territorial power plays launched against others is on-going, dynamic, performative and gamelike, it is, by its very nature, kinetic. Expressions like the action or the happenings connote for vernacular users a sense of events occurring, of things moving and happening, often with rapid shifts and changes in direction—of energy and life. Anyone who has experienced the verbal bobbing and weaving, the attempts to steal the conversational ball, the shots made against one's opponent, cannot help likening the action to that of basketball.

For the uninitiated, it is easy to assume that a contestlike orientation means that hostility or aggression invariably pervades all youthful interaction. This is not necessarily the case. Though the contest orientation grows out of a real need to survive at any cost, "the game," like other games and contests, is infused with high spirit, parries and thrusts, creative and resourceful gambits, and a pervasive sense of playfulness. As one young man put it, "Like the man say, 'All d' world a stage and you d' actor.' Be runnin' down your li'l' ol' hustle, get over. 'Nother dude, he be runnin' his li'l ol' game too. Gon' put you in some trick bag—he thank! Shoot on each other—'Nigger how come you smell so *damn musty?* Ain' you never hear 'bout soap?' Dude jam you, say, 'Nigger, you feel froggy? Den leap on over and lose yo' life!' Be righteously eyeballin' each other. Den, it be all over. Somethin' else be goin' down. Ain' nothin' to it.''

Many of the interpersonal games and fronts teenagers engage in allow them literally to play out some very real feelings of hostility, tension, and anger, as well as develop their expressive skills. There also is a very fine line between play and real expression of feeling. The secret of successful manipulative behavior is to know when, how, and in what guise to game someone—without getting jammed.

THE VERBAL GAMES

As already suggested, the game refers to the particular kind of contest one engages in order to manipulate, control, or coerce others. It is the modus operandi by which forays into another's social space are accomplished. What the following discussion attempts to do is illuminate some of the most visible and important games played and catalog the vernacular used to characterize and describe them. The subtleties and nuances of gaming are exceedingly intricate. What follows does not pretend to examine all the facets of gaming; it is offered as an overview of a complex phenomenon.

> Hey, Edie, you remember dat program—d' Name of d' Game? Right on. Like d' name of d' game down here it be runnin' down some fine lines. Like you talkin' to some young lady, tryin' to catch. Else you be blowin' on d' brother hard, fast and heavy. Some rootiepoot rank yo' play with yo' squeeze, righteously get on dat sucker case. "Don' be doin' me chump—lose some *blood* behind *dat* shit!"
>   Sometimes, you jus' be sittin' up dere in the pad, gettin' high, drinkin' some nice Akadama, crack jokes on each other. "Hey bro', how come you hair so nappy? Look like a cotton ball! Better get you some Madam Walker [hair preparation] walk all 'round d' edges." Shit like dat. Yo' rap can save yo' life too. Fo' real! To my mind a fiendish rap is what's happ'nin'.

Anyone who knows black teenagers knows the central role verbal interaction plays in their daily exchanges. The oral tradition is still pervasive in black culture. Because who you are (and very often how well you survive) depends so heavily on how well you talk, verbal dexterity is highly valued. Young people growing up in the black community play endless verbal games with one another, much as their mainstream white counterparts play games of war, cops and robbers, or cowboys and Indians. Like skilled musicians, children early on learn to refine their verbal skills, to develop their "instrument" so that it can play a variety of songs. "They learn the importance of banter, the power of the taunt, the pleasure of playing with words. They develop vocabulary and others skills in active contest situations for the purpose of winning a verbal game and gaining esteem from their group" (Abrahams, 1970, p. 17).

Words, then, are tools for power and gain. As the young man said above, a good rap can save your life. It can also get you a woman (or man), money or other material things, and recognition and stature. All these "commodities" are potentially purchasable through the power of words. Among teenagers who have limited access to capitalism and its payoffs, words buy you important things—and no one can take them away from you.

Because verbal excellence is recognized as an important and powerful way of manipulating others, young blacks early become connoisseurs of good and bad talk, of who *shoots blanks* and who *shoots a good shot*. And because many of the verbal contests are played out for others—or are at least within earshot of others—youths have an opportunity to feed back to the contestants how well they are doing.

> Like we was sittin' up at my momma house, sittin' up dere, doin' dis: "Boy! That ugly ass bitch, I hear you seein'. OOOwheee!!! She look like DEATH, boy! There's somethin' that didn't even *dissolve* good!" Now dat righteously funky. He done got down hard an' heavy. Ever'body crack up. "Man, he sho' did shoot a shot on him!" Sometimes dude jus' shoot a blank. His shit jus' off the wall—jus' falls off—don't stick, ain' no good. Nobody say nothin'.

The verbal strategies themselves are as various as the situations in which they are used. Because any given verbal exchange may incorporate several plays within the same conversation, it is hard to distinguish the fine edges. However, the vernacular vocabulary is an exceedingly useful way of looking at some of the main categories of strategic talk that go on between young blacks as they vie for position. Before going into that discussion, I would like to take a brief look at what is certainly the most common word for talk itself: *rap*.

A cover term like dude or brother, the word rap refers to all kinds of talk. Its specific meaning emerges only in context. Basically, to rap means to talk, to speak to someone. Probably one of the best characterizations of the term was told to me by a young pool hustler.[3]

> See yo' rap is your thing. I's like your personality. Like you kin style on some dude by rappin' better 'n he do. Show 'im up. Outdo him conversation-wise. Or you can rap to a young lady, you tryin' to impress her, catch her action—you know—get wid her sex-wise. Like, "Hey baby, you one fine lookin' woman. Let's you and me get better acquainted." You can school the brother wi' cho rap. Run down some heavy lines, tell 'im what's happenin'—like he do somethin' ain't too cool, you rap to 'im about, "Hey brother, that was some cold shot. Ain' no cause for *dat!*" Else you can righteously get on d' dude's case. Run down the basic fundamentals to d' dude. Talk about 'im bad. Callin' him a funky-ass-low-life-son-bitch! Sometimes you rap jus' be woofin', jus' playing aroun', shootin' jokes on each other—like d' momma's game. If you playin' wi' some sucker, you rap 'im around you little finger—hear where I'm comin' from? Send him on a hombug wi' yo' rap. Dude

rankin' yo' play wi' dis certain lady tell 'im, "Hey man, ain' nothin' here. Lemme tell you 'bout dis party over Wilton. Some fine young ladies, good weed. Outasight party." Dude go dere, ain' nothin' hap- p'nin'. Vacant lot. See, what it is, use yo' rap in all different situations. Jus' talkin'.

So the expression to rap means to talk, but it also means to talk with style, to invest your talk with your particular personality. In this sense, your rap is as important for its form as for its content. There are different kinds of raps that are mobilized for different kinds of contexts.

*Play.* As suggested, the element of play, both in a recreational and performative sense, runs through many of the verbal contests in which teenagers engage. In situations marked by confrontation and coercion, playfulness potentially counteracts emotionally charged content that could bring the contestants to blows. There are a number of verbal terms that characterize playful exchange. For example, the terms to *crack* or *shoot on* and *drop lugs on someone* generally refer to cracking jokes at someone else's expense. The idea of the game is to hurl quick jokes back and forth in an attempt to best your opponent. One evening I was with a group at a Teen Post recreation center. Wait- ing to play dominoes, two young men got to "cracking on" each other.

> A: Hey man, you look like a goddamn Christmas tree! You a regular caution sign! You righteously light up the whole street!
> B: Listen sucker, don't be buyin' my clothes in Woolworth like some five-and-dime nigger—five cent fo' yo' shirt an' dime fo' yo' pants!
> A: Hey homeboy, what chu doin' dere—beatin' yo' meat? Nigger's makin' whip cream!
> B: Ain' nothin' to it, punk! Hear tell yo' thang so small, need a tele- scope to find it!

Cracking on someone is closely related to one of the most popular verbal games played by young blacks: shooting or playing the dozens. Shooting the dozens, we have seen, is a ritualized speech event in which would-be combatants exchange a variety of insults directed at the other's mother. The dozens run the gamut from quick oneliners— "Your momma's so fat, she needs wheels to turn the corner"; "Your momma's like a doorknob, everybody gets a turn"—to rhymed coup- lets: "I don't play the dozens, the dozens ain't my game/But the way I fucked your momma is a righteous shame"; "Iron is iron, and steel don't rust/But your momma's got a pussy like a Greyhound bus."

The dozens, along with a variety of other verbal games, is liter- ally child's play—a training ground for more complex interaction.

"That's out! When I was young, go to a party or somethin', my part-ner make me mad or somethin', say, 'Man, what wrong wi' chu shoe? Got some big holes!' I used to do dat. I was in junior high, 'bout 7th, 8th grade. Used go home an' practice. 'Yeh, gonna get my partner tomorra.' " Even though many teenagers claim the dozens is a game they left behind in junior high school, the fact is that I heard the dozens being consistently played by young blacks in their late teens and early twenties.

There are two kinds of dozens: dirty and clean. One young man explained how the dozens gets started in a conversation and when they get identified as dirty or clean.

It's according to how the conversation starts. Yeh. We be sittin' round, get to talkin'. Then, righteous somebody get to sayin' somethin' 'bout some else's momma. "Aw, y' momma!" They be playin'. "You mom-ma's a dog!" Start d' momma's game! I shoot on my pa'tner, "You momma wash her hair with Babo"—shit like dat. Gets real dirty some-time—"Momma's pussy so big, airplane park in it!" They shoot on you great-granddaddy and you uncle—jus' through the whole generation. Like dat's dirty dozen—shootin' on d' moms, else on kin. Den gets to talkin' bout each other. You don' be sayin' somethin' bout the family, you talk 'bout him. You see somethin' you wanna talk 'bout, like you see his hair real nappy, you say his hair's like Brillo—jus' trippin' off each other.

We don't play d' momma's dozen too much. That starts confu-sion. Dat happen today. A lotta confusion, a lotta fightin'. Don' shoot on d' moms less'n you fittin' to fight. You know, when we fittin' to fight, maybe shoot on moms. But mostly we talk 'bout each other. We leave d' moms at home, 'cause she too old to be in the street anyway! Do dat among friends. Way of blowin' off steam, of releasin' yourself. You wanna few laughs. But, it's mostly done by friends. You usually cap with someone who don't take offense.

What this account of the dozens also says is that the dozens can move very quickly from verbal play to physical violence—particularly if one's mother and her sexual nature is hit on. It is important to note that most young people played the clean dozens and shied away from shooting on "the moms" unless they were attempting to provoke a fight. A final observation. The dozens, because of its highly charged emotional content, is a game played mostly among friends or people one knows. To shoot the dozens on a stranger or outsider is invariably to provoke a fight.

Though the element of play runs through much verbal inter-change, it is most evident in the games described above and others like them. There is, however, always a delicate balance between playful behavior and serious confrontation. Youths soon begin to learn through these games where the line is drawn. If they don't, they are seen as lames or outright hardheads looking for trouble. Verbal games not only provide young blacks with an arena in which to practice verbal strategies and sharpen their skills but are, in their own right, examples of manipulative behavior. By besting another through the force of your joke or insult, you have effectively put down that person. Invasion of one's psychological, if not literal, space has been effected and, in the process, the winner has expanded the scope of his or her own social space, has gained psychological ground. But given the fluid, dynamic nature of conversation and verbal game playing, one's claim on the territory is easily lost, gained, and lost again.

*Confrontation.*   Verbal play takes a more serious turn when an unexpected or deliberate confrontation takes place. Sometimes the game turns sour—the boast has provoked anger rather than laughter, the capping session has become too "cold." Other times some incident, a real or fancied affront, sparks words: "Like dude feel brother done did him. At a party or sumpin'. Dis cat's gotten down wid his ol' lady, get on his case for dat. Dude try to burn 'im for his stash, scream some cold lines down behind dat." Sometimes interference with a person's attempt to "catch" provokes a strong retort: "Like a pootbutt come. Like you tryin' to talk to a young lady. Messes you up, talkin' trash. You righteously blow dat sucker away. 'Listen nigger, don' step too far or you get jammed. So leave the scene, else you mouth gon' get you an ass-whuppin'—mos' certainly!' " Other times the verbal confrontation is not reactive but is deliberately initiated to provoke another, to vent strong negative feeling, or systematically to embarrass or humiliate: "To put some jive-ass sucker in his place. Talk about 'im so bad, they cain't hardly git a word in. Cuttin' 'im front a whole lotta people. Sucker keep his mouth shut then." And given the contest nature of much interaction, one might verbally accost others purely to test them, to see if they can take it: "I may shoot on d' dude just to see where he's comin' from, what his reaction's gonna be. An' if he's together, he'll come back sooner or later."

The number of vernacular expressions used to characterize verbal confrontation or put-downs are more numerous than any other verbal strategy. Like the classification of name terms, there is a hierarchy of expressions one can choose from, and the choice depends on the intensity or seriousness of the verbal encounter.

If you all sittin' around, everybody's trippin', call 'im names 'n like dat. "You *ug—ly* man! Big head"—like dat. Dat be like cappin', git cold. Like d' word say, you clamp down tight on someone. Depend on who be cappin' and what dey sayin'. Den you got yo' base. Like I told

Leroy las' night, "What were you doin' over dis young lady's house
after you tol' me you wadn't gonna *be* at d' young lady's house?" An'
he squared up and he said, "Man, you wants to *base?*" You get to
basin' more or less put a man or woman in dey place. Den you get down
*real* funky. Righteously blow d' brother's stuff away, jus' steadily
scream on someone like dey done sumpin' to you and you righteously
mad at 'em. Call 'im "sack o' mothafuckas," "trick-ass nigger." Tell
'im get out you face. Jus' righteously ride 'im down to the ground!

So verbal confrontation runs the gamut from the more or less
playful capping sessions to the more serious encounters, where you
*base on someone* or *get on someone's case*, to hard-core confrontation
where you *scream cold, hard, foul* or *stomp on someone.* Of course
each encounter also carries its own tone. Sometimes the intent is to
*bug someone*, to annoy or irritate; another time the attempt is to embarrass or humiliate; still other situations demand that you totally
undermine another to the point of "throwing blows." Knowing when
to use what strategy is part of learning the verbal game.

In most situations, the performance aspect of verbal confrontation is apparent. More often than not, third parties are present to hear
or overhear your words.

You be talkin' 'bout somebody. You jus' have all d' people 'round criti-
cizin' 'im in front whole lotta people. You laughin'. You *really* downin'
'im! Like dude get you angry, start talkin' 'bout 'im in front a woman,
sayin' somethin' wrong about 'im like, "You still got gon'rhea?"
Really you be frontin' off, showin' off in front somebody, tryin' impress 'em!

In fact, the expression to *scene on someone*, which means to undercut
another through your words or acts, connotes the sense of performance in process.

Corollary to the performative aspect of confrontation is the kinetic nature of the words describing the verbal strategy, as well as the
kinetic elements apparent in the actual situation itself. For example,
terms like to *blow away*, to *scream*, to *dump*, to *stomp*, to *cut*, to
*shoot*, and to *holler* all connote loud or energetic action. And anyone
who has heard verbal confrontations among young blacks knows that
these are not quiet or subdued encounters.

Finally, some of the terms used to characterize verbal confrontation—to *blow someone away*, to *jam someone*, to *cut someone*, to
*lean on someone*—are the same terms used to describe physical assault.
This is not surprising given the physicality of much black interaction,
whether it be verbal or not. Also, the line between verbal and physical
confrontation is narrow. Verbal harassment can quickly spill over into

physical exchange, and the dual use of assault terms highlights this dynamic. Edward Hall (1969), in talking about social space and appropriate distancing among given members of a species, indicates that there is a point when one's interpersonal space becomes so intruded upon that one is compelled to fight rather than flee. This "critical distance"—the zone between flight and fight—is very thin and, in many species, irreversible. Hall's discussion of social space seems particularly relevant to black teenage confrontation. It can be suggested that a verbal confrontation has been brought to such a critical psychological and physical point, when contenders are "eyeball to eyeball," that the options for further talk or flight give way to physical combat. This is a particularly compelling argument in a culture where proving yourself—acting like a man and not backing down—are important values. Young blacks engaged in argument seldom do so at a distance. The phrase, "We standin' jaw to jaw, toe to toe, eyeball to eyeball, ain't nothin' between us 'cept air and ain' much of that," suggests just how close the space is.

*Education.* There is a term in teenage black vernacular—to *school someone* (to inform, to explain something, to set someone straight)—that characterizes still another kind of verbal interaction. Here the encounter may have confrontational overtones, but the emphasis is on teaching a person how to act appropriately, to educate the socially naive or stubborn person to the ways of the streets. Again, the line may be finely drawn between confrontation and education. "I might be talkin' 'bout 'im and still tryin' to bring 'im up. I might be on dey case, tellin' the brother, 'You ain' nothin', you's nothin'.' You talk about 'im so bad, he's nothin'. Nex' time you see 'im, he's walkin' tall."

Education in this context is seen in practical terms, how do you "get over" in the streets. The majority of teenagers I met had universal contempt for school. School was seen as a place where teachers were apathetic, often prejudiced and students were rebellious and disinterested, where people learned little and attended infrequently, where you could cop drugs and get high. For many, the streets were where you got your real education. And many were distrustful of the so-called educated person, the person perceived to be a bookworm or a high-society type.

The sources of real education, instead, are those who have been around and know what is happening. And age is not necessarily the measure of experience or knowledge. "Like everybody in d' ghetto grows up fast. Take's a year or two in the streets and a dude could be sixteen, and act like he thirty or forty. I's all how you develop. I's jus' accordin' to who be around and how *dey* do it. I'z small, hang around

wid people from nineteen to thirty-five. I never did all my life hang
around nobody my age, 'cause it never could learn me nothin'.''

Central to the concept of schooling is to teach people their lines,
teach them verbal strategy. However, unlike more overtly performative interactions, sometimes you take a person aside to "run it down."
"Instead of basin' on him front the young lady, you pull 'im over to
the side and talk to 'im." The term to *hip someone* means essentially
the same as to school them, and it carries with it the connotation of
making someone hip—making them aware of what's happening,
what's important to know in order to survive.

Contrary to "talking trash," schooling someone often also carries the implication of content-filled talk. Unlike shooting blanks, to
school or hip someone connotes weight. "Like I like to listen to
brother got somethin' to say. You kin learn a lot 'bout wha's hap-
p'nin' from some dude really talks. Brother been around, dealin',
hustlin', gettin' over. Maybe heavy into Black Power bag. Dude run
down some heavy lines."

The instructional aspect of this kind of verbal interaction is seen
in other terms also—to *break it down* ("Break down the happ'nin's
for the dude"); to *pull someone's coat* ("Like you stop d' brother an'
like pull on his coat, say, 'Man, dat ain't too cool, lemme hip you to
what's happ'nin' ' ").

Though schooling someone may not be overtly manipulative or
confrontational, it still involves a vying for one-up position. Expressions like to *break it down*, to *run it down*, to *lay it on someone*, to
*bring someone down front*, all suggest operating from a position of
power in relation to another. And it is often used as a strategy that
turns the tables on others and puts them in their place. "If dis dude
gonna tell you 'bout black history, okay? An' you *know* wha's hap-
p'nin' 'bout black history, you gonna blow on 'im. You lay it on 'im.
You puttin' him down."

Breaking it down is also a way of invading psychological space by
convincing another person to accept your way of thinking. "You be
tryin' to git 'im like you. You gonna talk to him to try let 'im understand what groove *you* in and why don' he come from out dat bag he's
in up to yo' level." Like other verbal strategies, how well you get over
to someone depends on how well you've learned the verbal techniques
that allow you to be "heard."

*Deception.* The oral tradition in black culture is rich with stories
about people being outwitted or conned. For example, in the oral literature there is a famous toast, the "Signifying Monkey." The signifying monkey is a con artist who, by turns, bluffs, goads, and lies in
his attempts to outwit his protagonist, Mr. Lion.

The vernacular itself has a number of terms that characterize deceitful or overtly manipulative kinds of verbal strategies. The philosophy behind such encounters is, as one young woman put it, "If you cain't beat 'em, con 'em." The con takes many forms. Although the expression to *woof on someone* is also used to describe playing the dozens, it also carries the additional meaning of bragging, boasting, talking big, lying, tricking, or bluffing. As one young woman saw it, "See, like the wolf in 'Little Red Riding Hood?' He was dis slick dude, talking all kinds shit, disguise hisself. But somebody done bought his ticket—and goodbye wolf!"

There are two related expressions that refer to tricking others or calling someone's bluff. Both carry the image of the wolf. One is the expression to *sell a wolf ticket*; the other, to *buy a wolf ticket*. The first refers to boasting or bluffing your way through a tight situation; the second refers to the consequences if someone calls you on your attempted bluff. "I don't sell no wolf tickets to nobody. Git you head broke dat way. Say you and me's talkin' 'bout each other. You signifyin' and say, 'Looky here brother, I don' sell wolf tickets and I sho' ain' *buyin'* none.' So you lettin' him know you sho' ain' goin' for what he sayin'. Either he shut up or he be fightin'."

Of course, the ultimate end of the con game is to outsmart your opponent. A number of the terms, to *sham*, to *slick*, to *run a game*, and to *gigolo*, imply pulling the wool over another's eyes. Implicit in the verbal con game is taking advantage of another through some deception. This may mean conning others out of material possessions or their "old man" or "old lady." It may also mean to take advantage for psychological entertainment and satisfaction. There are a group of expressions that relate to this aspect of verbal manipulation that suggest sending someone on a wild goose chase. Terms like to *send someone on a trip* (*merry-go-round*, *hombug*), to *trip out someone*, and to *zoom someone out* are all movement-related in tone and, in fact, may literally imply sending someone a very long distance.

> Like, "Hey, man, gonna be some outasight party up at Hooper and 90th." Brother go over dere, i's nothin'. I's a dud, ain' nothin'. Buncha heads, no women dere. Else like somebody ask you, "Man, know where you can cop some weed?" Say, "Yeh man, over at such 'n such"—tha's 20 blocks away! Dude git over dere, ain' nothin' but a vacant lot! Send 'im on a *long* hombug.

> You send d' sucker on a big ol' goose-chase, tell d' dude, "Hey, man, i's dis new club up dere by Main an' 88th. Some fonky sounds, nice-lookin' young ladies, don' check no i.d.—yeh, i's okay!" Dude go on up dere—now da's a long ways from Compton, man. Dude get up dere, gonna get down, i's a church! Ain' no dancin', no broads, nothin'. Jus' a lotta singin' an' hollerin'. Now da's a righteous humbug!

It's easy to see that sending someone on a hombug can be funny to the sender. But, on a deeper level, it can operate to vent feelings of hostility or resentment—and give the initiator a sense of power or revenge. This vengeful aspect becomes more apparent when the ones being hombugged are whites in an all-black community: "Like some white boy he done got lost. Stop d' car—don' get out 'cause he be afraid. Say, 'How you get to Imperial?' Tell 'im, 'Take a right, den you take a lef' an' den you jus' keep goin' fo' 'bout two mile. Cain't miss it.' Now you done sent that boy to South Gate! Da's a righteous hombug!" Or with the police: "Like I build dis fire and I tell d' police, 'They had dis fire *way over* here.' But really's over here." Or with a suspicious husband: "Like I went out with this guy one time, and my husband called to see. See, he so suspicious. I told him I was going to a party. Called to see where the party was. So I gave him a fake address out in Long Beach somewhere and that was a *humbug!*"

In one way the verbal con is the ultimate manipulative strategy. It is more subtle than, say, verbal play or verbal confrontation in its reward, since the "sucker" may never find out he or she has been taken for a ride. But psychologically it is very potent and enhances your prestige as soon as you can tell someone what you've done. Many teenage conversations are punctuated with stories (and fabrications) of successful cons. In the retelling of your story, you lay claim to an expanded social space in somewhat the same way that you do when you crack a good joke, shoot a successful dozen, confront people and put them in their place, or school someone about appropriate behavior.

TALK AS PROCESS

There is an old song line repeated by black teenagers to characterize much verbal interaction: "It ain't what you say, it's the way you say it." Given the contest orientation present in much talk and the performancelike quality of many verbal situations, it is not surprising that talk is seen in terms of process. As the song says, what often counts is not necessarily what you say, but the mood, tenor, tone, and skill with which you say it. Verbal encounters provide the arena for testing others, proving yourself, and gaining recognition for how well you rap. Verbal interaction easily becomes an event, a happening, a space in which to perform—and this becomes apparent in the most seemingly innocuous situations. For example, the way you greet someone may become an opportunity to one-up another.

> Like cat say, "Wha's happ'nin'?" or people come up and say, "What it is." Dey say, "What it ain't." Den, "What's it gonna be?" Whole conversation. Hafta know a comeback. Da's when a cat wanna scene, get fiendin' on you. He say, "What it ain't." And you gotta know some-

thing to come right back the same. So one cat say, "Wha's happ'nin'?"
You say, "Me, brother, me!" Den he say, "What's it gonna be?" So he
tryin' keep hisself together an' on top, so he don't get ranked.

Some greetings are ritualized, virtually automatic non-sequiturs,
such as the following responses to standard greetings like "What's
happ'ning?" "What's the action?" "What's the scam?":

> You got it.
> Ain' nothin' to it.
> Ain' nothin to it, a baby could do it.
> Ain' no big thing.

Others are more creative and provoke the need for an equally clever
retort.

> I'm sly, slick, and wicked.
> You know better 'n I do.
> You, baby.
> Me.
> Me, try it you'll like it!
> Well, I guess it's life, brother.

In some cases, the greeting and response get very elaborate, and what
starts out as a simple exchange turns into a woofing session:

> A: Hey brother, tell me somethin' slick.
> B: You got it, brother. Me—the one, the only Iceman! Hey, what 'tis? I
> stays cool, I freezes showers, turns a tub of water to ice cubes. I'd
> shake hands wi' chu all but don't want you all freeze to death.
> A: Yeh, brother, you cool alright! But not as cool as me! Man, I'z so
> cool, I oughta be illegal!
>
> A: Hey bro', what 'tis?
> B: Playin' the game from A to Z. Fiendin' and leanin', wheelin' and
> dealin', cappin' and blowin', restin' and dressin'. I'm driving in a
> Cad with four doors and four whores, one pimp in the trunk,
> sniffin' cocaine and smokin' dope and drinkin' champagne.

There are two vernacular expressions that especially characterize
meaningless talk, talk as process—to talk shit and to talk trash (to
"bullshit"). Sometime ago, I was conducting a communication workshop with some community people from South Central and the East
Los Angeles barrio. We were talking about how people communicate
as well as the strategies they use to withhold information. One black
woman made the following observation:

> See, Chicanos they be real quiet, don' say a lot, don' tell you much
> about themself. Black folks, they be righteously talkin' all d' time. Yeh,

but lots of time, don' be sayin' anything, really. They ain' tellin' you 'bout theyself neither—just *seem* like they do. Like you kin talk a lotta trash and sister or brother *still* don' know where you comin' from. Do it with the Man all d' time. Say a lot, tell 'im nothin'! Like you be steadily talkin' shit and it kin get you outa some cold situations!

Christina Milner (1972), in her discussion of black pimps, has suggested that talking shit "is a linguistic recognition that words are worthless excrement compared to more significant aspects of communicative encounters" (p. 49). Certainly expressions like talking trash and *talking out of the side of your neck* suggest that words lie; but body language and other nonlinguistic vocal cues, such as pitch, rate, volume, intonation, less often do. Focusing on content does not get at the potential power of the process itself, that is, to manipulate others through a verbal barrage, solely to sharpen performance skills or to ward off physical violence. Though most young blacks acknowledge the "bullshit" element in much talk, they are also aware that the process of keeping up steady conversation, regardless of the content, can sometimes act as a survival strategy, a way of averting direct confrontation.

Like I was smallest for my age. A lotta people know I don't take no jive —I have had fights and thangs, but I ain't never really got whupped for my size. I takes care o' myself, but I can just scream so cold on somebody, dude just step back. Like dis big ol' dude from west side jammed me over on Hooper and 89th. I just steadily talkin' to d' brother, talkin' trash, jus' anythang. Righteously blow his mind! Dude move on off.

One night, Gregory an' me was walkin' down Central—Irvine swoop hard, fast and heavy! Pig tellin' me I looks like d' dude ripped off liquor store. I say, "Looky here man, you is mistaken, ain' even in d' vicinity!" I just blowed hard on the Man, talk whole lotta shit to 'im. Dude let us go. Like I'z sayin', yo' rap can save yo' life.

Furthermore, seemingly elaborated, overwrought, or boastful content may seem like trash to ignorant white ears, but to a black listener it is an integral part of black culture. Vestiges of fancy talk and other forms of elaborated dialog, such as "riddling conversation" used in the courtship process, attest to a long tradition of talk as process. One young woman summed it up: "I likes to hear a brother who knows how to talk. Don' hafta blow heavy, can sweet talk you too. Don' hafta make whole buncha sense, long sounds pretty."

The verbal game not only offers elaborate options and strategies for the would-be contestant, but provides a highly creative and intellectually challenging outlet for one's performative energies. Any discussion of verbal art in black culture is necessarily limited and impoverished set next to the real thing. The subtleties of body language, of intonation and facial expression, of gesture and stance, are impossible to transmit in words or even through pictures. What is possible is at least to highlight the range of verbal strategies that are played and something of the elaborate vernacular that characterizes the game.

There is another verbal strategy that has not yet been discussed in this section: verbal seduction. Because it is a male-female game, it will be saved for the next chapter. When talk gives way to physical manipulation and coercion, a different group of strategies are set in motion as well as a different set of vernacular expressions.

THE PHYSICAL GAME

The shift from verbal encounter to physical encounter is as much a shift of degree as of kind. Given the kinetic nature of verbal exchange, the performancelike quality of the situation itself, and the contest orientation of much interaction, the action implied in the phrases to *stomp*, to *jam*, to *come down hard*, gets reinforced or played out through some overt physical act. However, like their verbal counterparts, physical strategies get played out in a variety of ways depending on the intensity and seriousness of the confrontation, the initiator, the response he or she gets, the intent of the act, and the kind of verbal interaction that precedes or accompanies the act. Physical strategies also have their own special vernacular designations.

*Muscling in.* There are a number of physical moves that fall short of out-and-out fighting. These moves revolve around the concept of muscling in or strong-arming your way into someone's physical and psychological space. Applying muscle is seen, for example, in a number of sports-related terms—to *fire*, to *gun*, to *stuff*, to *stick*, to *slap one's shit away*, to *take one to the bridge* or *hoop*.

The expression to *bogart/bogard* is one of the commonly used terms to describe muscling into someone's personal space. The act and the expression are associated with Humphrey Bogart, a personality that many teenagers see as tough. You can muscle in on someone's sexual action: "Like, you be wid a girl. Dude come up, bogard you, get in d' way. Rank your play." You can also bogart in more physically overt ways: "Like, you be dancin', somebody try cut you. Move in on yo' space. Take up all the room." Sometimes actual muscle gets applied. "You at the end of the line, you jus' go on and push your way up to the front, bully in front o' somebody, and everybody that be in the front of you is now in the back. Dey say somethin', you gon' jam 'im." Sometimes you physically outmaneuver someone: "Sham on a person. Like he goin' through the chow line in d' joint. Dude in line drop his pencil, pick it up and somebody else got his place!" "Like a dude can be goin' to a party. If he hafta pay, he ain' gonna wanna pay, he gonna try to bogard his way *in* there.''

Implicit in the act of bogarting someone is the message that you can back up your muscle—that you can physically make good your claim over someone else's space. The expression to *bully* is a synonym for bogart. And, as the word suggests, your provocative move has muscle power behind it. Also implied is the literal intrusion on another's space—a manipulative move that also gains psychological ground for the intruder. This move is often seen in macho terms: ''Person jus' pushes everyone out they way. Be's a little bit mo' *masculine* than others—like Bogart. Named after Bogie who use let d' cigarette hang on his lip 'n git wet. So when 'bogart' a joint, you let it hang on yo' lip. Da's one way. Else you bogart, push people roun'— righteous gangster, like Bogie. He a cold dude!''

Of course muscling in on someone's territory can provoke both angry words and sometimes blows. But, before push comes to shove, there is often an extended verbal dance that gets played out.

*The Psychology of the Fight.* ''Like d' person really doesn't wanna fight you, but you get to loud-talkin' 'im 'n embarrassin' 'im in front o' his friends. Else you be bogardin' heavy. Not gonna sit dere an' take it, so he calls you out.'' Whatever provokes a fight, whether verbal harassment or physical bullying, the act itself is often prefaced by ''calling someone out''—a verbal challenge to fight. Anyone who has witnessed a fight between young blacks is struck by the pre-fight strategies that go on, an almost ritualistic performance. First, the opponents may base on each other for an extended period of time—testing each other through a battle of words and wits. The shift to actual physical aggression comes when opponents have, in a sense, felt each other out and find that ''talkin' ain' gonna do it—you gotta down his shit.'' Then, closure is demanded. This is done through any number of verbal challenges which are hurled back and forth:

> Well sucker, it's just me and you, so let's get
>   it on!
> Ain't no good feelings between us, so let's
>   thump.
> Ain't no air between us, we're toe to toe
>   now, so what we gonna do?
> Get along or get it on, chump!
> Get in my ass or get on!
> Let's go from the Y [refers to the Y-shape
>   fight stance—arms apart and body ready]
> Go fo' what chu know!

If you feel froggy, jump on!
In your ass!
Jump off my chest!
Open your chest and do your best!
Come out of you shit!
Come out of your coat and get down!

Some of these fight expressions are ritual challenges that have been in the vernacular for years; others are made up on the spot in response to the particulars of the situation. In either case, one sees strategic verbal exchange right up to the time the combatants throw blows. As one young man explained it, "You rap to d' brother, try make 'im see d' light. But when push come to shove, you come out you coat and get down!"

The psychological testing, the verbal display, the ritual challenges to fight, are very much like the pre-fighting behavior observed in other species. As Konrad Lorenz has pointed out, the human species goes through some of the same ritual dances as, say, the stickleback fish in maintaining and protecting claimed territory. And, like other species, humans engage in vocal challenge and display before combat. One teenager who had seen cock fights in Mexico likened fight rituals to the behavior he had witnessed between cocks before they fought. "Like dey circle 'round each other just like dudes gettin' down. Got dem little ol' steel spikes on and they be crowin' and carryin' on, righteously gettin' on dey case. Den dey get it on. I's cold, man. Cut each other wid dem spikes like cat do with his blade. I's a real trip!"

Fight vernacular used by black teenagers is extensive. Along with name terms, terms related to sex and drugs, and expressions characterizing verbal exchange, fight terms comprise one of the largest single categories of descriptive terms found in the lexicon. But fights are of different kinds. Some are pervaded by ritualistic verbal exchange; some are sudden and use the element of surprise for their success; some resemble a sneak attack; some are fought with fists, others with weapons; some reflect the playing out of a code of honor, others do not. Again, the lexicon reflects the differences in mood, tone, and stance that characterize each.

In particular, the largest number of fight terms deals with fistfights (to *go from the shoulders*, to *throw some blows*, to *go to blows*, to *get down from the Y*, to *go to fist junction*, to *thump*, to *cuff*, to *go from the fists*), along with vernacular terms that define the act of fighting itself (to *go down*, to *gunzle*, to *choose off*, to *box*, to *tussle*), and strategies used in fistfighting (to *throw a block/run, roll, throw sets on someone*—to hit a person with a series of quick double-fisted blows in an offensive move to incapacitate another before he can re-

104

taliate). A number of the terms for fighting warn the opponent, in no uncertain terms, just where he can expect a fist or knuckle to fall—*go upside one's head, get in one's eye, dance on one's lips*, and figuratively if not literally *get in* or *bust one's ass*. Finally, the endgame is literally to ground your opponent—to reduce his social space to next to nothing. So you attempt to *deck, drop, down*, or *dust* him with all due speed.

Many teenage fight narratives involve a western-frontier code of honor. A fair fight is seen as a one-on-one encounter—you *step out on the green* and others stand back, watch, give encouragement, make comments. And, finally, to the victor goes the spoils. The following narative is characteristic of accounts of fair fighting given by various teenagers:

> See, I was walkin' to d' student store. Two dudes came and jammed me. I know one o' 'em was playin', but d' other one was serious. He hit me in d' arm, the chest, d' legs. But d' other one hit me in d' face. "Why you wanna hit me in d' face?" An' he did it again. But the teacher stopped it, say, "Don't be fightin'." So I say, "Okay, you gon' git it after school. Den we get it on—fair fight." It got around d' *whole* school. All my pa'tners was dere, girl friend was dere. I would've felt bad if I woulda lost. He try tell me he goin' to d' band room. I say, "No, you gon' fight me today."
>
> I'z kin'a nervous 'cause I don't know if I could beat him. We walked down street car tracks and he didn't want fight in d' grass, he wanted to fight in the street. I had some slippery shoes on. I jus' hit 'im real fast like, knocked 'im down, didn't feel like jumpin' on him, 'cause wasn't no sense in it. So I let 'im get back up. Den he swing and I blocked his punch. Den white lady came round dere. She talkin' 'bout "Why you guys must be fightin'?" Den somebody called her a bitch in d' background. I think it was my girl friend, she say, "Bitch, why don't you let 'em fight? Dey ain' in *yo*' yard." An' she jus' went on home.
>
> Went around the corner, he want to fight again. Tha's where I really laid it to 'im. Crowd got bigger, I jus' felt good. Say, "Dat dude can *thump!*" Girl friend said, "I'ma give him a surprise when *I* get home! Dude Ali hisself!" I was dancin' around. He wanted fight 'bout two, three times. I didn't fight him the third time, 'cause wasn't no reason. It got around the school. "Yeh, you beat that boy's butt!" Den, I made friends wid him the nex' day. I didn't feel like be no enemies.

It is also characteristic of the fair fight that opponents often get together afterward, if not as tight friends at least as friendly adversaries.

In some instances, verbal and physical contests take on similar forms—the difference lies in the tools used to best your opponent.

Not all fights are fair, however. There are still other strategies used to overpower, outwit, or outmaneuver others and, in so doing, to wrest space from them. One way is to interrupt the pattern of the pre-fight verbal ritual by unexpectedly hitting your opponent. Terms like to *fire*, to *blaze on*, to *off*, or to *drive on someone* mean just that—to do unto others before they do you. "Like me and dis dude righteously basin' on each other. 'What chu wanna do?' Dat sucker fired on me right d' middle my word! No jivin'! You done jumped on a homeboy, fo' he had a chance to hit back—blaze on him!"

Another strategy is to sneak up on your would-be victim and catch him unawares.

> That's what happened to me. Dude creeped on me. I was fightin'. Dude was chokin' me up against the wall, and I was hittin' 'im, and his part-ner creeped up and stabbed me in the leg. His partner finally let me go and he was crawlin' through the crowd and his partner let me go. I guess he thought I'z dead. He's big dude. Had me up in the air, he let me go, and I fell on my legs. God damn! I seen him crawlin' through the crowd and I just got started limpin' over there and I hit 'im with a pipe.

Still another strategy is to gang up on a person and gain your ground by sheer numbers and fire force. Terms like to *jack up*, *jam*, *double punch*, *crowd*, and *move on someone* carry this meaning. All suggest crowding someone in a corner to take physical (and often material) advantage of him. "Like you and some brothers swoop on dis dude, jack 'im up, righteously jam him fo' his money, leather piece, watch—whatever he got. Sucker fight you, jus' double punch 'im. Usually too scared—or else surprise him, don't have a chance."

Probably the most aggressive behavior is when individuals go out purposefully *headhunting* or *gunning*—looking for an opportunity to start trouble. One of the most common arenas for starting a fight is at a social event, where they *turn it out*.

> Couple o' roughies, hardheads that comes into a party and don' wanna see it happen. They hafta start somethin', like get in argument wid a dude or disrespect a young lady. Git rough, jump on d' people, snatch the record player, snatch everybody's hat, rip off their leather piece. Get to thumpin' wid everybody! Turn d' party out. Jus' *end* the thing!

*Weapons.* The force of strong feelings can escalate a fistfight into confrontation with weapons: a knife (*blade, toothpick, flick, nig-ger flicker, shank slicer*), a gun (*piece, roscoe, my shit*), brass knuckles (*knuckles, brass*), chains, tire irons, or whatever else you can grab. "Busted for almost killin' dis dude. Me and dis dude was throwin' blows. Dude pick up dis 2 x 4 and was beatin' me wid it and I jus' had my little blade on me at the time—I jus' got 'im. Try to kill 'im. He jus' had me dat mad. Like you. You git so mad sometime, lose self. I jus' put a few cuts all over 'im.''

Among teenagers who had been directly or indirectly involved in escalated physical assault, one of the prime reasons given for turning to weapons is retaliation, an eye for an eye: You do me, I do you. "In the projects we had twelve-gauge shot gun. An' my brother ran down the streets. He shot it up in d' air, yellin', 'I'ma blow you away.' Dis girl done slapped him or cut 'im or somethin'. I thought he's gonna *shoot* 'er!'' Sometimes retaliation involves groups of people gunning for those who have assaulted a friend. "Like a whole bunch a low riders—they had messed up dis dude—beat 'im up, cut 'im, shot 'im. All his partners got mad. Get in their car—nothin' but hardheads— swoop on dey set, shotgun. Turn it out.''

The ultimate act of aggression that can be played out against your would-be foe is the act of killing (*wasting, icing, offing, chilling, sniping, snuffing*). For those teenagers who continually live on the cutting edge of survival, who often walk around with a life time's accumulation of feelings of resentment against the Man's control, the ultimate act of retaliation is to strike out and kill. The grim reality is that those most often killed are your own people, not the perceived oppressor. It's a "no win" proposition. "Dude gets crazy, offs a brother. Den pigs waste 'im. Dude dead, other brother dead. Honky pigs be sayin', 'Look dem niggers killin' each other.' Now ain't dat cold! White man, he kill all kinda people—Viet Nam—he send d' brothers over dere, get wasted. He been killin' our people since we slaves! All d' time on black people's back, dey jus' get crazy wid each other. Ain' doin' nothin' 'cept killin' our own same kind.''

*Upstaging.*     Not all physical strategies are coercive or abusive in nature. Some attempt to call attention to the person through the performance of some physically related feat—the demonstration of some particular skill. The expression to *shoot your best stick* means to do the best you can, to show off your finest skill. Though the phrase usually relates to pool, it has become generalized to a variety of other "competitive" activities: dancing, playing an instrument, sports, sex. Here the performer tries to outdo would-be rivals—to upstage them through the demonstration of greater ability. Some of the expressions that characterize an extraordinary performance, to *cook*, to *blow fire*, to *smoke out someone*, suggest that the person is generating lots of energy, lots of heat, and in so doing is taking lots of space. There are song lines used by young people to let someone know when their performance is "on" and when it's not: "When you're hot, you're hot; when you're not, you're not—so get down to d' ground and move it round and round or get along wi'chu song.''

The suggestion that a good performer demands literal and figurative space is even more apparent in other vernacular expressions for a "hot" performer, such as to *wail*, to *tear up*, or to *stride*. Though none of these performances are purely physical in nature—a good pool player attempts to outwit as well as outshoot his opponent; a fine musician brings great intelligence to the music—the action element does get forcefully played out. And the vernacular characterizes the physical impact those performances have on spectator and performer alike.

*The Physical Freeze.*   Perhaps the most overtly psychological of the physical strategies (though all games involve psychological maneuvers) is the freeze. As the expression suggests, a person attempts to one-up by giving another the cold shoulder. Here one does not necessarily confront or outperform another in the ways already discussed—you simply ignore the person. Sometimes, in fact, the response to provocative physical or verbal confrontation is to *shine it on* or to *chill another's action*. "Like when somebody wanna fight, jus' walk away from 'im. Blow dey mind. Don' say *shit* to 'im. Like somebody's blowin' on you, jus' don' feel like listening to 'im. Just don't say nothin' to 'im." Ignoring someone else is purposeful behavior. Sometimes you just don't want to be bothered and by ignoring you say, "Don't come into my space." Other times, shining someone on is a deliberate strategy to effect a particular result. "Like you have a broad—know she digs you a lot. You wanna see how much she does. You don't talk to her for a while, see what happens after that." An expression like to *fake on someone*—to pretend not to see another—implies the conscious deception involved in this kind of move. You cool down the situation. Ironically, though you do not overtly move to take space as in other manipulative strategies, you do, in fact, take it by doing the unexpected, by calling attention to yourself and your action.

Finally, there is a kind of manipulative act that, in a sense, freezes someone with a look. The power of the evil eye—a look capable of putting a jinx on another—has a long history in black culture, dating back to Africa. In African culture, people of power, shamans or witch doctors, could put a curse on a person by fixing their eyes on them. In contemporary teenage culture, the evil eye gets somewhat transformed —you stare hard at someone with the intention of "blowing their mind" and disrupting their behavior. In a manipulative sense, the evil eye, or the *coke stare*, accomplishes much the same purpose as it did historically—to jinx someone, to upset them and make them susceptible to your power.

There are other expressions for intently looking or staring at another—to *scope*, to *pin*, to *eyeball*—but none carries the ominousness of the act of giving someone the evil eye. In fact, terms like to scope or pin may be covert, so that the person is unaware of being looked at. Though these visual strategies vary in degree and intensity of impact, they all are potential approaches for manipulating or gaming on others.

### THE POSSESSIONAL GAME

One of the most flamboyant games in town is played out through the conspicuous display of material possessions. Whether it's your car, your clothes, your young lady or young man, your new hairdo, your jewelry, you *style* it. The word "style" in vernacular usage means to show off what you've got. And for teenagers with little money and few actual possessions, showing off what you do have takes on increased importance. As one youth put it, "It's identity. It's a big ego trip." Roger Abrahams (1963) has noted that "exhibitionism for purposes of attraction" permeates much black male behavior. Indeed "style of living is more important than life itself" (p. 37). In one sense, style is the person—it makes a statement to the world about who you are and how you wish to be seen.

*Dress.* Perhaps the most literal style you can display is in your clothes. Again, it is important to remember that much teenage behavior is performance-oriented, complete with lines, stage movements, and costumes. Your social costume takes on increased significance when you are vying with others for attention and space. It is your personal signature. Definitions given for terms like to *style*, to *front off*, to *fiend*, to *high sign*, or to *fonk*—all of which mean to show off or upstage others—invariably reveal the highly competitive and consciously manipulative aspect of, for example, dress. "You all dressed up and you have your apple hat on, your flairs, and your boots and you walkin' down the street, lookin' at all d' people lookin' at you. You lookin' good. You *know* you lookin' good, so you gon' style wid the lookin' good. Be more or less flamboyant!" Some see themselves as being "on stage" whenever others are around or even possibly around. "I'm always high signin'. Got to be clean and ready! I stay sharp while I'm at the pad too, so I high sign on couple cats if dey slide by. Stay sharp."

Because how you dress is a personal statement about who you are, many young blacks resent jobs where they have to wear uniforms. "I likes to get clean and stay sharp. Tha's why I wanna quit this job [groundskeeper aide for the County of Los Angeles]. I like to wear nice clothes. [What kind of job do you want?] Don't make no difference, 'long's I can wear some nice threads."

Not all teenagers costume themselves in the same way. It depends on the part being played. Many males still emulate the pimp. The pimp style, of course, gets personally interpreted by each individual but generally carries with it an air of flamboyance and elegance. "Right now, if I came off in here and I had on one o' dem fonky all-wool suits —three piece—cape 'n things, diamond ring and everything, I say I *would* be fonkin' on you. Frontin' my pimp clothes."

Another discernible style is the so-called gangster look. Though it is as sharp as the pimp style, it is often more subdued. "Like you dress down in you gangster fronts. Sharkskin suit, stingy brim, else fedora ace-deuce to d' side. Got on yo' executive shoes—thousand eyes— packin' your piece under y' coat. Righteous gangster!"

The Black Power movement has had an influence on dress, and it can be seen in what can be called the Afro style. "Got on your dashiki, some beads—maybe some sandals. Walkin' down d' street. 'Bhani ghani, brother—Wha's happ'nin'?' Got yourself a nice natural—all blowed out. Frontin' wi' d' Afro look."

Also there is a catch-all style that can be labeled the mod front. It essentially means that you are dressed in the prevailing style of the day —whatever that is or whatever you perceive it to be. One young man talked about the "mod bag" he was into during a conversation about an upcoming party:

> You see me mod to the bone tomorrow night. In d' full flesh! I'ma show you how I gonna get decked out and ready! I'ma have on NA-VY COAT! A NA-VY seaman's jacket, some blue navy pants wid black iridescent pattern, silk shirt—tight! Apple hat and some black boots wi' d' heels—they cold! Blow everybody's mind!

Of course there are idiosyncratic touches to all costuming, and some teenagers push costuming to highly dramatic ends to establish a reputation based on their unique dress. One young man known as Panama always dressed in white: white jump suits or white three-piece linen slack suits, white shoes, and a white Panama hat. Another, known as Cowboy, wore boots, levi flair pants, cowboy shirts, vests, and a Stetson hat. Still another, who called himself Al Capone, carried the gangster style to great lengths: black suits complete with black shirts and white ties. Though all costumes are not so elaborate— exceptions to the rule—the rule itself is still to be clean, tight, and ready.

There is a large vocabulary that defines clothes in general— *drapes*, *rags*, *pieces*, *threads*, *fronts*, *styles*—and some terms that talk primarily about specific clothing items, such as *vines* (suits), *sharks* (sharkskin suits), *silks* (silk clothes), *bennys* (coats), *brims* (hats), *kicks* (shoes), *lizards* (lizard-skin shoes), *leather pieces* (leather jackets), and so on. There is even a larger vocabulary that refers to being well dressed (*tabbed, suited down, decked out, ragged out, pressed, dressed tight, dressed down, dapped down, choked down*). Finally, there are expressions reserved for being extraordinarily well dressed (*clothed heavy, dapped to a tee, decked to death, fonked out heavy, clean/fonky/mod/ragged/tabbed/sharp to the bone, sharp as a mosquiter's peter*).

The cover term that is most often used to characterize the well-dressed person is *clean*. It carries with it the connotation of being not only sharply dressed—"sharp as a pin"—but physically clean ("he was clean—had his Sunday bath"), neat (clothes pressed or ironed), and dressed in your good clothes ("be wearin' good clothes, not raggedy shit"). And, in a real sense, clean is "untouchable." "You clean, nobody cain't touch you den. He's decked out clean, Clean, CLEAN! His clothes is *bad!* He's decked to kill! Da's what we [young women] tell 'im. Like if a dude is dressed clean and he's walkin' down d' street, I look at 'im, I say, 'Man, dat dude is decked to kill. He's clean as a PIN!' An' you better not touch 'im neither. An' don't tell d' nigger he ain't lookin' good, 'cause you get in d' biggest fight!"

Being exceptionally well dressed encourages a hands-off policy. The cleaner you are, the more space you often demand. Among teenagers who see getting clean and staying sharp as a desirable goal in life, there is a kind of respect for the person who exhibits a clean front. Of course, for those whose game is elsewhere, the sharp dresser can become a target—the object of jokes, threats and other forms of coercive behavior. But even among the hardheads—those who are into physical fireworks rather than costuming—there is a grudging recognition that to get clean and stay that way is an important mark of getting over in the world. "Dude dress nice, stay clean, brother maybe think twice 'fore he mess 'im up."

The ultimate in fine dress—particularly among males—is to get *silked to the bone*. The expression connotes not only the exceptionally well-dressed person, but a man who is so clean that he is wearing silk from his underclothes on out—"Silk underwear, silk tee-shirt, silk shirt, silk suit, silk nylons—you fiendishly down in yo' silks! You be sayin', 'I'm the greatest, more expensive than everybody else!' " Being well dressed is not only a way of upstaging others but of demanding attention and, therefore, space. So the more conspicuous the display, the more expensive the outfit, the more ammunition you have to game on others. And garments made out of silk (or more often passed off as silk), imitation, or sometimes real, alligator or lizard-skin shoes, "diamond" stickpins and rings, namebrand watches, all give you a look of affluence (and "costume power"), even if they're not the real thing. That's for others to find out. Many capping sessions revolve around exposing another's phony fronts. Nonetheless, real goods are appreciated and suggest to one's audience, "I've got some money to back up my fronts."

*Money.* Young blacks are very much aware that the ultimate name of the game in American society is money. You can get away with imitation clothes, but *long green* or *long bread* speaks loudly and for itself. The expression to *flash* defines fronting in general, but most often it refers to the noticeable display of money. Seldom do ghetto teenagers have much money. But when and if they do, they let others know: "Like dude maybe cop a TV, somebody get they purse took. Else, dude get his paycheck—he gon' show it around. Flash on people. Nigger's money funny, he still gon' try 'n flash!" The vernacular includes expressions that characterize the pretense of having a lot of money. A phony bankroll—a wad of money with maybe a large bill on top and a few singles in the middle (and sometimes paper on the bottom)—is variously called *a California bankroll, a nigger's bankroll,* or *a Chicago bankroll.* So, even in the case of monetary display, the person may pretend to have more than he actually does. Style may not replace substance, but here, as in other teenage encounters, it can go a long way toward claiming space for the performer—if not directly through what you have, then indirectly for how well you pretend.

*Cars.* We have already seen that cars play an important role in the lives of many black teenagers, both as status symbols and as mobile homes, territory on wheels. For many, the car also allows the widest range of conspicuous display. It is highly visible (and audible), it literally takes up more space than other possessions and can be shown off in a variety of contexts. And it allows one to simultaneously front off in a number of different ways. It is the most versatile possession.

Not everyone desires the same kind of car to style with. It depends on the kind of front—the image—you hope to cultivate.

> Like you got your pimp ride. Da's a blade, some kinda Cadillac—El D., D.V., whatever—long and sleeky lookin', black blade wid a rag top. All d' pimps got Cadillacs. They too common for me. I likes a Mark IV. Den you got yo' gangster ride. Could be a big ride, like a Cadillac—like my ride's a Lincoln wid d' gangster doors.
> Low-riders and gangsters they different. 'Cause lotta gangsters they ride around in big ol' giant cars. And low-riders they ride around playin' d' music loud, beautiful paint job on they car, freakin' up and down the street on dey lifts. So, I would call a gangster ride a big ride— Al Capone ride.
> Git one o' dem old cars—one o' dem '50, '60 rides. Throw a new motor off in dat car. Put black seats in dere, tints [windows]. You just

shine it up and put some wire wheels on and some diamond-shape back windows—got yo'self a fiendish ride!

Can identify certain types of cars with element o' people. Like car used in d' roarin' 20s. And d' dude tha's in the car—an' all of his partner's—got big hat or they sittin' in certain way—like gangsters.

Sometimes, gangster rides—along with a variety of other cars—are converted into low rides by installing hydraulic lifts. Teenagers who can't afford this may *heat the springs*, although the lowering of the front or back is not subject to electrical manipulation. "Have your springs heated, so you can go down. It bounces, but not as much as when it's lifted, 'cause when it's lifted, it dribbles. When you lifted and i's dropped, it dribbles real fast. But whe yo' springs are heated, you jus' bounce like dat [gestures up and down with palm] when you hit a dip."

Many teenage dialogs are given over to detailed discussions of the ways you can freak off your car and increase maneuverability through lifts, heating the springs, and the like. The primary goal in freaking off a car is to create a vehicle (literally or in one's imagination) that will take space from others.

Expensive cars are much desired since they take space by the sheer fact of their size and implied cost. But for most teenagers, such cars are way out of reach. So other car-related strategies for fiending, fonking, styling, or gaming are used—such as the elaborate attention given to car accessories or to the maneuverability of the car. There are a number of terms in the vernacular that characterize showing off your car—and simultaneously showing up another person. Terms like to *bounce*, to *dance*, to *drop your ride*, to *dribble*, to *jitterbug*, to *pancake*, to *fall*, to *scrape*, all describe some kind of showy effect obtained by playing with your lift system. The goal is definitely performative.

> If a person has lifts in they car, get downright fonky! Jus' fall 'n scrape. Make as much noise you can and lay down some sparks. And da's when you git downright fon-ky! You tryin' a make *them* look bad, frontin' *dem* off. Get beside a dude, let yo' lifts down on 'im. Drop it all the way to the ground. Bring it up. Dance wid it! Or you low-ridin', bouncin' down d' street. One dude may be low-ridin', but he don't have no lifts on his car and other dude do. Well, dey stop where dey's s'pose' be at— dey destination. Other dude drops his car to d' ground. Well, he done fonked on dat dude—'cause I use dat myself.

Sometimes, as suggested, a person makes his presence known through loud sounds as well as visible maneuvers. So a driver revs the engine, abruptly drops the body of the car so that sparks fly and a blast of sound hits the ear, or *lays rubber* or *lays wheels* by abruptly driving off to the accompaniment of loud exhaust pipes and screeching tires. "Like if you got a bad ride an' you be dribblin' down the street, you wanna make sure everybody see and hear you, lay some rubber, blow your pipes—jus' righteously make a lotta noise."

There are still other maneuvers that decidedly call attention to driver and car. One of the favorite strategies among the teenagers I met was to *swoop*. In car-related situations, this means a variety of things—to weave in and out of traffic; to abruptly maneuver your car in order to cut off another car; to cut across several lanes of traffic, either in front or in back of another car (the *Hollywood swoop*); to cut in front of other cars at an intersection and, in so doing, stop traffic and force cars to go around you; to serpentine over a dip, so your car bounces up and down (the *Slauson swoop*); to come around a corner at high speed, making a racket (to *cop a block*); to pull abruptly over to the curb and park (to *pull a quick park*); or to pull over to a particular curb to attract the attention of some young woman (*hoopdie swoop*). Whatever the strategy, the end is both performative and manipulative.

Often several cars *caravan*—join together to perform elaborate street and freeway maneuvers. "Like you havin' a caravan. Like when ever'body playin' 'follow d' leader.' Call it caravan. You be leadin', you be ridin' in dis lane, you make a quick jump over dat lane. Everybody swoops wi' chu. D' caravan got dis pretty down. One might swoop in front another car at a red light, and let d' other ones come. One go dis way, one swoop dat way, and one'll swoop *way out*. And let 'em all come in and den dey all fall back in line."

Strategic moves are not only made with the car itself, but by the driver and occupants in terms of the ways they physically arrange themselves in the car. Two of the most stylized types of physical posturing are to *lean* and to *low-ride*. Essentially to lean means to lean inward, away from the window, as if you are resting your elbow on a console or armrest—whether or not your car has one—while steering the car with your left hand (or, as a passenger, with your left hand braced against your leg or waist as you lean inward). Leaning carries all kinds of connotations. It is suggestive of what pimps do as they cruise around in expensive cars, checking on their prostitutes. "Pimpin', like in a Cadillac. You stylin'. I'm a Cadillac pimp! Jus' lean on yo' armrest, ride on. Check out yo' young ladies. Takin' care o' bidness." Leaning also suggests that you have an expensive car that *has* an armrest or console to lean on. "Like you have a Riv, a big, beautiful, expensive car with a console. You gonna *lean!* Mos'ly you lean in a Cadillac, because you *know* you in high class. Put yo' arm on d' rest and you *know* you look good!" Leaning also implies that you are involved in some illegal, dangerous, and therefore important activity.

"Jus' like all d' gangsters an' pimps have deir armrest down, be leanin' in, checkin' out d' action, smokin' weed, hidin' from d' police. Dat represent they doin' somethin' wrong."

Very often, low-riding accompanies leaning. In one sense, low-riding means to drive a car that has been lowered. But low-riding also refers to a particular posture assumed by the driver (and sometimes by the passengers) where a person sits as low in one's seat as possible, so that all that is visible is the top of the person's head and eyes peering over the steering wheel. Like leaning, low-riding is a strategy designed to call attention to driver and car. One young woman's detailed and humorous narrative sums up some of the more important dos and don'ts:

Leanin' tha's when a dude be leanin' *so hard*, like he layin' down in d' car. Da's what they do in their cars. They sittin' pretty and watchin' the girls. Lean like, "I'm jus' the man." But, it looks good when you got three guys and they be leanin' and the one in d' middle he sittin' some kin'a way and both of 'em up front—oooh! If they got somethin' to show for it. They mobsters, they kin forgit it. Some jus' high sign. Cadillacs da's all it is—a high sign. Some guys don't know you don' hafta *lean* in a Cadillac, 'cause it automatically stand out. You don' hafta make d' car look good by you doin' extra curriculin' things, 'cause it's *there*—specially a Rado. It's *there!*

But guys in low-ridin' cars lean and low-ride 'cause they know they gotta be fonky and they say, "Well, the car be lookin' good, I gotta look good." 'Cause guy'll tell me, "Joanie, get low." I say, "Get low, my ass!" I don't lean for nobody! Can you see me leanin'? Mm-Mm! Only way I be leanin', I be loaded or I be drunk. Be leanin' on some-body's shoulder. But leanin'—uh-uh.

An' now for a girl, I don't dig. Young lady don' look nice. *She* can be on d' armrest and sit straight up and maybe d' guy be leanin', talkin' to her. But some guy like to be stylin'—show his woman off at the moment. But for a woman to *lean*, uh-uh. She wadn't made for leanin' —strictly for guys. I's a game, really.

Almost any context provides the setting for the conspicuous dis-play of driver and car—around schools, parks, playgrounds, along main streets that traverse South Central, on freeways—any place one can be seen. Some of the best show places for teenage car devotees are the local drive-in eating places. "You go to Jack-in-the-Box, Imperial and Main, Central and Compton, McDonald at Florence and Santa Fe where blood and Mexican go, all d' funkiest rides be out. I say *all* d' funkiest! Sunday night."

One Sunday night, a young friend and I went up to the local Jack-in-the-Box. It was an extraordinary show. Cars of every make and model were out: low rides, high rides, gangster rides, an old Hudson,

Camaros, freaked-off Volkswagens, even old Cadillacs, cruised around the parking lot like great birds showing their colors. Tape decks competed with each other for musical space. Cars screeched in and out of the lot, leaving tire marks and sparks in their wake. The revving of motors and the blowing of pipes mingled with other noise. On occasion, a musical horn punctuated the scene. People were leaning and low-riding, styling their cars, their clothes, their companions. Cars with lifts dribbled, danced, and pancaked down the streets adjacent to the drive-in. The finale was the departure of one caravan of Volkswagens, a club called the Volksmasters. They formed a V-shaped phalanx and sped off in twos down the street in a criss-cross pattern like some military drill team. My companion summed up the whole show when he said, "Blood really gettin' down to d' ground—fiendin' and leanin', stylin' and frontin'—it be better 'n TV!"

These, then, are some of the games that black teenagers play out in their attempts to assert power over others, to control and manipulate their environment, to survive with style in a hard world. It should be apparent by now that the games are not played independently of one another—verbal contests may be accompanied by physical displays; fights are often preceded by ritualized verbal exchanges; fine-looking clothes are enhanced by good conversation and attractive companions; driver and car both perform for others. Though a sense of contest and performance permeates much teenage behavior and interaction, all games are not serious or deadly. Many are playful, though to the outsider they may appear deadly serious. Many are practical. Others are psychologically satisfying ways of playing out a whole range of "socially unacceptable" feelings and behaviors. Finally, these games are a way of taking space and establishing one's sense of power, status and prestige in the eyes of one's peers. In teenage culture, where "what you do" is often equated with "who you are," one-upping becomes a socially prized end in itself.

THE FRONTS

The games you choose to play depend, to a large extent, on the particular front you want to display. As already said, the front is the image, the persona you show to the world. In performance terms, it is the character (or characters) you are portraying, the role (or roles) you are playing out. To develop and sustain your front, you may use a combination of game plans—verbal, physical, material—to get over. Or you may rely on a particular strategy for your modus operandi. Though fronts overlap and make use of some of the same interpersonal strategies, there are still distinct and identifiable personality types that emerge. And these types use the same games in different ways. Among black ghetto males there are two prominent role models that seem to dominate the scene: the pimp and the badman.

*The Pimp.*   Where middle-class status, occupation, or office remain largely inaccessible and illusory, the mark of a person, particularly a young man, is what he is, his self and the extensions of that self. As we have seen, these include his personality, the clothes he wears, the possessions he displays, the women he claims as his own, and, not the least, his ability to rap. For many black men, no one epitomizes these qualities more than the pimp. He plays many of the games with consummate skill; they are his stock in trade.

There are many variations and permutations of the pimp front. Some, like the *slickster* or *con man*, rely more on verbal guile and deception than, say, on the display of possessions. Others, like the *dap daddy* or *doogie daddy*, the *cool dude* or the *cool cat*, emphasize sharp dress as well as skillful talk. His manner, dress, and conversational style are widely emulated. He has made it through wits, guile, and verbal mastery, more often than not at the expense of the white man— a fact not lost on young blacks.

The impact of the pimp and the pimp front is still so widespread in teenage interaction that it is hard to isolate all the areas of influence. A number of varied expressions are defined by young blacks with the image of the pimp used by way of example. A few are worth noting—such as definitions given for the expression to "fonk on someone," which may emphasize the fact that a car-related front may well include being seen as a lady's man. "Say some dude has one car, another car comin' down the street, he got one young lady. Other dude, his car *full* o' ladies—like a pimp an' his 'hos [whores]. Righteously fonk on him." "Ridin' down the street, got yo' curly-haired girl sittin' next to you, ride up. You gon' high sign your young lady. She just looks better—she d' star and you her pimp!"

Other situational definitions emphasize the pimp's possession of fine things and the speaker's identification with him. "You have on a nice suit of clothes, ridin' in a Cadillac, Lincoln, Riviera—whatever you got. You pimpin'. You stood on yo' armrest. Set to d' side. Just stylin'. Just lean, ride on. Wait for next young lady to slip outa nowhere. I'ma Cadillac pimp. Leanin' *hard* and *heavy*! Dat what pimps do. They put dey pimp rest down and just style." Finally, the pimp is seen as someone who *steps fast*, who knows how to take care of business. "Somebody be steppin' fast dey like a pimp, on their J.O.B., righteously takin' care o' business in d' streets. Pimpin' hard, gettin' over. Apply to hustlin' life."

The term pimp itself is often used to modify words or phrases that are seen as aspects of the pimp style. So there is a *pimp walk* or *pimp stride* (in which the walker bobs up and down and side to side as he walks), a *pimp rest* or *pimp post* (the armrest in a car, particularly a luxury car), *pimp shades* or *pimp tints* (lightly tinted glasses), *pimp fronts* (expensive clothes), and *pimp dust* (cocaine, acknowledged to be a favorite among pimps).

Finally, teenage vernacular is heavily laced with expressions borrowed from the pimp's vocabulary. Terms like *'ho*, *bitch*, *trick*, *John*, *turn someone out*, *put her on the block*, *stepper*, *mack*, *star*, *queen*, and *stallion* are just a few of these expressions.

For many young men, the pimp's game is the ultimate one. Because it combines wits, intelligence, and verbal skill with great style, it is a hustle many not only emulate in manner and dress but actually aspire to in fact. Many youths see pimping as the best job you can have. When I asked young men what they wanted to do, a number responded they wanted to be pimps. "I'ma be a *stone* pimp. Get me a Cadillac—a woman's gonna put me in one. She gonna step for me, make dat money." There is an expression, used as an epithet, to challenge a person who aspires to pimp status: "Are you good for the hustle?" (Can you really make it in the world as a pimp or are you a *wanna be* just fronting off, form without substance?) Because the art of pimping requires a great deal of street savvy and brains, those who are seen as pretenders to the profession are put down with particular vehemence. "Like some sucker frontin' off like a pimp—be jibbin' 'bout his 'hos. He nothin' but a fonky nickel-dime nigger, wanna be. You kin tell d' dude righteously down with the pimp hustle just be lookin' at what he do. Don't need to talk 'bout it, he *doin'* it!" Few of the young men I met actually had made it as pimps, but it doesn't prevent them from trying, at every opportunity, to "get across." Many a young woman has been approached by a would-be pimp:

> I went to Jeff last summer and it was *different* from Dorsey [a middle-class high school]. Buncha niggers over there think they pimps! All during class—after class too—you'd get notes sayin' "Job!" This dude asked me did I wanna be his "secretary." SECRETARY! At night? "Very good job, pays real well." Sucker gonna put me on the block, 'ho for 'im—that's his secretary.

The pimp is often seen as the complete businessman with the best game in town (the expressions "take care of business" and "be on your job" often imply pimping or pimplike activities). But pimping is recognized as hard work, a fact not lost on many. One aspiring young man saw it this way:

> If you gonna hustle, gotta do it right. Got to steadily stay on yo' job. Lotta dudes *think* they pimps, but their conversation just ain't strong

enough. Like you shoot yo' best mack to some young lady. Like you
mackin' hard and heavy and you rappin' hard and you *know* you rappin' hard. Shootin' your stick hard, but young lady ain't diggin' your
action. You can't sell, you can't buy, hear what I'm sayin'?

So there is often a great gap between the desire and the reality,
between form and substance. The fact that few young males make it as
pimps is, in one sense, beside the point. The point is that the pimp and
his front are important in teenage male culture. He is a real-life success
story and exerts influence on the content and style of much teenage
interaction.

*The Hardhead/Badman.* Certainly the bad guy is more accessible in both form and substance than is the pimp. Like the pimp and
his various alter egos, the *hardhead* or the *bad-assed nigger* or the *badman* has also been a folk hero both in the oral literature and daily lives
of blacks (see Roger Abrahams, 1970, for an extended and lively treatment of the trickster and badman in black folk literature). Whereas
the pimp gets over through wits, guile, and verbal skill, the hardhead
relies heavily on physical intimidation to get what he wants. He is a
man of brawn who uses his muscle to control others, a person given to
few words and much action. He is decidedly a man's man, not a lady's
man—a bird of prey rather than a peacock.

In teenage terms, the badman comes in many more guises than
the pimp does. There is the outright *hardhead, gorilla, cutthroat,
hoodlum,* or *mad dog* who actively seeks out situations in which to
confront or assault others— to headhunt. He is generally seen as a
person of little style and limited strategy. The expression to *gorilla
someone* means to beat up someone severely or to rape a woman.
"Like the slang say, hardhead gon' get down fonky on somebody. He
a righteous gorilla! Crazy-ass nigger be like animal—like in d' jungle.
Don't care 'bout nobody, nothin'. Cain't tell 'im nothin', 'cause he
ain't listenin', just righteously in yo' ass. Rip on young ladies too. He
crazy!''

Closely related to the gorilla is the *cowboy*. He too is seen as a
outright troublemaker, but is less overtly violent in his behavior. He is
more disruptive and disagreeable, a rowdy rather than a cutthroat.
There is a fine line between the two types and certainly they are synonymous in many contexts, but there does seem to be a recognized and
acknowledged difference between their outward behaviors.

See, a righteous thug, a cutthroat, he do you in a minute! He ain't
talkin', he jus' fire on you. He kill you dead. Now d' cowboy, he make
a lotta noise, get foul wi' chu. Turn out a party—get to throwin' things,
start a fight. Act crazy. Call attention to hisself. Jus' a varmint, a
rowdy. But he ain't gonna *waste* you!

119

The *gangster* shares some of the same badman qualities with the hardhead or gorilla—he can be a physically violent or abusive person, intractable and immune to any verbal strategies designed to dissuade him. But, unlike the out-and-out hardhead, he has style, courage, and a ganglandlike code of ethics. He is the tough guy of TV and movies. In addition to terms like "bogart," other tough-guy fronts are reflected in the vernacular to describe aspects of this particular badman's style. Gangster-related terms like *piece* and *roscoe* are used to identify a gun. The *Dillinger front* is a particular style of dress that attempts to emulate the gangster look. As mentioned, the *gangster ride* or the *Al Capone ride* is a car that looks like the black sedans popular in 30s and 40s gangster movies. Like the term pimp, the word gangster is used to modify various things associated with gangsters. For example, certain car parts or accessories, identified with gangster rides, are labeled accordingly—*gangster walls* (wide white-walled tires), *gangster doors* (four doors on a sedan), and the *gangster ride* itself. The term gangster alone means marijuana. Finally, gangster is an adjective that refers to something good or exceptional and, like many other synonyms for fine and exceptional in black vernacular (*fiendish, terrible, bad, tough, mean, wicked*), inverts standard white usage for the words. Bad becomes good.[4]

The gangster front, then, is not limited to a sheer display of physical power or force. It can incorporate a variety of props to interpret the badman image—a certain kind of car, a particular style of dress, a tough-guy sense of honor that acknowledges and respects another's physical courage and prowess.

> Like dude call himself Dillinger. He tough. Don' mess wid 'im less you think you kin whup 'im. Drive around, partners in d' car—dey righteous gangsters. Got a '64 Chevy, black, gangster walls, tinted window. Looks good. One time, me and my partner at dis party—Dillinger and his partners come by, gonna jam Joey 'n me. We get down. Thump wid 'im. We won too. Shook hands at d' end. Everything cool. We done showed ourself and Dillinger he don' mess wid us no mo'.

The low-rider is a front distinct from but related to the badman. Low-riders can be physically abusive, rowdy, and aggressive. But often their aggressive behavior gets played out through assertive and showy driving. They "assault" others with their cars, not necessarily with their fists or weapons. Even more than gangsters, the low-riders use the car as a central part of their front. In some ways the low-rider is like the frontier badman who is lost without his horse. And expressions like *sitting* or *riding a dago or a beast* reinforce the image of the man and his ride. Furthermore, the expression to *ride shotgun*, which means you and your companions are out to get someone or you're posturing *as if* you're out to get someone, is often associated with low-riders as well as gangsters. It again suggests the inseparability of the ride as part of the front. As we will see when we discuss local heroes, the low-rider is a kind of nomad. And like other nomads—Atila the Hun, Gengis Khan—the low-rider's car becomes a literal and figurative vehicle for preying on those who are less mobile. The image of *swooping in your ride* connotes a nomadic sense of moving in quickly on someone.

The variations on the badman theme described above hardly exhaust the front. Like the image of the pimp, the badman front includes a variety of permutations and combinations of behavior that overlap. What is basic to the various types of badmen is some kind of conscious show of physical force. There is a need to prove oneself, to demonstrate an ability to "dish it out" and to "take it"—even in the face of overwhelming odds—such as when you move to another territory, to another part of town.

> When I first went over dere see, weren't no friends over dere—I didn't know *nobody*. I walked in dere. At first I thought I'z gon' have a problem. I guess they gonna give me a blanket party, but I let 'em know ahead o' time, first one dat does it, I'z gon' sharpen up somethin' to stick 'em with. I don't care *where* I stick 'em. 'Cause they had dis big ol' guy—he was real big—me an' him had a fight. He whupped me, he kep' on whuppin' me, but I kep' on—everytime I see 'im—I jump right back on 'im, even if I get a whuppin'. Den, the last time, I whupped him. Den, everybody started givin' me respect den. 'Cause dey knew I wadn't d' type dat never quit. Somebody whup me, they might as well kill me, 'cause I'm gon' get back on 'im, when I do get right. Don't nobody mess wid me. Den, all my friends started comin' over. Whenever dey needed *my* help, I be dere now.

And within the gang structure, it is often an expected part of the initiation to prove onself. "Was baby Gladiator. Had to fight to get in, you know the one before me."

A great pride is taken in being tough. The more potential danger inherent in the situation, the greater the proving ground for one's "bad-assed" ability.

> Oh, I got a *beautiful* assault! Knocked a police officer dead up side d' car—got *to* 'im! Boy, I loved dat. Other pull his gun, couldn't get to 'im. He said he's gon' blow my black ass off. I said, "Bitch!" He got hot and pulled his gun. I just grabbed 'im in the throat and I said, "If you move your hand up a *little mo'*, I'm snatchin' dat throat out!" I took the fine art of self-defense. I would kill you *dead* in d' *streets!* You be surprised how fast I move. I more or less jumped on him. He was talkin' like dis, he thought he could git his hands down dere and give it

to me. Thing to do is always look at dat man's eye—he give himself
away! A cop ain't no fool! He'd a FLINCHED—I be on him!

I had another one. He messed around and got *his* ass righteously
whupped! It took six police to git me off dat man. I'm goin' to trial next
week. Possession of a deadly weapon. I had an ax handle that was
cracked half in two, but boy, do I know how to use stick and glue
fast!!!

For the would-be badman, the ultimate prize is to establish a
reputation among his peers. It is the final compliment and comple-
ment to his front. It means being known and carrying weight in terms
of physical power and the psychological impact it carries. Like the
pimp, it means you can and do command space and the potential
status and respect that accompany the ability to stake out territory for
yourself.

Like the frontier badman, the person who does establish a reputation is fair game for other would-be badmen out to ruin his reputation
and to establish their own. As one self-proclaimed cowboy put it,
"Ain't nobody *dat* tough, it's just in the mind. 'Cause somebody mess
wif me, they might have a reputation and I mess it up for 'im!'" So the
trappings of the frontier prevail both in teenage behavior and in the
vernacular used to describe it.

### BADMEN HEROES AND LOCAL LEGENDS

There have been a variety of badmen—as well as strongmen—
celebrated in black folklore. Whereas strongmen figures like John
Henry and Shine perform feats of great physical endurance with style
and courage, the outright badman awes and controls others through
sheer meanness. One of the greatest and meanest badmen in black folk
literature is Stagolee/Stackolee. He is the prototype bully and he (and
his alter egos) are central figures in many black songs and stories:
"Stagolee, he was a bad man, an' ev'body know/ He toted a stack-
barreled blow gun an' a blue steel forty-four." Stagolee's contemporary urban counterpart might well be the gang leader. And like badmen
of old, these contemporary figures become legends in their own time.
One such badman was a prominent figure in South Central during the
time I was doing fieldwork there. His story is worth retelling because
he epitomizes the badman front as it is played out in a teenage urban
landscape. Like the legendary badman, many tales were told about
him—some true, some fanciful, some boastful and filled with bravado. I've named him Dawson, and his story is told by those who
knew him or knew of him.

Dawson was reported to be one of the originators and the leader
of a well-known South Central gang called the Avenues—and some
claimed to be there where it all started.

We was the first one's start it. We started the Avenues 'round '70.
Started in d' 80's [80th Street]. Spread out. You heard a Dawson? He
one that started—him and Coyote and Davey Boy. Dawson and Coyote
in jail now. I's pretty big, we jump in the ride, go beat up somebody.
It's still there, but not like it was. 'Cause everybody know 'im now.
Word gets around. Cain't hardly go too many parties, 'cause people be
lookin' for 'im.

Unlike other gangs that might rely on weapons and sheer numbers to intimidate physically, Dawson and his gang cultivated their
physical strength as well.

Avenues get a guy look fairly big. Not really big—tall. Big in d' arms.
They strong. They be together liftin' weights. Dey big, some of dem got
19, 20 [inch] arms. Dawson he look like Hercules. They all have some
kinda knife—else a gun. Now dey carryin' gun. Dawson he keeps a
sawed-off shot gun and monkey wrench in his car.

As part of the badman front, Dawson and his associates drove gangster rides which were freaked off so as to identify who they were.

Like Dawson, his boys, they ridin' 'round in dese little Novas—great
big wheels an' things. Gangster ride. Instead of a solid paint job, it's
usually a prime color, some prime spots on d' paint job. An' anybody
see 'em, gonna know who they is. Got 'em hopped up.

The Avenues also became identified with a certain kind of costume.
"They put on a leather piece—else a trench—those brims, caps use'a
wear in Chicago. They walk 'round, you know 'em. High sign dey
front."

In the tradition of the out-and-out badman, Dawson and his
associates often started trouble just for the hell of it. "Tha's one o'
Dawson ol' games—turn out a set. Ever'time. When he's dere, he
turns it out. Ever'body know 'im. If he feel the party ain't too fiendish, well, 'Hey, man, lemme have yo' coat!' 'Hey man, I cain't do
dat.' POP! *Take* his coat."

Dawson and his boys would jack up people for watches, for
money, for whatever they had. And his reputation and his collective
muscle allowed him to do pretty much what he chose—at a party, at a
record hop or on the street.

One day he was comin' from Fremont. There was five or six of 'em.
Dawson and some other big dudes. He stopped us all, ask us to pull out
all our money. I didn't do nothin', but stand dere. Rest of 'em pull out
deir money an' give it to 'em. I had 15, 75 cent in my pocket and he say,
"Le's see yo' money sucker." Den he kick me in my balls. Den his boy
took it. After he took all d' money, den he let us all go.

But Dawson was best known for taking people's leather coats and jackets.

> He's big and like he'll go in a party and he'll put his arm out and just
> start collectin' leather pieces. Everybody know 'im and if they got a
> leather piece, they better hide it. He don' rip it off, he *takes* it! He takes
> what he wants. He says, "You wanna whup me, know where to find
> me!" He's a bad cat.

Not everybody thought Dawson was all that tough. There were
the skeptical, the contemptuous, the envious, who claimed they were
unimpressed with Dawson and his reputation. Many times when Dawson's name came up in conversation, he was put down by the speaker:
"He not bad. He's only bad when he have his little gang 'round. The
Avenues, the biggest ones, they all built. He might win a fight 'cause
he keeps a monkey wrench on his hand." Or else, "Dawson ain't
nothin' but a pootbutt. He ain't nothin'. He jus' another person."

As with any badman, there will always be those who actively seek
to challenge his position—those who are real or fancied despoilers of
the man and his reputation.

> I stood in between *three* guns—two in the back o' me, one in the front
> of me, and have an Avenue he tell me he gon' blow *me* away. His two
> hunchmens in the back of me they gonna shoot me with a gun! You see
> I'm still here! When the fool in front of me saw the two in back of me
> get knocked down—I got some outasight ace coons come from *no-
> where*. And when they come, boy, they be *bad!* I just told dis other guy,
> "I don't believe you. I'm givin' you the benefit d' *doubt!* Go on
> shoot!"
>    I hung Dawson up! Dawson ain't nothin' but a pootbutt! I already
> know! Have you ever more or less seen a person bait a trap for a per-
> son? And have you ever more or less have someone bait a trap like dis:
> A person is walkin', he's talkin' to a friend. While he's walkin', he has
> his head turned and you just downright steps over in front o' him while
> he turn his haid and lets him run into you—you fires on him! And steps
> offa him and say, "Punk, what you wanna *do?*" Only thing he said
> was, "Sorry brother," and went on about his business.
>    Dawson already knows me. See, I'm crazy. 'Cause whenever I gets
> violently mad it's altogether different. Iffen you think Dr. Jekyll and
> Mr. Hyde was somethin', they ain't nothin.' They was more or less
> what I call babies, Jim. He be cuttin' up people with knives an' things.
> Oh, I can get *real* mean. I kin get real mad, just hurt someone for the
> *fun* o' it. Dude gets outa hand and swings at me and I be laughin' at
> 'im, carryin' on—dat's what makes 'im hot. Then I drop my hands and
> say, "Hit me," and he got nothin' but hell on his hands.

Not all those who had run-ins with Dawson and his gang could boast of such a single-handed victory. Some retaliated with collective force of their own.

Some associates dey's walkin' up here. Dey *clean*. Couple dudes from d' Avenues look at 'em, call 'em pimps. Dey don't like to be called pimps. Dey say, "Ain't no pimp!" One call Davey Boy he took cigarette out his mouf, put in his pocket and burnt a hole in dude's pocket. Fought them, got Davey, dude got Dawson. Beat 'em up, kick 'im in his balls. Dawson guy got his gun—he big, carry a piece too—then other got his rifle.

Three kids from Avenues got stabbed. Just some dudes tryin' get revenge from d' Avenues, takin' they coats and stuff. They don't come on this side of d' tracks. People on dis side jus' don' like no big bullies comin' over here an' tryin' take over. Make everybody scared. Dey big, some of dem.

We *all* know Dawson. He try to take a watch from me. I walkin' down d' street, jam you up in d' corner. Try to take ma watch! So, he *took* it. So I went around d' corner and I got Johnny boy, my cousin. He [Dawson] scared o' him [Johnny]. But he dead now. He died in Viet Nam. So, I brought him back and around dere. He made Brad [Dawson] gimme my watch.

Dawson he ain' so bad. My cousin, Titus Hanes, is badder. He taught Dawson everythang he know. People don't know what dey talkin' 'bout. Dey jus' say what dey hear. Cousin's little nigger, but he's *big* and Dawson's bigger den him, but Hanes is too much for 'im.

Invariably, Dawson was compared with old-time local badmen, such as Treetop or Alley Oop.

Around '65 Tree Top got shot. Dat was one o' my pa'tners right dere— ol' Tree Top. Da's when I was goin' to junior high school. Tree Top he always be up dere. He had a nice '57 Chevy. He got shot. [Is Dawson as tough as Tree Top?] I think Tree Top—no Dawson, he just a little tougher den Tree Top, I think. See it's hard to say. Different style, different front.

When I left South Central for the first time in 1971, Dawson's whereabouts was shrouded in rumor. Some said he had jumped a Black Panther and the Panthers were out to get him and he was in hiding. Others said he was in jail again for assault with a deadly weapon. Still others said he was in the jail hospital because some people had jumped him and severely beat him up. Whatever his real story, the rumors abounded, and like the legend that he was, there was a sense that he would persevere, no matter what. "I heard he shot some cat. Finally got convicted for it. I heard he got stabbed and shot and hit on the head and still kickin'. So I guess you jus' cain't get rid of 'im like dat!''

## POWER OVER SELF

Perhaps the most important form of power is power over oneself. This is particularly apparent in an environment where manipulation and control over others have been raised to the level of a fine art, where contest and game playing are often the rule, not the exception. To lose control over yourself means to lose control over the situation —to lose psychological and sometimes literal ground. Like a cracked dam you become vulnerable to a variety of pressures, until the force is so great that you break. Someone has "blown your mind," got to you.

The state of one's mind is central to the concept of control. In teenage terms, a person is seen to have a weak mind or a strong mind. Essentially, a weak mind connotes the lack or loss of control over one's emotions, and by extension over one's psychological and social space. The previous discussion of game playing suggests the myriad ways a person with a weak mind can be got to—through verbal play, through physical or verbal confrontation, through material ploys. Not all games carry the same psychological impact and one can be got to at different levels of emotional intensity. But the person who is perceived to have a weak mind is seen as the easiest "game."

In addition to expressions like to *mind fuck*, to *blow* or *mess one's mind*, there are other vernacular expressions that characterize someone who can be (or has been) got to—*messed up, not with it, out of it, raggedy*. The vernacular also reveals the particular ways a person can be made vulnerable—through love, through drugs, through sexual invasion. Though more will be said about love and sex in the next chapter, it is significant to note in this context that the terms depicting the state of being vulnerable in love are all suggestive of a person who has lost self-control—who is controlled by others. For example, expressions like *pussy-whipped*, to *be strung out behind someone*, to *be on a tight leash*, to *have a ring through your nose*, or to *be a turkey on a string* mean to be deeply infatuated or in love with another, to be obsessed with someone to the point where he or she dominates your actions and thoughts. "Woman she just got yo' nose! Like you strung out behind a girl. She's doin' you wrong and you know it, but you just can't cut 'er loose—'cause she's got you on a tight leash. They say, 'Man, you ain't nothin' but a stone, hope-to-die, strung out nigger! She blow your mind. Playin' d' fool!' ''

Interestingly, to *be strung out* also means to be obsessed, controlled by some drug, often heroin. The act of breaking away from another's control (or drugs) is literally characterized by the expression to *cut someone (something) loose*, to break one's addiction.

Essentially, the weak-minded person is not only seen as subject to another's dominance, but as someone who is childlike or childish—lacking maturity, "lame." Like the child, the weak-minded person is subject to the manipulation, control, and authority of more "mature" or less ingenuous companions.

A weak mind among males is also equated with appearing or acting feminine. One of the most severe testing grounds for a male's sexuality is in prison. Here one of the prime tests of whether or not you have a weak mind is how you handle homosexual advances.

> They had some bad guys up Tracy [Youth Authority institution]. I didn't never care 'bout nobody talkin' 'bout me—I base on 'em in a minute! Long as dey didn't put they hand on me. Too many put they hand on me, den I git mad. Third week, had to fight in order to not be broken to punk. Only the strong survive. Dude'll turn you out if you let 'im. Make a punk outa 'im. Fuck 'im. Make a bitch outa 'im. 'Cordin' what kinda mind you got on you.
>
> If you ain't got no good mind, naturally, they know you weak-minded. They be a lotta weak-minded people up dere. Some of 'em come in kin'a feminite. Brothers be talkin' to 'em just like they women. It'll bug 'em for awhile. Finally, gets to 'em. Turn 'em out.

To *turn someone out* means to introduce someone to something new and often illicit. In sexual terms, it means turning a male into a homosexual (*punk*) or a woman into a lesbian (*bulldagger*) or a prostitute. As the previous narrative suggests, being turned out implies a lack of self-control, and domination by others is often seen in macho terms as being feminine and susceptible.

The antithesis of the weak-minded person is the cool individual. Though the word cool connotes a variety of specific things, depending on context, its most common connotation is to be in control, to be emotionally invulnerable. "Like d' word say, you cool—you ain't hot-tempered or jumpin' 'round, like you got a hotfoot. Like some pootbutt runnin' off d' jibs. You cool—calm, together!" There are a number of vernacular expressions that characterize the state of being and staying cool. Expressions like to *be together*, to *have it together*, to *be uptight*, to *have your game* or *program together*, and to *have it covered* all suggest being in tight control of your words and actions, to be well-armored against invasion of your psychological and social space.

The object of staying cool is to *maintain*. In the vernacular, to maintain is short for maintaining your cool. It suggests that the cool person is seldom caught off balance. Terms like to *let your game slip* and to *lose your cool* mean that you are losing a grip on yourself and the situation and you need to *tighten up your game*. One is particularly struck by the imagery of containment that runs through much of the vernacular dealing with mental control. It seems contradictory to the concept of exerting power by taking social space from others. But one can take social and psychological space from others through a battle of wits or wills as well as through more aggressive stances. The best offense is a good defense.

The key to maintaining one's cool is to know when and how to act in a variety of situations.

> Like with the police. Dey don't bother me, 'cause I stays cool. Rootie-poots dey be gettin' in trouble, talk off-the-wall. Most of dem dey get busted by d' pig. After dey get busted, they gonna talk shit. "You mothafuckin' dis and dat!" 'Stead of gettin' hot jus' be cool. Get in d' station be cool, keep yo' game together. When your lawyer get dere, *den* you call 'em a bunch s.b.s.

Again, the lame pictured in Chapter Two suffers from not being cool —a person who acts "crazy," doesn't know how to dress, or, most important, talks too much or at the wrong time.

> Like some dudes jus' run off d' jibs. Talkin' lotta jive, jus' always talkin'. You can go wid a partner and you kin just stand, just scope and scene on everything, everyone. Some cats dey be talkin' every second. Sometime, you have better fun wid a person, get over wid d' young lady, if you jus' be cool, be standin' 'round, see wha's happ'nin'. Everything cool.

Though your rap can save your life, you also must know when and how to use it.

Survival, finally, is the ultimate name of the game, however it is played out: "To get down, to communicate, to pry on someone, to blow dey mind, to jam 'em, to bullshit 'em, to con someone, to use your mind to overcome them. Dat's how you get over." And the end-game is to *get over*, to *get across*, to *make it*, to *step fast*—to get what you can, to be successful at what you do. As the expressions suggest, being successful means, on a literal or psychological level, to move along, to get to a new place where life may be better. "Dig. All life is a game. You constantly gamin', tryin' get over with your conversation, your fists, whatever you got. All d' time you be out dere on d' streets, you tryin' to whup the game—game o' life."

The discussion in this chapter has attempted to highlight how black teenagers use confrontation, manipulation, performance and its trappings, and creative play in their daily encounters with each other. It is suggestive, hardly definitive; no account of human interaction can pretend to be otherwise. Though I've attempted to catalog vernacular vocabulary as being associated primarily with one game or another, it is important to say again that terms get used and applied to characterize multiple situations. And like the terms themselves, game strategies combine in a variety of creative and fluid ways, as the context develops and the participants move to play it out.

# 4. playin' the game from A to Z

## male-female interaction

ONE OF THE MOST spirited arenas of teenage interaction is the "play" between male and female—a complex drama in many acts. As with most interpersonal behavior, there is an intricate and often contradictory set of attitudes and beliefs, preconceptions and expectations, that underlie and shape it. Like the contests already discussed, the battle between the sexes is suffused with a sense of performance, competition, creative manipulation, and power management. But there is a vital additional ingredient: the male-female game is decidedly sexual in nature. And this sexuality introduces into the game a unique cutting edge, a special electric tension that often accompanies the polarized state between male and female—regardless of culture, geography, or class.

## ATTITUDES TOWARD SEX, LOVE, AND MARRIAGE

Elliot Liebow, in his candid and compassionate work, *Tally's Corner* (1967), made the following observation about the interplay between the sexes that he witnessed in a Washington, D.C., ghetto neighborhood: "Men and women talk of themselves and others as cynical, self-serving marauders, ceaselessly exploiting one another as use objects or objects of income. Sometimes, such motives are ascribed only to women: 'Them girls . . . they want *fi*nance, not *ro*mance.' But more often, the men prefer to see themselves as the exploiters, the women as the exploited" (p. 137).

Though Liebow was involved with adults, his observation addresses some important teenage attitudes as well. Among children who grow up fast and are exposed early to the hard conditions of ghetto living, the need to survive—to take what you can get—is an integral part of making it in the white man's world. In male-female relations, taking what you can get is often translated as sexual exploitation. As one seventeen-year-old saw it, "Women either gonna be a Chesterfield or a Camel. You gonna be a Chesterfield and satisfy, or be a Camel and take that mile walk."

Many teenage narratives about male-female relations revealed the sentiment that one is either used by the opposite sex or does the using. Though exploitation often refers to sex, it also is put in financial terms as well. "I'm gettin' a Cadillac. A woman's gonna put me in one. Put 'er on d' *co'ner*, so she can sit on her stuff and bring my money home! Don' hafta be rich. She kin make money—whatever she wanna do. Just take care o' me." Though the statement is as much bravado as actual fact, the sentiment expressed is one that reflects the desire felt by a number of youths. As Liebow has pointed out, women, and men too, are often evaluated in terms of their moneymaking ability as well as for their sexual accessibility.

Corollary to the exploitative and manipulative aspect of much teenage interaction is the feeling that members of the opposite sex—including one's current mate or lover—cannot always be trusted. This is seen as particularly true in matters of sexual fidelity. There are a number of expressions in the vernacular that characterize infidelity—"getting it on" with a variety of people other than one's mate or moving in on someone else's mate. For example, expressions like to *creep*, to *burn*, to *gigolo*, to *tip*, and to *trip up on someone* all connote sexual infidelity, being somewhere you shouldn't with someone who is "off limits." Promises of fidelity are often treated with undisguised cynicism (or at least a large grain of salt)—particularly by females. "Like dude tell you, 'You my main squeeze, my one-an'-only.' He say he don' want nobody else but you. He don' wanna *look* at another young lady. But, da's a lie—less he dead, underneath and buried! Right on! And den he *still* be lookin' up!"

If young females see males as out to get as much as they can from a woman, teenage males also experience being taken in love and for money. When I asked one young man if he had a special young lady, his reply—like the young woman's above—expressed male sentiment about getting "strung out behind someone": "No. Cut 'er loose. She was kissin' on somebody and sittin' fron' o' me too! An' one she was kissin' on say I better not hit her. I say, 'I'm not gonna hit her—but what *chu* wanna do?' I hit him. I spen' my last five dollars on her one night, an' I was drunk, high as a kite. I spend it on her. Den, she gonna act d' fool. Next thing, I was out like a light. I wake up d' nex' morning feelin' nice. Not fo' long. She had my money and she done spent it on some pants. She bought her some levis. Cain't be trusted.''

As the story also suggests, males feel that females cannot be trusted in matters of love because, as many see it, they are so easily won over by a slick-talking man. "Like you have a young lady. She's your main bitch. You at a party, some dude come over an' he gets to rappin' to her. And his conversation might be strong 'n fas'. He talkin' big words. She jus' sways over to 'im. Can't trust 'em, 'cause dey have weak minds.'' Indeed, males often see young women in much the same way as females see them, as "lame.'' That is, they are weak-willed, childish, and easily coerced and conned by the right man. "I had that woman's mind. I had that woman's mind goin' crazy. The right man knows just what to say to a ripe woman. You will *have* her where you wants her—to do whatever you want. 'Cause a ripe woman's mind is weak to a certain extent. 'Cause if you mo' or less love a woman the way she needs to be loved, therefore, she will get all satisfaction outa anything you wanna put in front o' her. Da's gonna be yo' pup-py!''

Feelings of suspicion and distrust sometimes extend to members of one's own sex as well. Where competition is often the name of the game, there is always the chance that you will be the one burned—and sometimes by friends as well as strangers. As one young woman put it when I asked her if she had close women friends: "I used to. You know, Edie, I used to take on to girls real close as sisters. But I been outdid by so many girls. Because I never did have a sister—a for real sister—and when they needed something, I always gave it. Or if they had a misunderstandin' at home, they could come to our house. But one time, my partner Nadine, she did me an injustice. Creeped on my ol' man. Where now I don't take to females tightly as I used to. 'Cause I'm a woman and she's a woman and she don't wanna see me get over.''

Males also voice varying degrees of distrust toward other males when it comes to their women. Many of the verbal games already discussed revolve around vying for the attention of a female who is known to be going with someone. "Like my friend did me. Like man, he burns his own partner for his young lady. He be talkin', 'Man, dis broad ain' no good, you don' need her.' But all at the same time, *he* wants her. Creeps on his partner. Steals her away!''

Another motif that runs through much teenage dialog is that of jealousy and revenge. Indeed, one of the greatest single causes cited

for fights resulted from jealous or angry lovers responding to someone
"bogarding" his or her territory. "Mos'ly, fights start 'cause of a
broad. Those niggers always get they head too bad. Be lookin' at
somebody else's woman. See a nice lookin' young lady—maybe look
better 'n his—he wanna go over dere and rap to 'er. He jus' can't *look*
and *admire*, he wants to try to play chicken an' steal somebody's old
lady. 'You can't take my broad!' Lotta cold words come down. An'
dat's when the fightin' starts.''

Fighting over one's mate is not restricted to men by any means.
Females can become quite aggressive in defense of their "property":

> I got cut over my baby's father. His wife, me an' her got into it and she
> cut me. She cut me behind d' neck and on the shoulder. I had 14
> stitches. Guess she couldn't dig it dat her husband was takin' more at-
> tention to me than he would her. Well, she cut me one night. She ask me
> to talk to her. I didn't object to it. She say, "C'mere, I wanna talk to
> ya." So I went around dere and talked to her. She say something to me
> like, "You been in my husband's car?" I looked at her, I said, "Nah."
> She say, "Wha's yo' name?" I say, "My name is Sandra Joan Mitchell,
> but mos' people call me Joanie—why?" She say, " 'Cause I found a
> Mother's Day card in d' glove compartment and it had yo' name on it."
> I say, "Well, honey, i's mo' den one Joanie."
>
> She was tellin' me somethin' and as she was talkin' to *me*, some-
> body else was sayin' somethin' to me about, "C'mon, go git in d' car."
> I say, "I git in d' car whenever I *feel* like it." And she thought I was
> talkin' 'bout her husband's car and we got into it.
>
> We got to fightin' like cats an' dogs. So, she broke a bottle and she
> hit me with the bottle.
>
> After d' hassle, she came lookin' for her husband. Over to my
> mother's house. Stupid woman went and shot herself in d' finger. She
> tryin' to load d' gun and shoot at him [her husband] and [he] kept tellin'
> her, "Girl, you're gonna shoot yourself in d' finger!" "Nah, I ain't!
> Nah, I ain't!" She think she bad.
>
> After den, she wants to be my friend, but I still didn't trust her. She
> went an' left him. She couldn't have him without me and her both
> havin' the same man, she went to Fresno and da's where she is now.

Not all—or even most—jealous encounters are as highly charged as
the one Joanie relates. Yet perceived territorial rights, whether claims
on a neighborhood or a lover, are not easily or silently relinquished.

It is not particularly surprising to find that some of the expectations and attitudes around male-female interaction and sexual involvement should affect attitudes toward love and marriage. It is significant
to note the negligible number of favorable vernacular terms that deal
with love and marriage, when compared to the vast lexicon dealing
with sex and sexual exploitation. When asked about their feelings

toward marriage, most males and a large number of females voiced less than positive sentiments. Many saw marriage as a form of incarceration—something that restricted your action with the opposite sex, burdened you with responsibility, tied you down, took the fun out of life. A vernacular phrase popular with both sexes—*you don't have papers on me*—is expressive of much teenage reaction to marriage. When one person becomes too demanding of another's time or seeks to impose restrictions on another's activities or drops hints about marriage, the response is often:

> "You don't have papers on me, we ain't married, so don't be tellin' *me* what to do. You don't have no laces, no chains, no strings. You don't own me." 'Cause I tell a nigger dat in a minute! Like las' night, I was talkin' on d' telephone. This dude gets to talkin' trash. I say, "Wait a minute, hold it! You don' have no papers on me, so you cain't tell me *what* to do, *when* to do it, *when* to go, *when* not to go. If you had some [papers], you *still* wouldn't be able to." I have to keep 'im in his world. If you *not* together, niggers try to take advantage of you.

Love, in vernacular terms, fares little better than marriage. Expressions that characterize the person stricken by love—to be *on a tight leash*, to *wear the ring*, to *have a ring through your nose*, to *have your nose wide open*, to be *a turkey on a string*—all picture the individual as little more than an obedient animal, being docilely led around by another. Love is seen in the vernacular as an addiction, an obsessive habit. Indeed, the same expression, "to be strung out," applies to being addicted to love as well as to drugs.

But underneath the veneer of cynicism surrounding matters of love and marriage there is a hard fact of life that many teenagers acknowledge, a fact that often discourages marriage: a sober recognition that marriage without a source of financial support is like pushing a rock uphill. "Yeh, we talks about marriage a lot. But I just don' have d' money. Go through all dem changes. But you cain't keep it together if you bread too short. But, I wanna do it! I wanna keep 'er. She all right. Good woman hard to find." Couples that wanted to marry often said they didn't because of lack of money or a job to support them. Young blacks who live in the ghetto have no middle-class parents to start them off financially or find a job for one or both of them or provide them with a rent-free apartment until they get started. Many of the teenagers I met were on their own, and educationally unprepared or underskilled to compete in an ever-shrinking job market. No dowries or nest eggs were there for them. "I am more or less prepared to get married, because I think I know enough about life to keep my marriage the way I want it. But, I can't be gittin' married with no money. My old lady she on welfare. When we get married, what dey gon' do, Jack? Dey gon' cut her loose. Cain't even see her on welfare.¹ Ain't got no job—gettin' some trainin' at skill center [in Watts], but jobs—any kinda jobs—they be hard to git.''

Many were acutely aware of not only the economic problems that tries the best of relationships, but of the emotional polarity between male and female and the charged atmosphere that surrounds much male-female interaction. For many, there was a sense of inevitability, almost a fatalistic acceptance that the male-female game had always been played that way, so "take it slow and go for what you know." For others, there was a sense of wry humor that pervaded the contest between the sexes. "Don' be gettin' too excited. I's *just* a game anyway. Gotta pay to play, so might as well enjoy it."

Yet, in the face of both emotional and economic reasons for caution in relationships, teenagers also talked of their desire for long-term, stable ties. Expressions like *TLC* (tender loving care), to *have an understanding*, and to *have a thing* or *something going* attest to that. The sense of doing battle with the opposite sex, of fatalism, pushes up against a deepseated traditional and romantic notion of love and an unspoken belief that maybe there is that one-and-only. "See, like what it is. Say, 'Nigger he cain't be trusted; woman she's no good.' Still, you be hopin' dat ain't true. Like you tell yo'self, 'Nigger ain't gonna stay home,' but all d' same. Like the story 'bout the bumblebee and d' turtle. Bee be jumpin' from flower to flower, but d' turtle he always stay at home. Well, like d' story say, you might have yo'self a bumblebee, but you sho' hope fo' some dat turtle!''

## THE GAME

It is against this complex backdrop of attitudes about sexual involvement, love, and marriage that the sexual game itself gets played out. In the context of male-female interaction, expressions already discussed (the game, the play, the action) take on decidedly sexual overtones. The endgame in much male-female exchange is to *catch*, to *catch action*, to *pull*, to *get over*—essentially to win over another with your words and actions with the intention of *getting down, getting it on, doing the do, doing the thing*—having sex.

A primary strategy used in getting over to a young woman or man is *the mack:* seductive conversation that blends together coercion, flattery, put-down, confrontation, and manipulation, in a steady stream of sweet talk marked by quick shifts in mood and tone. The skilled mack is high performance. It is a verbal-kinetic game that, at its best, combines the imagery of the poet with the movement of the dancer and the improvisation of the jazz musician. On a number of occasions I was personally treated to the more or less forceful mack of

some young man. One such encounter is worth noting because it highlights some of the multiple strategies used to "blow a young lady's
mind" with the intention of getting over.

> You beautiful, you married? You very smart, you know. Jus' bein' here
> wid you is sufficient. Don' need nothin' else. You gonna tell your old
> man what you doin'? [He knows what I'm doing.] He know you more
> or less studyin' social life? Well, I wanna know when you comin' back
> here.
>
> See, I kin jus' set up here and just trip you out by sayin' all dat. See
> how I come down and jus' set quiet. I'ma tell you now. This is what I've
> been doin'. I'm just fuckin' wi'cho mind. Tha's all I'm doin'. I'm right-
> eously fuckin' wi'chu. You just cain't understand it. [Yeh, I know,
> you're just too swift for me.] Now you wan' me be like dat? Slick an'
> swift? You couldn't even *catch* my mind; you couldn't even keep up wid
> me. I say I fuck wi' chu, I think I have you a nervous wreck! [Sounds to
> me like you're running your line down.] Hey, you cool, you got a strong
> mind.
>
> When*ever* you get it in yo' mind to where you need a young man to
> more or less talk to you 'bout anythang or *every*thing what he can talk
> about, I be dere. Tell yo' old man he ain't doin' somethin' right, all I
> kin say. You let 'im hear it! He have a fit! I tell 'im! "Man, you better
> get to be a swing daddy and learn how to do yo' thang, 'cause if you
> *can't* do your *thang*, somebody gonna do it *fo'* you!"
>
> He's okay for you because you more or less overpower him by yo'
> mind. I know dis. You mus' have some kinda hold on him. You need a
> natural-born man. Someone gonna love on you in the proper way. Tell
> that boyfriend of yours, if he cain't handle you to jus' send it on here to
> me!

Though the mack is often associated with the pimp front (a synonym for pimp being *mack man*), and has been seen by writers as a
male expressive form, it is used with consummate skill by females to
accomplish similar ends. As one young man observed, "You find a
whole lotta young ladies dey see a dude they dig on, they gon' try to
rap to *him*. I knows a lotta 'em dat macks hard and strong. Conversation be together too." One example of a female mack came up in a
conversation with a young woman who was talking about how she
almost joined the Muslims because of her interest in one of their members. "I almos' got hung up in dere one time. This was this *fine* dude
used to come to my sister's house—ummmm *hmmmm!* He was fine as
wine! Tall, nice natural, wearin' dat nice suit. Sweet daddy! Comin' to
d' house wid dat paper. I say, 'Well, yeh, I'll take d' paper—just to
see you every week!' One time he come inside. He got to runnin' dat
shit down to me. I'm admirin'. 'Damn yo' paper, baby! What about
you? Are you married? You some fine-lookin' man. I *know* we can
take care of some righteous bidness together! You come 'round later

and we have some real fun! Won't need yo' papers den!' '' The mack is an integral part of male-female exchange and is often engaged in as a matter of course—as much for playful practice as for actual payoff.

As with other manipulative strategies, there is a great deal of competition and jockeying for position in male-female exchanges. Not only do males and females maneuver to gain a one-up position, but potential contestants vying for the same person's attention engage in a variety of cooptive strategies aimed at undercutting their would-be opponent. There are a number of expressions in the vernacular that characterize one person's attempt to interrupt, impede, or totally sabotage another's action—to *cock block*, to *c.b.*, to *rank someone*, to *mess up/rank someone's action/style/game/play*.

The various strategies used to rank someone's play are highly creative and sometimes totally outrageous (and very funny). Sometimes two people will try to outwait each other—with the result that neither one gets over[2]: ''Like somebody wanna do they thing and neither one o' you gonna give up. Ain't neither one gonna move. So you both jus' gonna set dere and *cock* block and neither one o' you gonna get nothin'.'' At other times one person will try to outwit or outmaneuver the other: ''Like you rappin' to some fine stuff, dude come up, say, 'Hey, man, so-'n-so got some bad weed. Yeh, in d' john. Better get some 'fore it gone.' Go dere, nothin' happenin'. Come back, dude mackin' on d' young lady. Nigger done ranked yo' play!'' Sometimes the cock block is more overtly disruptive: ''Like dude talkin' to a young lady and you say, 'I'ma rank the nigger, take his stuff from 'im.' Come up 'n tell d' broad, 'Dat dude, you know what? He mess wid a dog.' Gonna make d' young lady kin'a look at you kinda funny. Or like if she older, den you say, 'Ah, man you ain't but so-'n-so age.' Or tell broad he married. Say somethin' wrong about 'im like, 'You still got dat clap?' Fuck up his pussy. Intrude rudely.''

Young women use many of the same strategies to rank another woman's play, but some are uniquely female. ''Like I be rappin' to dis fine dude, sister come up, say, 'Hey, Jolene, hear you pregnant?' Else, 'Girl, you on yo' period? You sho' smell fishy!' Da's cold. Bitch done ranked yo' action. My partner did dat to me at dis party. I'z blowin' hard 'n heavy. She ask me, 'Do yo' husband know you here?' Den another sister, she rank my sister. Tell d' dude how Clara she done lef' her babies by deyself—shit like dat. Now ain't dat somethin'!''

So competition and jockeying for position and control take many forms. However, not all sexual maneuvers are overt or waged directly against or in the presence of your opponent. Often advances take a covert form, as when someone *creeps* on another. The expression ''to creep on someone" has multiple references, as do its synonyms, to *tip*, to *burn*, to *gigolo*, to *rip on someone*. It can mean to catch someone unawares by sneaking up behind them, usually with the intention of doing physical harm. It can mean deliberately and slowly to follow another person—usually in a car but also on foot—with the intention of making a play for them. But, as already suggested, the most common meaning relates to some kind of covert sexual move, making a quiet play for another's mate or lover: "*Creep* on a *nigger's woman!* One of yo' partners got a broad and you jus' creep, go over dere and don't let nobody know—on the quiet side. Tha's like committing adultery. The husband goes to work, you gonna creep on over on your toes." It may refer to cheating on your mate or lover[3]: "Like if you got yo' woman. Like you goin' out wid another woman—and another woman. You jus' creepin' all *over* d' place." Or it can mean to lie about your whereabouts: "Creep on yo' old man. You say you goin' out wid d' girls to d' movies. Really, you be out wid 'nother brother."

At the most general level, to creep means being somewhere you're not supposed to be, say at a young woman's house against her mother's wishes. "Like you go over a girl's pad. Old lady don' dig you. Else it late. You hafta creep!" Sometimes the tables get turned and the would-be creeper finds his or her mate or lover creeping too—"checking out what's goin' down" in equally devious ways. "Say, for instance, your best friend and your old man is together. Well, you done creeped up on 'em. You done caught 'em in d' act of doin' the thang. Like you may set it up—trick the dude. Tell 'im you goin' out, creep on back to d' crib, rank his play. Bust in, call 'em all kinda name— dog, dirty mothafucka, fonky nigger—turn bitch an' him out *into d' street!*"

But finally, if your conversation is strong enough, your action forceful enough, your covert moves successful enough, you reap the rewards of conquest. You can show off your newly won prize, much as you show off your car, your clothes, and other valuable possessions. As already indicated, terms like to *style*, to *fiend*, to *fonk on someone*, and their synonyms, connote whatever you have that is of value—and a fine-looking young man or a foxy-looking young woman is definitely seen as a prized possession. What constitutes a desirable "catch"?

## DIMENSIONS OF MALE AND FEMALE ATTRACTIVENESS

### THE MALE PERSPECTIVE

*The Stone Fox.* One of the primary measures of a female's desirability is her physical attractiveness. And whatever else is considered, the more physically attractive she is to the beholder, the greater her sexual appeal.

There are a number of vernacular expressions that characterize the desirable young woman, and many connote the focus of the particular appeal. I have already pointed out that, despite acknowledgment of black as beautiful, some males still appraise a woman's desirability in terms of the light hue of her complexion: the lighter her skin tone, the more attractive she is often seen to be. Terms for a light-complected person—*high yellow, melted butter, mellow yellow*—were most often seen in a positive light. They were also most often used to designate an attractive female rather than a male. "Now da's a fine-lookin' chick. She easy on d' eye and sweet to d' taste—just like it say, she melts in yo' mouf!"

The texture and condition of a woman's hair—as in many cultures—are also ingredients in her sexual attractiveness. Though both males and females admired an attractive person with a "fonky" *natch, natural, Afro, 'fro,* or *French rolls/corn rolls*, there was still an appreciation of the woman (or man) who had *good hair* (hair that is loosely curled or wavy and approximates Caucasian hair texture). While a number of vernacular terms relate to the care and maintenance of the natural or Afro hair style, there is an equal if not greater number of expressions that characterize the *process* (hair that has been chemically straightened). Though the process is more of a criterion of attractiveness among older blacks than among younger ones, it was still not uncommon to hear teenagers talking about getting their hair *conked, fried, pressed,* or *gassed.* In fact, during the 60s one of the popular hair styles among young men was called the *Kennedy swoop,* another *the Elvis.* "Like wi' dem Kennedy boys—dey got dey hair fried, dyed and swooped to d' side. Pimp do a lot too. Look good too!"

It was often as much the care taken with one's hair as the style or texture that attracted many males. As one young man summarized it, "Don't care how the young lady wear her hair. She kin get down with a fonky natural, corn roll wid dem ribbons, else she kin have a righteous process. Don' matter, long as she lookin' good wid d' hair."

A woman's body is also an important component of her desirability. However, what young black males mean by a "good shape" is culturally influenced and differed, in particular aspects, from white mainstream standards of sexual desirability. Black males, like their white counterparts, give a great deal of attention to the size of a woman's breasts. There are a number of vernacular terms that refer to a woman's breasts as big, tasty, touchable, and formidable—*grapes, apples, dairies, knobs, guns, headlights.* Generally, terms associated with small breasts, like *boobus*, are used in a derogatory sense. The male's regard for large breasts is also seen in expressions like "It's what's up front that counts" or in the keen attention given them in the following dialog:

A: Did you see that fine bitch in that nigga's car?
B: Hey yeh, but that nigger didn't catch shit, his bad-ass ride did all the catchin' for him.
A: Yeh, that car was bad, but his bitch was badder. Did you see the guns on her, man? They were damn near as big as Pam Grier's 38's. Damn she looked good! I'm gonna dream about her tonight. I could play with those big rascals all night long!

The shape and size of a woman's legs, thighs, and buttocks also figure prominently in her attractiveness. By contrast with mainstream culture, black males consistently put a high premium on women with full-fleshed legs and buttocks. The term *butter*, for example, refers to both an attractive woman and to a full derriere. A common expression for male appreciation of a woman's buttocks is to exclaim, "Look at all that butter!" The expression *butter baby* refers to a girl who promises to be amply endowed—as one young man put it—"from her headlights to her hocks."

The size of a woman's legs are as important as her buttocks. Terms for legs, *hocks, ham hocks*, or for thighs, *hammers*, suggest that males appreciate ample legs and thighs on women, whatever else may turn them on. In fact, expressions like to *get some leg/big leg* and *soft leg* refer to having sex and generalize from the desirability of a woman's legs to her whole body.

Women are also described in terms of car makes and the body type each epitomizes. This is not particularly unusual when you consider that a fine catch is a prized possession. As one young man saw it, "Women dey like a Porsche, a Mercedes or a Cad: Porsche it round and built low to d' ground. Mercedes is not too big an' not too small. Jus' fine to look at and bad to ride. Now d' Cad—da's my favorite. I's big, black—and beautiful!" Finally, any and all sexually desirable parts of a woman's anatomy—legs, thighs, breasts, or the vagina—are referred to as *g* or *goodies*.

Though there are a number of expressions used to describe the attractive woman, there are three particular characterizations that stand out in teenage vernacular which add still another dimension to the overall view males have of females. The first set of terms for a sexually attractive woman are all shared with the pimp—*main 'ho, main bitch, bottom woman, star*. As already stated, the connection with the pimp front is not accidental. It reflects male identification with and appreciation of the pimp's life style, not the least of which is his ability to charm and control women and reap financial gain at their expense. Though males often talk about desirable women in pimp terms, it is usually among themselves. Though they may refer to a woman as their star or their queen when they are sweet-talking her, they seldom in fact say "main bitch" or "main 'ho" to the young woman's face. First it shows a lack of respect. "Hell no! If tha's the case, ain't gonna be sayin' my 'main 'ho,' 'cause dat's a bad way o' sayin' it—'main 'ho.' You mean my 'ol' lady.' Other way git you in trouble." Just as important, it won't score many points with a young woman. "Like a nice-lookin' young lady walkin' down d' street 'n you scopin' on her. A nice broad wif a body. 'Da's a good-lookin' bitch.' 'Cause we call all young lady bitch or 'ho. But not to dey face. I don' call none o' my women 'hos when I be callin' them. Bite your head off for dat!"

A second set of terms characterize the desirable woman in animal terms. Expressions like *bitch, stallion*, and *fox* see a woman's desirability linked to her sexual appetites as well as her sheer physical attractiveness (and her assertive sexual power, as seen in the image of the potent horse). Though these terms refer to any attractive woman, whether sexually accessible or not, they also imply a strong sexual appetite. The bitch in heat, the wild stallion, and the sensuous (and voracious) fox are all images of women that come up in male conversation. Like males, women are characterized as having strong sexual (animal) appetites. How overtly she exercises her appetite is another matter. Also connected with the sensually and sexually lusty image of the young woman is a level of fear and respect for her very appetites. At the same time a young man is turned on by a foxy woman, there is some trepidation about his own ability to put his "money where his mouth is." "I's like you mack hard, fast an' heavy. Stone fox—she look good and she *ready*. Don' be half-steppin' wid dis young lady, 'cause if you mouth can't cash yo' check, you gonna hear 'bout it!"

Finally, there are a set of terms that are used interchangeably to characterize a sexually attractive woman and a variety of drugs—*stuff, main stuff, golden girl* (very fine cocaine), *silk and satin* (any combination of amphetamines and barbiturates). These drug-related terms suggest that desirable women get you high and make you feel good. And desirable women are addictive. "'Cause I seen it. A brother he wants dat young lady so bad, he like a junkie. 'Gimme dat stuff!' He do anything to get her." As we have seen, the image of addiction in the vernacular runs through many aspects of the male-female relationship.

*The Chickenhead.*  If the stone fox represents all that is attractive and sexually appealing in a young woman, the *chickenhead* and her counterparts epitomize all that is not. The term chickenhead generally refers to an unattractive, unkempt young woman. In more specific terms, it characterizes a female with very close-cropped hair: "A lady who don't have much hair. A bald-headed girl—no hair, look like a chicken." Or it refers to a young woman whose hair is unruly or just generally uncared for: "It mean a lady, she got a chickenhead. Maybe her hair stand up on end. Say, 'Hey chicken!' " However, not all short-haired young women are seen this way: "If they have a small natural and a pretty face, it's fiendish!" The term is reserved for the unkempt or unattractive young woman. Other synonyms for chickenhead are *duckhead, hen, thunder chicken, nail head,* and *short nails.*

The degree of "nappiness" is also subjected to evaluation. Women with particularly tightly curled or so-called kinky hair are referred to as *BB heads* and *fuzzheads.* The condition of one's hair is an important aspect of appearance in both males and females. A dozens remark that was passed on to me took its force, in fact, from denigrating the kinkiness of a person's hair: "Your hair looks like 50,000 ants raising their fists in the air!" So a young woman may get labeled as unattractive if her hair is messy, too short, or very nappy. And, at least for a number of young men, she will be seen as unattractive if she dyes her hair red or blond or uses greasy hair preparations. "Like a girl she don' look good, she look like a skag. She have all dat red stuff in her hair."

The young woman who is generally unkempt—whether it be her hair, her clothes, or her make-up—is characterized in the vernacular as undesirable "merchandise," "ill-made goods." Expressions like *raggedy, raggedy Ann, tackhead,* and *tackyhead* carry with them, among other things, the image of badly made goods. "Trashy-lookin', a female that don't look right. She dress all funny, her hair all messed up, just messed up, period! Cain't even give her away, she so bad!"

Other derogatory terms for women liken their unattractiveness to animals. Terms like *dog, hound, bear, beast, bat,* and *boogabear* characterize the woman as an animal, as do terms describing the attractive woman; the difference is the animal being identified. Still other animal terms are used to characterize the ill-kempt woman. For example, *skunk, skank,* and *bait* refer to a female who smells badly. There is a corollary expression used to identify the young woman who seldom or selectively bathes, *p.t.a.* used when a female only washes "pussy, titties, and armpits."

Though full-bodied women are seen as sexually attractive, there is a subjective point at which the voluptuous becomes the obese (*hully*). The heavy woman is also likened to certain animals, *cow* and *heifer.* Young women who are perceived to possess big appetites are labeled *pig, hog, pig mouth, pigger.* Other terms for obese women, *Bahama momma* and *Judy with the big bootie,* also suggest excessive girth and unattractiveness.

Finally, unattractiveness is often characterized in terms that suggest physical pain (*she is hurtin' for certain, scab, ruin't*); or disease (*scurvy*); or the effects of prolonged drug abuse (*wasted, tore down*).

Though the vernacular vocabulary graphically pictures many of the unattractive attributes ascribed to young women in a very direct way, still other equally important attributes are discovered through the subject of dialogs rather than vernacular definitions. One of the undesirable qualities often conveyed in the variety of derogatory names given women is that of being mannish or unfeminine. One of the major criticisms leveled at women who "got out of line," (that is, wouldn't listen to a male) was that they were acting like a chicken-head. In this context, the term meant that women were acting like men. A number of attributes are associated with so-called mannish behavior—for example, physical or verbal aggressiveness (not out-spokeness) as well as a masculine way of dressing. "Like d' young ladies on d' west side dey feminite, nice and soft. Dress nice. On east side, dey sack mouth you. 'Nigger, if you don't like it, well git in my ass or git on!' Fight you in a minute!"

The counterpart to the "bad-assed nigger" is the "bad-assed bitch." She is not only seen as a *hard mouth* but a *gang banger* and is perceived to be as physically tough and intimidating as any man. The following narrative describes the appearance and behavior associated with such a young woman. The context was a fight between the male speaking and a chickenhead.

> She *was fat!* She was *fat* and she was *tall!* The first hit almost killed me. She hit me and knocked me from the closet all d' way on the bed. Oh! And they was a lotta people over the house. I couldn't let it look like I was bein' whupped, so I just started beatin' her with lamps and chairs, curtains and telephones. Everything I could get my hands on, 'cause she was rumblin'! She hit ha-rd!
>
> Oooh! I finally got out the house and I hit 'er in the head with a great big rock. Pow! She grabbed 'er head and came back tryin' break my door in. She pushed it open, an' I kicked her back out. [What started it all?] I was talkin' 'bout her 'cause she was fat. Shit! Dat chickenhead is cold! Skag!

Skag is also a put-down term that does considerable work in male conversation. Generally, it means an undesirable woman. In particular, it is attached both to the sexually promiscuous female ("Skag's a tramp! One o' dem disgraceful young ladies! Take anythang she can git—the leftovers! Go wid anybody."); and to the young woman who won't "put out" ("Skag who dey call a girl. Like if try to play hard to get when you talkin' to 'em. Call 'em a skag."). One young man summed up all the unattractive characteristics of a female when he gave me his definition of skag. "Tha's what you call an UGLY LOOKIN' WOMAN! A skag is a thunder chicken, a garbage mouth's buzzard, a fonky low-life bitch! A person that looks like a man! Woman ain't got no sex appeal—whatsoever! She could pass for a man—any tuna thing. Skunk! Bait! Tramp! 'Nigger, you momma ain't *had* you, somebody *found* you!' "

At the same time that young males put down the so-called skag or chickenhead, there was a recognition among many that the tough or hard woman gave what she got. They admitted that the way a woman related to a man depended on how he treated her and if he showed her respect. As one young man saw it, "Woman anywhere would be tougher if the young man mistreated her. I mean you kin live in a desert, but if you treat the lady nice, she gonna be feminine. She's gonna be there."

Also, the same class of females who were put down as chickenheads in conversation (ones who were seen as physically or verbally abusive) were often respected and admired in fact. And terms used by males to "base" on a female among themselves were often absent from direct male-female conversation. Since an important ingredient of youthful male behavior is to demonstrate machismo, it is not unexpected to find that much male banter about women is filled with bravado and verbal posturing, often at the expense of the female. So she may get characterized as weak-willed or aggressive, sexually voracious or prudish—whatever suits the flow of conversation.

Still, those expressions that characterize the unattractive woman greatly outnumber those that compliment the female. Though vernacular vocabulary, as mentioned, tends toward put-down rather than praise, the sheet number of derogatory terms of reference for women provides interesting commentary on how females get seen and talked about by males.

### THE FEMALE PERSPECTIVE

*The Sugar Daddy and the Fine Brother.* The qualities of attractiveness sought in a young man by a woman are not radically different from those already discussed for males. However, males seem to put more emphasis on physical attributes like figure, hair texture, complexion, and desirable parts of the anatomy than women do. This is not to say that a young man who is "fine as wine" is not sought out as a desirable catch. "Like go to d' Polish Hall, they givin' a dance— Educated Gents. We go over dere. Some fine-lookin' dudes over dere. Nice clothes, righteous-lookin' natural. Got some fiendish-lookin' men! Good complexion—sorta honey color. Da's why I goes der for.

[Really good-looking men?] Oh yes! Mos' definitely! Like to catch one o' dem sugars for myself!'' But in general there is a wider range of male qualities seen as desirable when women evaluate men.

Though the vernacular vocabulary represented in this book is dominated by males—both in point of view and in the sheer number of terms generated—females offered their own variety of terms to characterize the attractive male. A motif that runs through a good number of them is the sense that the desirable man is both sweet (in his talk and action) and "delicious" or "tasty" in a sensual-sexual way. Terms like *my sweet, sugar, chocolate candy, sugar honey, sweet daddy, sweet poppa,* and *sugar daddy* reveal the female's sensual sweet tooth. A desirable man not only satisfies a woman's appetite physically but also emotionally. And one desired ingredient of emotional satisfaction is sexual fidelity. "Don't be hoppin' from hole to hole like some damn jack rabbit. He righteously be at home wi' chu.'' In women's usage, terms like *home squeeze, main squeeze, daddy one,* and *main man* connote sexual fidelity (or the desire for it) as well as intimacy.

Young women talk much more about emotional satisfaction than men do. The desire to be cared for—emotionally, sexually, and financially—is implied in the image of the sugar daddy and the sweet poppa. As one young woman put it, "I want a sweet daddy. He gon' do his thang, get righteously down to the ground and move it round and round! Oooowheee! Lemme at 'im! But a lot d' brothers dey thank all you gots to do is put it in, take it out. Uh uh! Ain' gonna do it. Young lady like TLC with her J.O.B.! Hear what I'm sayin'? Woman like her man to pet her up, make her feel good. Like Aretha say, she wants 'Mr. Feel Good!' Bring home d' bread, 'n butter *and* d' meat! Umm hmmm!''

Financial earning power is also attributed to the good man. Though young women, like men, often view the male in hard financial terms, their view seems tempered with a more immediate need just to be taken care of. Many ghetto females have seen their mother as the principal or only wage-earner in the family—when and if she could find work—and they have also seen the toll that perpetual labor and birthing and raising of a family have left on her. They wish for more. One young woman spoke for many when she said:

> See, Edie, my mother she work all her life for other people. She clean houses in Beverly Hills and she raise all d' kids [seven] all by herself. My daddy, he left' when I was fo' and we never did see 'im no mo'. D' men she be with, some okay, but dey be takin' her money, buyin' alcohol, gamble—ain't no good. Like me, I wants me a nice respectable man— don't smoke, don't drink, don't be runnin' round, carryin' on. Got his-

self a regular job, so I don't be supportin' him. He takin' care o' me.
Now da's nice!

Many of the terms used by young women to describe the attractive male are the same as the prostitute uses with her pimp. Whatever else he may represent, the pimp is seen by some, at least, as taking care of business—the sexual, emotional, and financial needs of his women. As one young woman bluntly saw it, "He's on his job and he takes care o' bidness. Better be on yo' back den on yo' knees. I rather work fo' *my* man den work for *the* Man."

However, in the 60s and early 70s, another male image vied for center state. That was the "together brother." Whatever his physical attributes, the brother was one who not only respected women for who they were—for being black—but, as many saw it, had more to run down than sweet talk and a flashy front. His prototype was the black militant. "Yeh, I met dis fine young man at d' meetin' [a meeting of US]. Now dat brother righteously to-geth-er! Into some heavy knowledge—not jus', 'Hey baby,' dis and dat shit. Made sense too. About our peoples and gettin' into d' culture bag. Brother look good too! Down in his dashiki, nice Afro, beads. Get behind *dat* brother!"

Undoubtedly, the Black Power movement made females (as well as males) more conscious of a new kind of image, another level of attractiveness. Here now was a young man who was *blowing black*, *blowing change*, and was working for political and social change. Though many young women did not subscribe to the political philosophies of the various militant groups, they found their male members most attractive.

Not surprisingly, several young women singled out Muslim men as among the best catches because they were seen to epitomize the nice young man. They didn't drink, smoke, gamble, or carry on with other women. In addition, they were considered well-spoken as well as soft-spoken. There was a recognition among most of the women I talked to that, indeed, a good man is hard to find.

*The No-Account Nigger.* Certainly females, like males, talked about undesirable men in terms of being physically unattractive (*raspy*, *rasty*, *geeky*, *bad news*, *corroded*) or socially inexperienced or inept (*puppy*, *dunce head*, *square brain*, *junior*, *candy butt*). But their main vernacular and narrative focus was on the male who displayed excessive appetites, whether for sex or drink or drugs or gambling or fighting. A number of terms were used to characterize the young man who could not be trusted when it came to his particular "weakness" —*dog*, *dog nigger*, *dirty dog*, *Mr. Do-you-wrong*, *no-account*, *bad-*

*ass, no-account nigger.* And the appetite that most often got singled out for review was sex and womanizing.

Though young women talked about how attractive the sexually faithful man seemed, few expected fidelity. For many females, promises of sexual fidelity were treated with a skeptical eye, a wait-and-watch attitude. Implicit in much female talk about men is the belief that men just cannot be faithful, just "can't help themselves"—that they need to have multiple sexual encounters to be satisfied.[4] Indeed, the labels assigned to sexually active males underscore this supposed sexual voraciousness—*stud, rogue, cum freak, flesh hound, cock hound.* However, the image of the insatiable male serves a practical purpose for at least some young women I talked with. It serves as a rationale for keeping men at bay, for providing distance between male and female (when a young woman chooses to) by dismissing men as merely animals. Many women voiced the sentiment that men were childish in their sexual appetites. "See, dey cain't help deyselves. Dey like little kids—'Gon' get me some candy.' Dey eyes bigger den d' stomach. Like a woman she knows what she want. She don' need to eat all d' candy in d' store. She kin jus' pick one da's right."

But many of the same young women who put men down for their "evil ways" also indicated an attraction for the "natural-born man," one who smoked, drank, raised hell, gambled, and womanized. He was "for real," despite everything. He was likened to "sweet, Sweetback the bad-assed nigger," or "Honky-Tonk Bud, the hip-cat stud," or "Pimpin' Sam, the sweet-lovin' man," of folk tale, song, and movie. Still, as one young woman summed it up, "Nigger's still a nigger. Give you lots of lovin', be gone nex' day. See where he put his money—not his mouth."

Like their male counterparts, young women's references to undesirable males or male traits were not always congruent with their behavior toward men who exhibited such traits, as the above suggests. Again, what may be a way of labeling and talking about men with other females is not always or necessarily a way of addressing or behaving toward them in person.

## SEX AND SEXUAL BEHAVIOR

One of the primary areas of discussion and vernacular focus among those I met was sex—expressions for intercourse, sexual anatomy, unconventional sex, homosexuality. The majority of young blacks I talked with were sexually savvy at an early age. As Diane Lewis (1975) has pointed out, in "Euro-American culture, children are viewed as asexual . . . in Afro-American culture . . . children are considered sexual beings. They learn about sex, menstruation and birth while very young, so that there is a continuity between their lives as children and as adults'' (pp. 234-235).

Also, like children in preindustrial societies who shared close and multipurposed living space with their elders, black children are often privy to intimate aspects of their elders' lives, including physical intimacy. By the time they are adolescents, a number of youths have witnessed adult sexual activity, and many have had sex themselves by the time they are in their mid-teens.

In addition, adolescence is a time of intense sexuality in many cultures. Youthful sexual encounter and exploration become commonplace as young men and women play out their attraction and feeling for one another.

For many teenagers, then, sex is a known quantity early on. And sexual candor and ease with one's sexuality is the rule, not the exception. At the same time, there is an underlying strain of decorum that also operates in sexual matters, a traditional view of sex. This is manifested in a variety of attitudes toward what constitutes appropriate sex and toward homosexuality.

### ATTITUDES TOWARD SEX

The fact that the majority of terms in this study came from males is particularly apparent when we turn to sexual vernacular. It reflects a decidedly male point of view. As such, it provides a vivid picture of how males see themselves in matters of sex but, equally important, how they see women.

Many of the same expressions are used for females in general and for the female genitalia (*pussy, cock, tail*), and for the act of sexual intercourse (to *get some pussy/cock/tail*). At one level, this merging of a woman's sexual parts with intercourse reflects the general male viewpoint that women are strictly sexual objects with interchangeable parts. This view of women is reflected also in mainstream white male sexual slang, where sayings like "If you put a bag over their heads, they're all the same" graphically reinforce the image of women as objects.

There are also a number of vernacular expressions that extend the image of sweetness—of a delicious and appetizing sexual partner—into the area of sex itself. As mentioned, the sexually desirable parts of a woman's body are called *goodies*. Expressions like "I'm gonna get me some *jellyroll, jelly, jam, sweet potato*" reflect a sense of sweet-tasting sex, of nourishment, of being fed. " 'Yeh, she got a sweet cock!' You'll find some dude'll say dat. 'Man, lemme tell you somethin'. See that broad right dere? She got a sweet *pussy* on her!' "

Women, too, relate sex to the sweet-tasting with terms like to *get some sweet*, to *get some brown sugar*, for sexual intercourse or love making; or when they identify an attractive male as *sweet potato pie* or *sweet sugar*.

It is also very common in general American slang to find food images used for sexual anatomy and intercourse, as well as the references to sweetness. It suggests that sex, like food, is necessary sustenance. But sweetness also implies a dessert rather than a dinner, as it were. It is rich and delectable, and you not only like it but you *crave* it —a decided difference. There is that sense of longing, of addiction, that once again presents itself in the vernacular and is reflected in teenage conversation. Sex can become a delicious habit and the stronger your appetite, the greater the craving. "Like my ol' man, he's so fine. I call 'im sugar, my sweet—'cause he's like candy—I jus' wants to eat 'im up! *Umm hmm!*"

Another image that recurs is that of the animal. This image is seen in terms of intercourse like *pussy*, *pussycat*, *bird*, *chicken*, and expressions for a woman's genitalia like to *do the pussy* or *skin the cat*. Women are pictured as wild animals to be tamed (and "ridden"), in expressions like to *mount*, to *hump*, to *hump ass*, or as domesticated animals—pets or, in more derogatory terms, barnyard animals. Women are quick to point out that the female animals the males are so fond of noting have their male counterparts—the *rooster*, the *tomcat*, the *bull*, the *dog*, the *alligator*. As one young woman put it, "You got cock for d' rooster, pussy for d' tomcat, and you got dat heifer for d' bull. It take two to tango!"

Women are not only characterized as land animals but as fish— *trout, fish, tuna fish*. Here the characterization reflects the male attitude toward not just the woman herself but to her vaginal scent, particularly when she is menstruating. "Tuna, that be some stanky pussy. She on d' rag!" The fact that a woman's vaginal scent is often perceived negatively is reinforced by terms like *stank* and *stink pot* and the expression *stink finger* (manual stimulation of a woman's genitals). Sometimes, however, expressions like *tuna* and *tuna fish* relate more to the tastiness of a woman, "tender meat" to be *snagged* or *hooked*. As one young man enthusiastically put it, "Sweet tuna! I'm Charlie Tuna, I'ma gonna git me a piece that *nice meat!* I don' care! Dark meat, light meat, ain' no difference to me. Pussy's pussy!" These contradictory images of the woman as both delectable and distasteful seem to reflect, once again, the attraction and rejection, the praise and put-down, that underlie so much male-female interaction.

Reinforcing a depersonalized image of a woman are those terms characterizing females as literal body parts. Expressions for intercourse—to *get a piece*, to *get a piece of ass/tail*, to *get some leg*, to *get a shot of leg*, to *cut a side* (of beef), *fresh hide* (for a new sexual partner)—not only view the woman as dismembered body parts but as a slab of meat, a *side of beef*, the cut-up heifer or cow or pig. There appears to be a great deal of disdain and hostility (and implicit sadism) toward women connoted in such expressions. Indeed, the aggression imbedded in the sexual vernacular is even more clearly seen in terms used, for example, to characterize any place designated for sex—a motel, a front room, a bedroom, whatever—as *killing floor, slaughter house, whip shack*. And some of the same terms used to characterize physical assault are also used to connote sexual intercourse—voluntary or otherwise—such as to *rip off/on someone*, to *jam*, to *jack up*, to *throw*. The sexual act, in this context, is seen as still another battlefield, perhaps the most intense, upon which male and female wage their intersexual contest. Though these terms are usually used by males to describe male sexual conquest, they are also used by at least some females to connote turning the tables on the male. "A young lady rips off a dude. The dude get loaded and he's too loaded to do anythin'. So she gets to playin' and she make it hard. Therefore, she get on over him. So she rips him off too—'stead o' *him* rippin' her off."

Women are characterized in the lexicon not only as dissected body parts, pieces of meat, but as receptacles for the male organ and its "discharge" or "waste." A favorite expression among young males for sexual intercourse is to *lay some pipe*, and the male who frequently engages in sex is called a *plumber*. One young man ran down a whole stylized rap when I asked him to define the expression plumber: "Yes, I'm d' plumber and I'm here today to lay some pipe! What has the hole the plumber's gotta put his pipe through? Who's gonna flood yo' hole, fill yo' canyon up? Me! 'Cause I'ma stone-hope-to-die, fonky plumber!" So young men talk about the vagina as the *canyon*, a *hole*, a *gash*, a *slit*, a *pole hole* ("your penis' sheath"), something into which you put your pipe. Young women, from their part, do not take kindly at all to this braggadocio on the part of males. One outspoken young woman voiced the sentiment of many when she said, "Nigger talk! That what he call his penis—pipe. Nigger talk about, 'I'ma plumber.' Ain' no plumber here. I don't believe in layin' no pipe. Righteously 'unconnect' dat nigger's pipe he be talkin' dat shit 'round me!"

Women are also seen as something to be plucked or, maybe more cynically, to be fleeced. *Pluck* refers to an attractive female and to *pluck* means to have sex. Terms like *fluff* for vagina and *cotton* or *bush* for female pubic hair suggest a woman's soft or furlike parts and, at the same time, her vulnerability at the hands of the male who "plucks her *trim* (vagina) clean." From a female viewpoint, being plucked can also suggest being well satisfied by your male. "I say,

'Hey girl, I met this *fine* dude last night.' They say, 'Oh, so you done got plucked.' Say, 'Yeh, I was sho' *plucked* when he lef' me.' ''

Finally, sex, as with so many other forms of interaction, is characterized in especially kinetic terms. Terms like to *boogie*, to *cha-cha*, to *jam*, and to *jazz* for intercourse and *scat* for vagina all suggest sex in musical or dance terms. Indeed, the term jazz connoted sex long before it was taken over to describe a particular kind of music. Other expressions for intercourse—to *lay up/back/low*, to *give it up*, to *get down to the ground and move it round and round*, to *jump up and down*, to *knock it out*, to *be uptight* (in the sense of up tight against another's body)—all suggest the strong kinetic element in sexual vernacular.

If the woman is pictured through the vocabulary in receptive or passive terms as a hole to be filled or a receptacle, young men characterize their penis in aggressive action terms. Expressions for intercourse, to *grind*, to *pile*, to *mash the fat*, suggest this quality. The male sex organ itself is seen as a tool for penetrating women: to *dip the fly*, to *poke*, to *give her the jam pot*, to *do the thing*. This view of the penis as an instrument of penetration also implies that it must be stiff and erect. Virtually all the terms for penis, *rod*, *pipe*, *stick*, *pole*, *bone*, *tube*, and *joint*, characterize the penis in its hard state.

Like the terms for the vagina, the penis is also referred to as a piece of meat: *beef*, *meat*, or *tube steak*. However, the implication is different. The "hunk of meat" is now positively valued and related to the size of the penis—the bigger the piece of meat the better. (The vernacular term *dinosaur* for penis suggests the extent of youthful fancy.) Males see the size of their penis as not only a mark of manliness (as is the case in many other cultures) but also as a potential vehicle through which to satisfy (and control) women. "Some dudes y' know, dey ain't too big, can't righteously take care o' bidness. The bigger d' better. See you like the plumber who lay his pipe. The bigger dat pipe, the more it gonna fill up dat hole. 'Cause *who* has d' key and *who* had d' lock? Person has to unlock, understand? Pop dat lock! Need a big key. Who has the combination to that lock? Person dat got dat combination gets in dat safe!" So young men see themselves as having the key to the lock, the combination to the safe, the thing to make women happy.

As in other areas of male behavior, there is a good deal of bravado and fronting off in the dialogs about women and sex. We have already noted that what is said among males differs significantly from what is said to females, if you hope to get over.

Females also evaluate males sexually, especially in terms of their potency or sexual staying power. Terms like *high waters* (erection) and

153

*muddy waters* (loss of erection) are graphic examples. Women also use vocabulary that addresses itself to the size and shape of the penis— *string bean* (skinny penis), *puppy* (small penis). As one young woman put it, "Like you wants righteously get down wid cho' man. If you got yo'self a li'l ol' puppy, you in fo' some muddy waters. 'Cause yo' puppy, see, he jus' be barkin', but he ain't got no bite. Hear what I'm sayin'?"

Overall, the vernacular is not very complimentary in its charac- terization of women. But the picture is not one-dimensional. For the talk also praises certain attributes of both the young man and the young woman at the same time that it puts each down. This pervasive push-pull relationship again needs to be stressed. It reflects a complex and often contradictory set of feelings that affect the male-female ex- perience, and highlights a basic polarization between the sexes found not only among young blacks but in many other cultures as well.

### ATTITUDES TOWARD UNCONVENTIONAL SEX

One motif that runs through much teenage dialog is the attitude that sexual relations are a natural, ordinary part of life. The term na- tural itself is not only a positive intensifier, as in "a natural-born man," but also conveys a sense of being yourself, of "letting it all hang out," of being free. The expression *layed to the natural bone* means to be naked and carries with it a sense of bodily freedom as well as psychological freedom. In a sexual context, it can refer to satisfying sex, having a *natural* (good) *feeling*, or *getting down to the natural thing*. Or it can refer to a good sexual partner, *a natural man/woman*. And anything that interferes with the natural course of sexual events, something that might make a man temporarily impotent—too much liquor or too many drugs—is seen as *messing with nature*. Also, the word fonky, which in other contexts means giving off an offensive body odor, takes on a positive meaning in the sexual context. Here it often identifies the good smells connected with good sex. So sex is viewed by many teenagers as an integral and basic part of life.

But doing what comes naturally doesn't necessarily mean doing what is unconventional. In the case of black teenagers, sexual preco- ciousness does not necessarily correspond to sexual exploration or sophistication. As with other areas of sexuality, there is a strong puri- tanism that pervades discussions of sex in general and the perfor- mance of the sex act itself. At the same time that young males brag about their past and future sexual conquests and boastfully preview how they're going out to catch some "cock," they are by turns shy, embarrassed, defiant, or sometimes totally euphemistic about sex when directly questioned, especially by a woman. For example, when I asked young men for the definition of poontang (vagina), the responses ran the gamut from a kind of defiant bravado ("You gon' fuck! Yeh, I want some o' dat sweet pussy—you wanna fuck?"); to long pauses, hesitations, or laughter preceding a response; to indirection and evasion ("Sorta nickname for a girl. I know what it is, but I don' wanna say [laughter and a pause]. So you want me to jus' go on and tell you what it is. Well, it means what's under a young lady's clothes. Well da's what it mean—to me!"). Of course, my being a woman didn't help the ease of response. Decorum ran up against bravado.

With few exceptions, sexual intercourse means vaginal-penile contact. Oral sex, anal intercourse, and sex during a woman's period, if not outright taboos, are certainly not seen as desirable experiences. Why are they considered unacceptable sexual behavior?

*Oral Sex.*[5] Attitudes toward oral sex were decidedly negative among the teenagers I met. Again, this attitude was particularly apparent among males whose responses to questions about oral contact with women ran the gamut from embarrassment—"[much laughter, then a long pause] Dat's to—well a—[more laughter]. Oh, I don' know, well a—pussy. Yeh, I know what it is. I don't eat pussy"—to outspoken rejection—"Oh, I don't do that! I know what you mean. Naaa, *man!* Da's eatin' pussy. I ain't gonna eat *none* o' dat stuff! I gonna get up and walk away!"

What came out of male dialogs was a general feeling that oral sex was basically unnatural, not right. When asked to define an expression that referred to oral sex, a number of young men first defined it, then said they didn't do it or that it was wrong. The following response is typical: "Eatin' pussy. I don't do none dat canyon stuff! Da's sex in d' wrong way. Dat's when you put your mouth where it shouldn't be." It is not surprising that one of the expressions for oral sex is to *do the nasty.*

But underneath this somewhat puritanical response are other reasons for the distastefulness of oral sex. Some see oral sex as the white man's trip. "Whitey does dat. Tha's when a white person say he gonna eat some damn tripe!" Oral sex is not only seen as a white trip but, more significantly, as a lack of white male sexuality. "Like white boy, he don' know *how* to righteously do his thang, so he gon' eat some pussy 'stead o' doin' it right!"

This view of oral sex as somehow wrong is intimately tied to still another male feeling that oral sex is not masculine, is not what real men do. And taking their lead from their reading of the pimp's behavior, many males claim that they don't "eat" on principle. "I cain't even say I won't do it, 'cause I be tellin' a big lie. I gotta get my mind alright. [Maybe the young lady would like it?] I hope not. I like to *stroke!* [Don't good lovers do things beside stroke?] Nah! Pimps they don' be doin' it neither! It jus' ain't what a man s'pose' be doin'. It ain' right!''

Certainly the element of machismo is a complex factor in male attitudes toward oral sex. It is not seen as masculine, in part, because it is not directly connected to the male, his penis and his pleasure. It focuses attention on the woman and *her* potential pleasure. Few males see oral sex as an act of giving pleasure to a woman and thereby getting pleasure through her enjoyment.

But beyond the element of machismo and manipulative behavior are deeper reactions to performing oral sex: it is seen as repugnant because of a woman's genital smells. What is often a tag to reasons given for not performing oral sex is that the woman's vaginal scent or taste is nasty or fonky. "I don't eat none dat tuna. It stank! Ooowheee!'' It raises another issue as well: fear, apprehension, and suspicion of the unfamiliar. Though a lot of male teenagers talked brashly about sex in general and others aspects of sex like oral contact, many also admitted that the woman's sexual anatomy is a relatively unexplored and sometimes frightening territory. As one teenager put it, oral sex is a "trip into the unknown.''

It seems that oral sex, because it is generally untried and unknown ("I ain't ready for dat yet"), is often suspect and therefore discounted. One young man's response to the expression to *eat someone out* was not an uncommon one and highlights how we all often dismiss or condemn what we don't know first-hand or what we may fear. "Nah. I don' even use that *bullshit!* Like I *hear* it, understan' me. I read books and shit about dat, but I jus' don' dig it!'' So oral sex for many is surrounded with mythology, coupled with a sense of repugnance.[6]

I think it important to reiterate that sexual precocity does not necessarily coincide with sexual exploration or sophistication. At fifteen, sixteen, or seventeen—even much older—there is a lot yet to be explored and tried. And with all the talk about sexual exploits, there were still a number of teenagers who admitted they had not yet experienced sexual intercourse, let alone oral sex. As with many cultures, male sexual experience—or, as is often the case among the young, the facade of experience—is an important myth to be maintained as part of the masculine ethic.

Women's responses to oral sex were qualitatively different than those of the men. A far greater number claimed to have engaged in oral sex, as compared with the males interviewed. Though some were shy and embarrassed about the subject, there was much less outspoken rejection of oral sex and less condemnation. At most, it was seen as "not nice'' for a young woman to do or receive, but not necessarily as something repugnant. "See you don't be doin' that, less you married. It jus' somethin' dat a young lady don' do, if she respectable."

Many young women were more willing to perform oral sex than have it reciprocated. This ability to give more readily than to receive is not especially unusual when you take into account the male attitudes toward cunnilingus. Some young women admitted that they believed, as many males did, that their genitalia had a bad smell. One young woman spoke for many when she said, "Like you know, Edie, I wash good! But I jus' don' feel right 'bout no pussy-eatin'. Don' know, it make me uncomfortable—but I gives head in a minute."

Intimately tied to this negative sense of one's vaginal scent are both male and female attitudes toward sex during menstruation. There are a variety of expressions, from the euphemistic to the graphic, that refer to a women's menstrual period—to be *on the rag, red Mary*, to *ride the white horse, the red dog/red knight is on the white horse*. There are also a variety of graphic expressions to characterize sanitary napkins—*rag, diaper, jellyroll, jelly sandwich*. The majority of males interviewed saw sex during menstruation as taboo. In fact one of the specific examples of a male's being "cock-blocked" is to find out that a young woman is having her period. "Like you goes over to a girl's house and she happens to be on her period. Think you gonna get some. He's blocked!" Generally, the male response to a woman's period is one of distaste, as evidenced in some of the smell-related terms depicting women. As far as engaging in sexual contact during a woman's period, male feelings are strongly negative. "Nah, ain' no way I'm gonna fuck some young lady's on d' rag. It all messy and it stink! My sisters dey smell like ol' trout when they ridin' the rag!"

Young women, again, tend to reflect and respond to the male image of them as "unclean" and undesirable. Few young women claimed to desire sexual contact of any kind during their period, and even those few who did were not very comfortable about it. "Like my ol' man, he cool. We gets it on fair weather an' foul. Understand? But I don' much like to do d' thang den. It *is* kinda messy and you got dat kinda fishy smell. But we do it." Women, then, are not particularly encouraged or motivated to have sex during menstruation. They are seen (and often see themselves) as somehow dirty (which also translates as bad, smelly, messy), and therefore undesirable to the man. Here again the male's point of view seems to inform the female's.

Some women are not only ashamed of their vaginal scent, but are apprehensive about what might happen to them as a result of oral contact. These fears ran from an apprehension about contracting venereal disease from oral contact to suspicion regarding the male's real motives. "Now, some dudes you know, dey righteously dig eatin' pussy.

But some o' dem niggers—WATCH OUT! They wanna get you all excited, turn you out! You be ho'in' for dem.''

Given the less than enthusiastic endorsement of oral sex—especially on the part of males in relation to females—it might seem surprising to find such a sizable set of terms in the lexicon that define the phenomenon. Not only does one find the more prosaic expressions to *eat pussy* and to *give head*, but those that are graphic (to *eat a fur burger*, to *have a sack lunch*, to *eat some pie*); euphemistic (to *dive/ yodel/sneeze/grin in the canyon*); poetic (to *sip/drink at the fuzzy cup*); and funny (to *blow some tunes,* to *brush one's teeth*, to be *a gorilla in the washing machine*).

Why all the attention—humorous and poetic—to a reportedly distasteful phenomenon? Perhaps because whether or not oral sex is condoned, condemned, enjoyed, or avoided, it generates a lot of heat among teenagers. And when something is important—either negatively or positively valued—it will give rise to or perpetuate language to characterize it. One need only think of the large sets of slang terms associated with, say, disease, alcoholism, and death to see that humans inevitably give much linguistic attention to the very things they fear, abhor, or disdain.

*Anal Intercourse.* If there is strong feeling toward oral sex, it becomes more intensified toward anal intercourse. A sizable vocabulary is associated with it, and again the terminology ranges from the graphic (to *get some brown/tight/round eye*, to *dog fuck*, to *pack peanut butter*) to the more euphemistic (to *ask for/buy the ring*, to *take on some backs*, to *throw a buttonhole on someone*). Some vernacular terms, such as to *get some booty* or to *get some duke*, can refer to intercourse with either a man or woman: "Brother use it both ways, understan' me? If dere's a lady around, he talkin' 'bout some pussy. Like if he jus' basin' to d' brother, he talkin' 'bout fuckin' from behind.'' But for the most part, the terms are associated with homosexual contact.

Few dialogs or references centered on anal intercourse with a female—except when describing unconventional acts like *making a sandwich* or *running/pulling a double train* (two men engaging in simultaneous sex, vaginal and anal, with the same woman). And the act of anal intercourse itself is generally condemned by males as what punks do, as something unnatural and unmanly. The outstanding exception is when one is in jail. There, having sex with another male is at least understood, though still not really acceptable.

Dat happen a lot in jail. Turn a dude into a freak. Make a woman outa him. Like some men thank they women, I cain't stand dem punks. Yeh,

they make me sick to d' stomach! [Ever been hustled?] Yeh. He got
knocked on his butt! Mostly dey have 'em off in a place call P.C. [Pro-
tective Custody]. Dey don' let 'em run, 'cause too many people git
killed over 'em. 'Cause people have life, don' never get out, so dey have
to mess wid a dude. Only reason dey do dat. If dey gon' get out sometime, they probably wouldn't do it. But dey know they ain' never gon'
get out, so dey hafta do somethin'. Some dudes lookin' like women.
Ever'time I look at one, I get sick. My friend jus' happen be biggest one
up dere, so nobody mess wif 'im. But you ain't got, do wha'chu got.

When and if a women is available for sex, anal intercourse with other
males again becomes proscribed. "They use dat at the place all d'
time. But I don't be usin' it on the streets too often. Too many woman
walkin' aroun' to be usin' brown eye. 'Cause there's too much that
*stuff*. So they always have it in jail—where there's no woman."

It is no surprise that anal intercourse, and its homosexual association, would be condemned by young males who ascribe to the machismo ethic. What is more interesting is that it is at least tolerated in
jail, ostensibly because women aren't available for sexual satisfaction.
But at the same time that most teenagers put down anal intercourse,
there is a curious interest in it among some, particularly those who
were incarcerated for any length of time. This curiosity was manifested in extended dialog about jail and homosexuality there, as well as
tales about anal intercourse. It has been said that the reverse side of
the ultra macho coin is homosexuality—for example, the sexual overtones in sports like boxing and football.[7] I am not suggesting that the
statement is necessarily true or accurate in this context. But it does
seem to be the case that we are often drawn to the very things we out-
wardly condemn or dismiss. And certainly the number of expressions
detailing anal intercourse reflect attention to it. Whether that interest
is acted upon beyond prison is another question.

*Homosexuality.* By far the strongest negative response centers
on homosexuality itself. This is particularly apparent, once again,
among males in their attitudes toward lesbianism and male homosexuality in particular. There are several vernacular expressions for a lesbian: *bull, bulldike, bulldagger, dike, jasper, lesbie, butch*. Male attitudes toward lesbians vary. Some young men are intrigued by them
and seem to admire their show of masculine behavior.

Bulldagger. Lots o' dem daggers where I stay. Like dis one come by d'
parole office. She was comin' by, she had on her hair her stingy brim—
ace-deuce to d' side. Had on her bad-boy bell bottoms, had on her twin
knit, her black shoes. I say, "What's happ'nin' brother!" She say,
"You got it." I say, "Lemme get a cigarette from you—MAN." 'Cause
she like when I call her *dat*. Throws me out wid a cigarette, go on down
d' street. She okay—righteous *man!*

Others are fearful of lesbians and what they perceive to be their "super macho" power. "See them real masculine women. Righteous bulldikers. I don' fool roun' wid 'em. I don't get too close to 'em. Don' say nothin' to 'em. Don' be 'sociatin' wid 'em. Dey too tough. Dey blow you away in a minute!"

But not all lesbians are seen in such patently masculine terms. One young man recounted the experience of his brother who was going around with a lesbian and didn't know it, until he saw her kissing another woman. "There's a lotta lesbie women roun' here. My brother use have a woman, use be like dey say, gay. You hardly know 'em, 'cept dey have dem little dots on their hands. Some stone fox too. Dey real fiendish. Jus' don' like men!"

Though males tend to stereotype lesbians as either butch or fem, their reactions to them are various and run the gamut from distaste to admiration. Among young women, the lesbian tends to get equated more with the stereotype butch, and becomes a real or fancied source of harassment and fear for many. One very outspoken and assertive young woman told of how even she was intimidated and frightened by an encounter she had with two "bulldaggers":

Looky here, they be some *strong*-ass old witch. They are good protectors, though. But, boy, I be scared to git *wrong* wid one of dem. 'Cause, they believe in offin' or hurtin' you so bad. Two of 'em followed me one day I came from d' cleaners. I was expectin' too, wha's so cold about it. Expectin' my last child. An' one o' 'em was walkin' in front of me, had been to the cleaners. Had a butch, you know. So, den all a sudden, dis Cadillac was comin' by wid dis guy—a *real male* from birth! But, it had one over in d' car wid 'im. So, this other one say, "Herbie!" Car stops, jumps out. They standin' over dere shootin' d' shit.

So, I gits in front. Rushin'. I'm puttin' RUSH on it right den! Shit! Pretty soon dey say, "Hey lady." My heart say, thump. "Nah, dey ain't talkin' to *me*." But I'm knowin' ain' nobody else on d' street but US—we three! I was *so* scared, boy. They say, "Hey lady, wait a minute!" I say, "When next time dey speak, there's gonna be a 'better.'" They sho' nuff did. Say, "You *better* wait!" I say, "Oh, God iffen I don' wait, what's gonna happen? Gonna jack me up either way." So, I say, "Nah, nah, I can't wait, I'm gettin' too close."

So den, it was two girls comin' down d' street. So, they was just quiet, didn' say nothin'. Dose two girls went on further, they call me again. "Don't take another step, 'cause I'm countin' on you, you better wait!" An' shit, I was close to dat corner. I looked back to see if dey was comin' and they was walkin' fast. I took off runnin'.

It was in d' summer time too. Boy, I was hot, tired, blowin' ass. And, I was scared to go home. They was lookin' for me, lookin' at d' house. [Why?] I didn't take time to find out!

Women also make a distinction between what they perceive to be a natural woman and a lesbian, who is unnatural. In fact expressions like *real women* for a heterosexual woman and *freak* for a lesbian are terms used among women and reflect this categorizing of female sexuality. Some women express a sympathy for the lesbian—that her lesbianism is a "sickness" she can't help. If only she could experience a "real natural-born man," she would be fine. This attitude, along with other aspects of female response, reflects a decidedly traditional point of view, which in no small part acknowledges the masculine point of view.

Yet what is intriguing is that a sizable number of young women know of or have friends or acquaintances who are lesbians, or themselves have experienced a homosexual encounter. Female homosexuality is almost never discussed in works dealing with black culture—which suggests that it somehow doesn't exist or that it shouldn't be acknowledged even if it does. Of course, the majority of work on black culture has been written by males about males. Though much more investigation needs to be done on black lesbianism, my own experience and data indicate that there is much more to be learned about female sexuality and interaction.

Male homosexuality, unlike lesbianism, provokes an almost unanimous negative response from males. It is unnatural: "Don' nobody like no punks. Mos' everybody gettin' over here. Don' wanna be tied up wid no punks. Go out and get some scat, catty-cat. They wanna fuck!" Furthermore, it is repugnant: "Like some men dey jus' like bitches. Dem punks is righteously fucked up in dey haid. Dey more like women den a young lady. [Ever been hustled?] Nah, no punk gon' *ever* touch me!"

Teenage males identify homosexuals with a lack of manliness and label them in "feminine" terms: *sissy, punk, sweet, swish, funny, fruit, girl.* As one young man saw it, homosexuality resulted from boys being kept in the home and therefore away from a male-dominated environment.

All's up dere [at a gay bar on Central Avenue] black punks. I hate 'em! Don' see how nobody can turn theyself out to be somethin' like dat! I think it mostly in the house, way people treat 'em. Keep 'em in d' house. He done got so if he go out on d' streets, none the brothers out dere wanna say nothin' to 'im. Li'l *punk!* Stay in d' house all the time. He can't help it, I guess. He got so sissify, he probably git to talk wif girls. They probably get to be his friend. Den he say, "I got all dese girls fo' friend, might as well be one myself." Hell wid 'im. Don' mess wid me.

In a slightly different vein, there is an expression in the vernacular, "to freak off," which in sexual terms generally calls attention to the unconventional character of certain sexual behavior. It generally describes unusual or seemingly bizarre sexual behavior—and included in that category are oral sex, anal intercourse, homosexuality, as well as masturbation, manual stimulation of another, and group sex. As one teenager said, in rather embarrassed and euphemistic terms, "Freak off mean indulge in some previous activity a little bit different from [long pause] . . . You know, d' usual sexual process." As already seen, the term freak is used to identify both the male homosexual and the lesbian, and the phrase to *freak fuck* means to engage in oral sex. The connotation of the word itself is to do something unusual or weird.

In addition to the term freak, the expression to *turn someone out* can mean to use unconventional means to introduce someone to any important first experience. Often the reference is to an unusual or first sexual experience. "My sister was real swingin'. She gave me an unusual birthday present. She got one 'er partners to freak off wid me when I turn thirteen. Her partner was twenty-three. She turn me out— but she broke my heart!" Whether the term freak and its derivations are being positively or negatively ascribed depends on the context and reference. What is of particular interest is to see what and who gets labeled freaky, and why. Again it tells us something about the sexual attitudes, myths, and mores of a group.

Teenage attention to sex in general, and to unconventional sex in particular, is also reflected in the content of jokes, dozens, and other verbal contests. Many put-downs turn on accusations of homosexual activity, oral sex, anal sex, and a host of other sexual activities. Sometimes these are maneuvers carried to great ends. For example, the expression to *ride pussy/punk/the bitch's seat* defines a manipulative ploy whereby a young man finds himself outmaneuvered by other males and forced to ride in a car "on the hump," where the woman is supposed to ride.

Of course not all teenagers—male or female—reacted negatively to unconventional sexual behavior. There were young men who claimed to enjoy oral sex with a young woman they particularly liked or with one who was willing to experiment sexually. One young man explained his philosophy of attraction, affection, and attitudes toward sex in terms that made good sense to other males I spoke with.

I's different feelings about different people. You jus' don' have feelings about some of 'em [women]. There gotta be something to draw me in dere if I'm gonna freak off wid 'em. Otherwise, I jus' go an' jump up and down. But I don't get too much enjoyment outa jumpin' up and down. But some young ladies they 'shamed half d' time. They embarrass' and scared. Wid me, I'm a tryer. I wanna see, I wanna experience dis and dat. There's a lotta talk go 'roun' 'bout if you go down an' eat and all dis, you git 'em wild, strung out and put 'em on d' corner and all dis. I's a lotta talk. And some girls *hide* it and they afraid of it.

Other teenagers talked about "giving head" in positive, if sometimes competitive, terms. Here the battle of the sexes gets waged in bed. "I's alright! Like I'm with my woman somewhere, go on and give a showdown—like who can take the most, without gittin' outa bed. But I always hafta quit—she can bag it better 'n I can. I always hadda quit when it come my turn to go down again. It depend on the young lady and the mood I'm in. It's a trip!''

As already suggested, though male homosexuality is publicly condemned, some teenagers are curious about it—and some have had some homosexual encounters (both oral and anal sex). One young man, recently released from the Youth Authority, who had been incarcerated for the majority of his seventeen years, told of his own experience with homosexuality on the outside. He was explaining the expression "to get some duke."

Get some duke is to have intercourse with a female impersonator. I been around them. I use to live with one of them. Black dude, too. We had a sexual relation sometime. He was jus' kinda queerish. He liked dudes. He said, "You have your women and your girlfriends and I'll have my men." And I say, "Well, da's nice." He gave me money an' stuff. First time I met 'im, I thought he was a broad, but he didn't play. He brought me out a roll of red devils. They were out of cigarettes. I asked him for a cigarette and he brought me a $25 bag [of marijuana] and told me to smoke what I wanted. He jus' liked to look at me. He said I looked good to him. I jus' couldn't live like that, so I finally split.

The dimensions of male and female sexuality and sexual behavior reflected in the previous discussion are, by no means, all-inclusive or solely limited to black teenagers. The vernacular focus on sexuality pictured in this chapter reflects not an unusual or unnatural obsession with things sexual, but an ordinary and age-old attention to sex and sexual attraction among the young everywhere. It is the particular tone, tenor, and expression given to these phenomena—through teenage dialog and vernacular definition—that I have sought to illuminate. The picture provides at least a partial view of the complex interplay between the sexes—how young males and females perceive themselves, their roles, and their relationships.

# 5. pills, pot, and pluck

# the

# vocabulary

# of drugs

ONE OF THE LARGEST single areas of teenage concern was drugs: who was dealing, where and how you could score, what types and quantities were available, how potent or pure the stuff, what you were using alone or in combination to turn you on, what kind of high you were experiencing and what it felt like to come down. As is the case in many urban centers—black, white, or otherwise—drugs are within the grasp of the youngest buyers if they have the money to buy them or the wits to get them in some other way. Not all the teenagers I met took drugs or smoked marijuana. But the impact of the drug experience on teenage culture in the 60s and 70s was so far-reaching that large portions of conversation invariably focused on the drug scene. If young people took drugs or smoked marijuana they talked at great length about their experiences; if they didn't take drugs, they rationalized about why they didn't; if they were undecided, they weighed the pros and cons in light of the experiences of others. And whether they were users or talkers, many utilized an exceedingly rich and intricate drug lexicon to relate their experiences and feelings.[1]

## THE DRUGS

Hey, baby, what you want is what you get. You wanna fly high in d' sky? O.C. got d' ticket for you. How 'bout some reds? Or dese here whites? Now, they keep you real wired—hummin' and strummin'! How 'bout some weed? Got some dat fine Nam shit. Hey, dat stuff'll get you so high, you be walkin' in d' strat-o-sphere! Hey lemme throw you out with a j. You try it, you never want nothin' else. No? Well kin you get behind some skag? Like dey say, "A little dab'll do you"—and den some! Dat ain't yo' stick neither, huh? Say, fine young lady like yo' self, I know, you got a real sweet taste, you go fo' d' "sophisticated lady" right? Like little coke get you tight, blow your mind and make you RIGHT!!

Girl, don't you wanna score *nothin'*! Say, white girl like you probably dig some nice acid—git chu psychedelic to d' bone! You be trippin'

for days! . . . Say, baby, you a hard lady to get over to. How'm I gon'
stay in business if you don't help?

This exchange between O.C. and me was one of several drug raps
I got involved in from time to time. Certainly O.C. was particularly
well-equipped and proved he was able to deliver the goods. Not all
young dealers—or would-be dealers—stock such a wide range of
wares. But the goods are there. Though many drugs were available,
the greatest traffic revolved around barbiturates, amphetamines, and
marijuana. And the vernacular reflects this focus. It is extremely elaborate and reflects the keen attention given to pills and pot.

### BARBITURATES AND AMPHETAMINES

Barbiturates are known in the vernacular by a variety of names,
and many of these names call attention to the soporific effect barbiturates have on the central nervous system: *downs, downers, stums,*
*stumblers, slow-em-ups, fender benders, stumble bumbles.* As one
young man put it, "Dem stums git you so messed up you be fallin' on
yo' ass! I always call 'em slow-em-ups. They righteously slow you up!
Git loaded, go out and drive, you *definitely* gon' bend some fenders!"

A variety of barbiturates was available to the teenagers I encountered. Those that were commercially produced and distributed were
sometimes identified by their brand name. So, for example, secobarbital, put out by the Eli Lilly Company for one, was known simply as
*Lillys.* More often, barbiturates were identified in terms of their color.
Amytal (amobarbital) was called *blue, blue angel, blue heaven;* Nembutal (pentobarbital), *yellow, yellow jack, yellow jacket;* and Tuinal
(amobarbital and secobarbital), *rainbow, christmas tree.*

The most popular barbiturate among those I talked with was
secobarbital, known by the trade name of Seconal. Its popularity was
attested to by the great number and variety of terms used to characterize it. Some vernacular terms identified Seconal by the color of the

capsule in which the powder was encased, identifications that ranged from the literal to the metaphoric—*reds, red devils, red man, red lady, red boots, red tennis shoes*. Other terms associated Seconal with its commercial identification number (and potency)—*F-40s, Lilly F-40s, F-60s, F-66s*. Still other expressions likened Seconal to "candy" (itself a vernacular term for heroin or pills of any type)—*M & Ms, gum drops, ju jus*—or some other kind of "food" that nourishes you—*apples, yum yums, jellybeans, jiblets*, or *hors d'oeuvres* (so called because they are served at parties and other social events).

However labeled, people tended to identify Seconal with the pharmaceutical company that produced the compound. As one teenager wryly put it, "Now dat dude Eli Lilly, he one d' most popular cats down here. *Every*body like him. He d' only white man dat done ever make you feel good! Lilly a fonky drug company!"

Not all pills, of course, were commercially prepared compounds. This was particularly true of barbiturates. In some cases, they were secured through prescriptions and then sold on the streets. One young woman dealer made the rounds of doctors' offices during her pregnancy, got prescriptions for Seconal, and sold the capsules for a street price of $5.00 a "roll" (three capsules). Most reds were purchased from drug dealers, from friends and friends of friends who, in turn, got the barbiturates through black market connections in Mexico and Canada. Though this contraband was often from commercial drug companies, the commercial powder was extracted from the original capsule and mixed with a variety of substances—such as baking soda or sugar—to dilute it before it reached the streets.

Knowledgeable young people made a distinction between commercially prepared barbiturates, such as Seconal, and dealer compounds. The commercial capsules were called *prescriptions* or *prescription reds*; the dealer mixtures, *borders* or *border reds*. In addition, pill-wise teenagers distinguished between commercial and noncommercial compounds by the shape of the capsules encasing them. Lilly's own goods were called *bullets* or *bulletheads* (as were other undiluted compounds, barbiturates or otherwise); the diluted dealer compounds were referred to as *blunts, round heads*, or *flat heads*. One pill-savvy young woman broke it down in the following way:

> Bullets they uncut red devils—any kinda pill dat's uncut. Could be red devils or Truinal or yellow jacks, blue heavens or pink lady. Doesn't have to be reds. 'Cause they're a lotta pills in capsule form. Like if you get 'em at the pharmacy, you get 'em in bullet shape. And blunts are the ones they're round at the end—they bigger than F-40s, but ain't as strong. Look for d' little number on bullets. Dat tells you dey uncut too.

Though a number of commercially prepared amphetamines (known generally in the vernacular as *ups*, *uppers*, and *pep-em-ups*) were familiar to young blacks and used by some of them, the one that was most often referred to was the compound Benzedrine—variously called *white*, *benny*, *bean*, *chalk*, or *wake-up*. The amphetamine Methedrine, which proved to be very popular among white teenagers in the 60s, had limited appeal among the blacks I encountered. And this is reflected in the vernacular. Only two terms—*speed* and *meth*— were used by blacks to describe the drug. Though some young blacks had taken speed, it was generally considered to be a "white trip."

In general, amphetamines were talked about much less often than were barbiturates or marijuana. When amphetamines were brought up in conversation, they were often seen as something you took in conjunction with another substance. "Some whites and weed, tha's a nice high. Jus' be feelin' mellow. Don' be hongry [which marijuana encourages and amphetamines discourage] nothin'. Jus' good. Last a long time too."

Both barbiturates and amphetamines were referred to as *candy*, *jellybeans*, and *vitamins*. As many put it, jellybeans come in all colors, and so do pills. Like candy, they are a "goodie" that satisfies your sweet tooth and, like vitamins, they make you feel good. As one young man summarized it, "They pick you up, they bring you down— they make you feel better 'n it is."

Teenage interest in barbiturates and amphetamines not only focused on the kinds of pills available—as well as their source and potency—but on the quantity or unit of measurement in which they could be obtained. A single pill was referred to as an *ace*; two pills, a *deuce*; three to ten pills of similar or varying strength or type, a *roll*, a *rack*, or a *set*; a bottle of 500 to 1000, a *jar*. A common way of asking someone for a given quantity of pills was to say *throw me out with* or *kick me down/out with* or *lay me down with* (an ace, deuce, roll). Few had ever scored more than a couple of rolls at a time. As one youth explained, "Don't hardly see no jar. Money ain't long enough. White boy, now he kin cop a jar. He got d' bread to buy d' whole candy store! Me, I jus' cops a few jellybeans here and dere. Take care o' my sweet tooth—dig?"

MARIJUANA

The most popular and widely used substance among black teenagers is marijuana. Fully 85 percent of those I met over the years said they had tried it; approximately 65 percent claimed to use it regularly. Its immense popularity is reflected in the striking number of terms used to identify it—*grass*, *weed*, *gunny*, *bush*, *herbs*, *tea*, *gauge*, *juana*, *maryjane*, *boo*, *shit*, *pot*, *smoke*, to name a few.

Great attention was given to the classification of marijuana according to its assumed place of origin, its ingredients, and its degree of potency. This penchant for detail was especially apparent among young connoisseurs of marijuana. So, for example, discussion would often move from general terms for marijuana to detailed comparisons of the various types available—from *catnip* (inferior, diluted, or bogus marijuana), through the stronger mixtures like *black mo'/moat, black gungeon, Chicago green, Jamaica* or *Panama red, Acapulco gold, Mexican green,* to the most coveted weed of the late 60s, *Nam black* (marijuana brought back from Viet Nam or other parts of Southeast Asia).

> So many gunnys. Like you got sucker weed. Say I wanna buy a bag. This cat come to me, gonna sell me some catnip—it *smell* like weed, it *look* like weed, but it *ain't* weed. Else some dude gonna burn you wid dat sugar weed. It moist and damp and green. Cut wif sugar. When you light it, it burn out. It git you high, but it don't last like the regular stuff.
>
> Now you got yo' black mo', it be dark, dark weed—buried an' moldy an' it turn black. I's pretty good, but it don't compare with that Nam shit. Oooo*wheeeee!* That's some good weed! Partner brought some back—two army sacks full o' weed. I's not strong, ain't harsh. You taste, say, "This stuff ain' no good, man." And POW! Cain't move! I was *out* before I took three, four hits. I was gone! Layin' down, da's all I remember. Got bad in d' haid. I jus' close' my eyes, next thang I know, I done flaked!

Along with this intense interest in the kinds of marijuana available was a keen and detailed attention to quantity or unit of measurement, for a *pinch* (approximately one or two marijuana cigarettes), through a *match* (a matchbox full), to a *can* or *lid* (one ounce), to a *brick* or *key* (approximately 2.2 pounds). Again, it was the real marijuana connoisseur who demonstrated the most detailed knowledge and used the most extensive lexicon around units of measure, as the following reminiscence between two teenagers demonstrates:

> A: Man, in them olden days you could score a match. No more. Don't even see no more can or *lid!* It be baggies [plastic food bags used to hold various quantities of marijuana] now!
> B: Yeah, me and my partner tried to cop [purchase] a ten-cent bag [$10 worth of marijuana] last night. Dude told us he don't sell no more ten-cent bags. "Inflation, man"—that's what he told us. It's quarter [$25] bags nowadays or fifty cents [$50]. And shit, you're not getting any more weed than before! I'm gonna start *dealing* myself! I have this friend who deals and he said he'd turn me on to his connection. Make some bread.
> A: I hear ya, man. Next time, I'ma get me a whole fuckin' key. Me an'

some brothers gon' trip on down to *T.J.* [Tijuana] and score a righteous brick o' shit. Yeah, then I'm gonna have a righteous stash for
days! Can you dig it!

To the uninitiated, a marijuana cigarette is a marijuana cigarette.
You may call it by one of its many vernacular names—*j, jones, joint,
smoke, stick, number, toke, reefer, skoofer, skoofus, skroofus*, or
*dubee*—but it's all the same. To the afficianado, however, a distinction is made between a "regular j" (a pinch or so) and a variety of
other sizes.

Now you got your toothpick. Dat be a real skinny joint. Ain't much
weed, but you got some dat Nam stuff, dat's all it take. Or could roll
one o' dem stencils. They out-grown joints. Lotta weed—I mean *long!*
Joint 'bout five papers rolled up—they have long Zig Zags [cigarette
papers] now too. Else you kin roll it real fat. One o' dem bombs—like a
stogie, big old tuskee. Mexicans use dat as a joint.

Finally, the ritual surrounding the preparation and act of smok-
ing a marijuana cigarette carries with it its own elaborate vernacular
vocabulary. Unlike the taking of pills, which may or may not be accompanied by ritual, "firing up a j" is often a social activity with its
own set of rules for appropriate behavior.

Like partner say, "Looky here, man, I got some fine weed at d' pad.
Me an' you, man." Fall by d' pad. Brother git his stash, little ol' Zig-
Zags—all kinda colors—licorice, cherry, strawberry. Outasight! Roll
you some righteous bombers! Fire up, pass around, git d' crutch out fo'
d' roach. Eat it. Drink a little Akadama, jus' kick back, watch color
TV. Cool it for d' rest of d' day.
    What I cain't stand is like you gettin' high with some partners,
everybody take three hits, pass it around. Some rootiepoot he take
'bout *seven*. Bogard d' j. Be greedy. Everybody else tryin' take equal
shares. He hoggin'. Else some nigger leave, come in after he done hit,
hit again. In other words, he double clutchin'.

As with vernacular descriptions for pills, marijuana is characterized by a variety of metaphors. Probably the most common way of
seeing marijuana is as the wild and natural plant it is (*weed, grass,
bush*); or as a kind of spice or herb (*the herb, tea*); or humorously
linked to soul food (*collard greens, turnip greens, greens*). "It be
called d' herbs or grass—or Mother Nature, 'cause it righteously
Mother Nature's *own* tobacco!" Other times marijuana is identified
in terms of the effect it produces (*joy, happy grass*); still other times,
vernacular expressions reflect a corruption, abbreviation, or play on
the word itself (*maryanne, maryjane, mariwegee, maharishi, 'wana*).
Finally, the fact that a marijuana cigarette is not quite the conven-

tional cigarette is reflected in terms like *off-brand cigarette, cigarette with no name, brand X, no-name brand, no-brand cigarette.* Its dubious legal status is even more prominently acknowledged in terms like *gangster* and *gangster sticks.*

But whatever it's called, marijuana is ubiquitous and figured in the lives and conversations of most of those I talked to. As one teenager saw it, "Dat's your friendly weed, your friend in need. Make you happy, keep you mellow—Mother Nature own medicine—hear what I'm sayin'?"

HARD DRUGS

The drug vocabulary reflected a keen awareness of and involvement in barbiturates, amphetamines, marijuana, and the behavior surrounding their use. The same was not true for the so-called hard drugs—opium and its derivatives (morphine, codeine, heroin) or cocaine. Though several terms were used to characterize heroin—*H, skag, boy, horse, stuff, junk, smack, shit, dog food*—neither the number of terms nor their level of descriptive power came close to the cache of terms related to marijuana and pills. Cocaine had even fewer vernacular labels than heroin—*girl, snow, coke, sophisticated lady, golden girl.* Though there were vernacular terms for codeine and morphine (*cubes* and *morph*), few came up in discussion during my time in the field. One additional expression—a wry euphemism—was used to refer to either cocaine or heroin: *C and H pure cane sugar from Hawaii.*

Terms describing the preparation, handling, and ritual use of hard drugs were also limited to the most commonly known expressions—to *fix* or *geeze* (to inject drugs, usually heroin); *spike, point, blunt* (hypodermic needle); *tracks* (needle marks); *Jones, habit* (addiction); *hooked* (addicted to). As often as not, these traditional, heroin-related terms were used to talk about injecting amphetamines or barbiturates. When statements were made about getting high, they most often centered on pills and marijuana, not hard drugs.

Though some teenagers had "chipped" (occasionally used one or another of the hard drugs) or "snorted" cocaine (through the nose), they did not admit to being habitual users. Of the total number of black teenagers I spoke with, less than 10 percent admitted to frequent or habitual use of hard drugs—this figure in stark contrast to admitted use of pills and marijuana.

A variety of reasons was offered by young people for their lack of involvement with these drugs. Certainly, one significant factor was lack of money or other resources. Many, for example, would have been more than willing to snort some coke, but it is known as the rich man's drug.

Man, coke is bad! I mean bad! Get you some dat golden girl, one sniff get yo' nose *cold* and your head *clear!* Cocaine is outasight! But, dig. Ain't in my league—'cept when I'm dealin'. Money's long den. You gotta have d' bread to cop. See dem white boys over dere in Beverly Hills dey got dem rich mommies and daddies, so dey kin cop all they want. Brother down here gotta hustle to get dat kinda bread. It's a nice high, though.

Besides lack of money, other reasons were given for the lack of involvement with hard drugs—no interest or opportunity, fear of being busted for possession, tracks, or marks. But the one reason that came up over and over again was a fear of becoming hooked. Many voiced the feeling that life was tough enough without being "strung out on smack." And though, as one young man put it, "heroin can righteously ease your troubles," a majority of those who brought up the topic of heroin in conversation wanted to put distance between it and themselves. One acknowledged heavy user talked about his habit and the price he had paid for it.

Never *did* dig pills. My stick *was* heraron, but I cut it loose, 'cause I got two case of marks and one case of sales. I sold to d' police. Dey tryin' to send me up, but I brought a lawyer and beat d' case—'cause I was makin' money den. So I'm out on parole now for another case of possession.

    Ten dollar a spoon. Jus' think for three year, I been spendin' from $20 to $80 a day and jus' think if I could've put that in the bank every day when I was rippin' off, hustlin' or doin' this or that, that would've been in the bank and I would've been half a millionaire.

Still another teenager summarized much feeling about hard drugs when he said:

Pills and weed—da's fo' me. Nice high, cheap high. I kin git 'em—one way or d' other. Irvine ain' gon' swoop and bust me fo' none o' dem tracks on my arms. Don' need that shit. Green ain't never gonna be long enough to support *dat* habit. Ain' gon' break my momma's heart wid a few little ol' pills and shit. Junkie he a fool, a sucker! He got a hunger he ain't *never* gonna fill—till he dead!

A number of teenagers had directly experienced the grief and pain of having an addict in the family. The wound cut deep and left a harsh scar on all involved. One young woman responded to my question, "Does your mother work?" with the following story, which I heard, in one version or another, more than a few times.

She baby-sits now. She used to have a job, but den she quit. She got sick. My brother he got busted for murder and that got 'er down. He's oldest, San Quentin. You hear about the cab driver what got killed on

64th and Central? That was my brother. He's on death row now and he was s'pose' get appeal in December, but he didn't want it. He done give up. He don' mind dyin'.

He was a junkie. He didn't do it just for the money, he did it to git the money to git 'im some more stuff. He probably stay in there a long time. He's been up dere three years. He [father] took it bad, but he was stronger den my mother. She never did come back, really.

### HALLUCINOGENS

If hard drugs took up little space in teenage conversation, the whole class of consciousness-altering drugs, popularly known as psychedelics or hallucinogens, took up even less space. Popular vernacular expressions for the most commonly known psychedelic drugs—mescaline (*cactus*), peyote (*button*), psilocybin (*magic mushroom*)—were virtually nonexistent in black teenage vocabulary. The single exception was lysergic acid diethylamide (*acid*, *LSD*), and even in this case terms were used infrequently. Fewer than a dozen terms were used to characterize this whole area of drug use and its related activities. On occasion the expression "to trip" was used to refer specifically to the effects of LSD, but mostly the term was applied to the effects from pills or marijuana.

This sparse usage is particularly striking when compared with teenage white terminology. If one looks through Eugene Landy's *The Underground Dictionary*, which deals rather extensively with contemporary drug terms, one will see a substantial number of entries describing and defining psychedelic drugs and related behavior. Why? Simply put, hallucinogenic drugs were not an integral part of the black experience. The psychedelic experience that fueled so many anti-Establishment actions and attitudes on the part of the so-called flower children, hippies, long hairs, and countercultural dropouts of the 60s was preeminently a white middle-class phenomenon.[2]

Black teenage response to the use of psychedelics was overwhelmingly negative. Their use was seen as part of whitey's trip and provoked responses of disdain, outright dismissal, and, most important, apprehension and fear. One teenager summarized much general feeling when he said, "Dey say all you need is one time. Boy! You *never* come back off it!" Less than a handful of blacks had experimented with a psychedelic drug. The experiences of two young blacks who had "dropped acid" are worth retelling because they provide some insight into possible cultural reasons for the aversion to these drugs. One young woman passed on the following story:

I've taken one acid trip, you know, to see what it was like, but I didn't like it. I was at home, there was this party going on, and me and my old man dropped some acid. It was a real bad scene. I started talking a whole lotta *trash* and then I started crying because my brother wouldn't be my friend. He got mad at me. And I said, "Just say that you'll be my friend!" And he wouldn't. He just looked at me like I was crazy. Kept telling me, "C., be cool, you ain't actin' right, be cool! Your mind is weak. You talkin' like one o' them crazy hippies! Get yourself together, girl!" Then, I started crying. I *really* started crying.

Another story was related by a young man who lived in South Central:

Me an' my partner we was trippin' on some acid. Went over to the pro-jects [Hacienda housing project in Watts] lookin' for a party. But my head wasn't right. Started seein' things—polices everywhere. Heard sirens, and man, I freaked! Started runnin' through the projects, yellin', "Pigs after me! They after me! Gon' jack me up! They gonna blow me away!" Spent the whole fuckin' night hidin' from the police an' Bear [a member of a rival gang who had threatened him], hidin' from everybody! . . . Acid jus' ain't my bag. Mind gets crazy with that stuff! Gimme some *reds!* Gimme some *weed!* Gimme some *pluck!* Now da's a nice high. Relax you, make you feel mellow. World look good den.

Generally black teenage response gives support to two important cultural factors that have worked against the use of psychedelics. One is the possibility of losing your cool, of losing control over your en-vironment and personal behavior. The grapevine has it that acid makes your mind weak; you become particularly susceptible to being taken advantage of. Survival—psychological and physical—is jeopar-dized and that is a high risk to pay, even for the best trip. Another is the accompanying fear and paranoia brought on by becoming vulner-able in a world which, for many young blacks, is already sufficiently distressful and dangerous without being exacerbated by mind-altering drugs.

## EFFECTS OF USING

Rivaling the vocabulary used to describe pills and marijuana was that used to describe the effects of the drugs themselves—from the first "rush" to the last "charge." It is particularly interesting to look at the kinds of visual pictures that the vernacular uses for the effects of getting high. It tells a great deal about the experience itself and its impact on the user.

One of the metaphors that recurs in dialogs about getting high is that of the trip. Many expressions—*trip, trip out, get off, fly, trip on, get high*—suggest not only the feeling of soaring (as in a plane or spaceship) but of taking some kind of literal trip, with the adventure and new experience implicit in travel. There is also an important aspect of getting away from it all in such expressions, of leaving boredom, pain, frustration, and struggle behind you. And certainly the escapist aspect of taking drugs is evident in much teenage conversation. "Like you say, 'Man, I'ma git down dis weekend. Pull to a set and right'ly get *loaded!*' Else get you some pluck, jus' lay back smokin' a reefer, you trippin'. World look good den. Everythang be cool, mellow. You flyin' high as a kite and free as a bird! *Nobody* kin git you den."

Once someone turns on he or she can run the gamut from feeling pleasantly high, relaxed and expansive (*mellow*), to being agitated (*wired up*), to losing motor and emotional control (*ripped*), to passing out (*flake*). Most of the terms focus on the last two stages because the implications of losing control or passing out are far-reaching for young blacks schooled in "keeping their head right."

A number of images relate to the excessive effects of drugs. One is that of being paralyzed—*frozen* and *ossified* suggest total immobility. Another visual image one gets is the feeling of being weighted down, slowed down—*stoned, loaded, having the slows.* "Man, when I'z loaded, my feet dey move *real* slow. Like dat Frankenstein. CLOMP, CLOMP. Da's how I feel sometimes behind reds—or some bad weed. Man, you stoned to d' bone!"

Still another picture is that of being cooked or overdone— *toasted, fried.* One of the most potent and frequent images is that of being physically destroyed, mangled, or injured. Terms like *ripped, tore down, twisted, ruint,* and *hurt* provoke the feeling of devastation. And certainly when young people talked about the consequences of drug excess, they referred to it in terms of real dangers to their physical person. One young man, who had recently "cut reds loose," told how he almost literally destroyed himself:

> I use'a drop pills til dat incident happen. Almost croaked off dose thangs. I was already drunk offa wine. Drunk dat wine Silver Satin, bit o' lemon. Drunk dat. Was already fucked up. I turn round, drop dem pills. Had 12 o' 'em in my pocket. Bulletheads—uncut, come from d' doctor.
>
> Las' thang I 'member, thang start to changin'. My friend he was tryin' to help me and I was unconscious. Police they come, foun' me. Took me to d' hospital. Come in Friday night, come round on Sunday. I couldn't see nothin'. I was blind to the world. I cut 'em loose!

There is another set of expressions closely related to the destruction metaphor in the vernacular. They have dual meanings: to be physically assaulted or to assault oneself. So the expressions *jacked up, wasted, ripped, messed up, fucked up,* or *gone* refer to destruction at the hands of others or self-destruction through excessive use of drugs or marijuana.

It is also interesting to note that terms like *ruint, hurt,* and *destroyed* refer not only to potentially distasteful or devastating drug experiences, but also characterize an ugly woman. As one young man put it, "Man, when I'm wasted, I feels like dat chickenhead look— HURT!" It seems no accident that the term skag for heroin also refers to a distasteful woman. And finally, as mentioned elsewhere, you can be hung out or strung out behind drugs or strung out behind a woman (emotionally hooked). Given the polarized stance between male and female, it is hardly surprising to see the excessive aspects of drug use also associated with the perceived negative aspects of male-female relationships.

The desired end in getting high is to turn on and then "maintain." The response to those who can't carry off their high ranges from humorous disdain to outright contempt, sometimes even hostility. One of the most significant factors influencing teenagers is the importance given to keeping your cool in a variety of situations. As one young man put it, "Most important thing to be cool. Maintain! Just like dude's trippin' after get high. Cain't hardly cool it. Jus' be stumblin', walkin' up and down d' street, just staggerin'. Cain't hold d' high. Drops whites behind reds, so I won't go to sleep—flake. I'm righteously wired up now. Looky here. I can control everythin' I do. I don' do nothin' I can't take care of."

"Keeping on top of the game" is a highly touted virtue, as we have seen. It becomes even more important in relation to drugs, where the game is essentially illegal and the penalties severe. Here, keeping yourself together takes on literal as well as metaphorical meaning. Given the great importance of maintaining under the influence of drugs, it is not unusual to see a general aversion to mind-altering drugs.

Implicit in the act of keeping your cool is the concept of a strong or weak mind. The mind controls the body. If your mind is vulnerable or subject to manipulation, you can't maintain control over your body and it will get you in trouble.

Like them little ol' '40s, they will set you on your ass and have your mind in a daze. I tell you dis, if anything go down wrong, you sure will get *fonky* wid a person. 'Cause dey will make you mad even, get deep in someone's ass. You mind get weak and yo' fists get fonky. A fool can't take too many dem suckers and think he can control his mind. If his mind is not strong enough, he *cannot* do it. I don't worry 'bout it. I don' let nothin' overtake me.

But beyond the disdain for those who show a weak mind around drugs, there is a kind of connoisseur's disgust for the waste of a good thing. Where money is tight and a roll of reds may sell for five dollars, someone who flakes generates some strong feeling. "Cap mean to flake. Dude went to sleep on his high. Pretty square. Don' need to get high if you gon' sleep on it—waste of time and money. Punk ass! Gets high an' flakes! Why get high when you gonna flake? Can't have a front den." You can't have a front, and that controlled face to the world is paramount.

Much of the feeling around maintaining reflects the manly stance that underlies much young male behavior. Different standards apply to male and female in terms of many areas of behavior, including the area of drug use. While maintaining your high is sometimes tangential to views of female behavior, it is central to the idea of being a man. This link between maintaining and manliness becomes clearer when we look at attitudes toward the drug neophyte or nonuser—one of the many faces of the lame.

We have already seen that the lame are considered social cripples. Not only do they lack experience of the streets, but literally or figuratively they are like children. One young man made the connection between inexperience around drugs and being a child when he was talking about fake marijuana. "Mostly younger kids get hung up behind dat phony marijuana. Don't know no better. You kin trick people dat don't know wha's happ'nin'—maybe a little kid, maybe a dude with a childish mind. We did a boy like dat. He ain' never been high. So we gave him catnip and he jus' sittin' up dere, smokin', swearin' he was gettin' high. Weren't nothin' in it! He just ain' growed up to what's happenin'."

There are a number of negative behaviors that are associated with the lame and the childish mind—and many of them are ascribed directly to the inability to maintain a drug high. Some can't get high without passing out, either through lack of experience with the drug or lack of restraint. "Git a big ol' car wi' chu one day, an' one cat has be a li'l punk and flake! Jus' nod out. Ruin it for the rest. Punk got so loaded, he out—like a *light!* Put a match to their ear, burn 'em fo' dey wake up! Dude righteously fucked up, rocked out. You think 'bout a rock. Rock come tumblin' down. Pootbutt jus' fall to d' ground, just like a rock—OUT!"

Sometimes drugs (particularly amphetamines, cocaine, and marijuana mixed with cocaine) can cause people to have the opposite reaction: instead of passing out they talk too much. "Like some little rootiepoot get high, run off at d' jibs. Talk whole bunch a shit. Talk outa style. Like a lotta people run off at the jibs when they runnin' offa whites. They cain't control they mouth. Act the fool, won't shut up! Damn kid stuff!"

For some, barbiturates have the effect of making the user irritable and subject to physical aggression.

> That's why they called red devils—they make you mean like d' devil. I use to drop pills. Cut 'em loose. Dey put you on some weird trips. Like to fight all d' time. Git in arguments. 'Bout a month ago, me an' my friend walkin'. We start talkin'. He had said somethin'. Den, I got mad. So we started to *fight*. Dey git you real mean, take too many. You know, I'm already mean when I'm sober, why I wanna buy me some red devils for?

For others, drugs create temporary impotency. They "mess with nature." "Like you git a young man high. His thang git hard, den it go down. He jus' drop entirely too many reds. Mess with nature. Don' know how to handle his high."

Drugs create not only physical impotency but verbal impotency as well. Among teenagers who value verbal dexterity as a prized commodity, lack of it generates lack of respect. "Like you kin get righteously fucked up. You cain't talk, you cain't talk to no women. You mind ain't together. How you gon' get over when you can't hardly keep yo' eye open. Young lady get on you case. 'Why don't you be cool?' Don't act right."

So the people who are unable to maintain physical and emotional control over themselves or in relation to others when on drugs often get derisively labeled rootiepoots, lames, punk asses. But the lames are also potentially dangerous. Their manner and actions may attract attention. They do dangerous things and, therefore, create dangerous situations. And the police—or other antagonists—are never far away. As one teenager observed, "Like you walkin' down d' street. Nigger cain't keep it together. He staggerin' and weavin'. Black and white creeps on down. You gets busted on a hombug! Da's why I don' be wid dem chumps. Dude cain't keep his high together ain' gonna be runnin' wid him—he git you in trouble ever'time."

For all the talk about appropriate and inappropriate behavior around drugs, there is a big gap between the ideal and the real. In fact, many who regularly use drugs have more than a few times exhibited lame behaviors.

> Everybody gets to actin' the fool one time 'nother. Brother tell you different, he jivin'. It's dem pills, man. Goofy pills! Ignorant pills! Dem *madman* pills, dey make you wanna fight! Else you talk too much. Get loaded at a party, you jus' flake. Cain't *nobody* wake you. Dem *poot-*

*butt* pills. Make you a righteous pootbutt. An' it ain't just little rump-kin neither. You see lotta dudes and dey know better!

Just because many teenagers fall short of the ideal—to always have their game together—they vent a great deal of their annoyance and self-anger toward convenient others. The lame becomes the scapegoat for many of the feelings about inappropriate drug behavior (as well as other kinds of behavior). The "other dude" is also you—and most young people are keenly aware of this fact. More important, the image of the lame is a reminder of what proscribed behavior looks like, and the trouble it can cause you and others. "So be cool, don't play d' fool an' everythang will be all right, uptight and outasight. Hear where I'm comin' from?"

## THE USERS

Me, I'm a red devil man. I drop an ace an maybe an hour later, I'll drop another one—and a couple of whites. They'll have me stummin' *all* through the night. A couple of reds and a couple of whites, they'll have me feelin' good *all day!* I won't have *no* problems.

I likes the herbs too. Had some bad herbs, straight from Nam. If you get it, it's not cured. They jus' snatch it up, put it in they combat sack. It's dark and you take maybe three hits, you don't want *no* more.

THC, synthetic, is sumpin' else. Outasight! I don't care if my parole [officer] hear me, I think THC the best narcotic they ever had. It make your mind remember, it make you keen. You have to drink hard liquor behind it. And when it hits you, ever'thing jus' glow—everythin' is beautiful, ever'thing that you touch is outasight and everybody you talk to, you blow they mind. You could say somethin' to 'em and they wouldn't wanna leave. It's some beautiful stuff.

I had some stuff from Nam. Looky here. It had me goin'! I thought the room was goin' round and round. Freaked out. But it was one o' dem freak-outs where if I sit dere and meditate and lay back, everything wanna move on, jus' like on a rollin' coaster—a merry-go-roun'. Had hash, little opium. It was outasight! Whoooooooo! I done had straight hash and opium an' weed cured in opium. That Viet Nam ain' nothin' *but* opium! Hash ain' nothin' but grown-up weed. But i's cold!

The above comments are those of two regular users. But all who use are not regulars. They run the range from those who "kick back on weekends with a rack or some smoke," to those who "chip for the high, once a week," to "your righteous pillhead. He don't drop 'em no mo'. He *chew* em! He be downin' so many, drop a roll, five minutes later he drop another roll. He be chewin' 'em like jellybeans!"

As with any "recreation," some play the game seriously, others once in a while, and there are varying levels of interest and involvement as a result. There are also different levels of sophistication and knowledge about drug use. The connoisseurs among the users are those who use frequently and have experienced a wide range of drugs, alone or in combination.

> I tried 'em all. Sometime, I cure weed in coke, embalmin' fluid. You get a *nice* high. You cain't smoke too much embalmin' fluid—no more 'n half a joint, you wasted. It *can* kill you if you smoke too much. I sell a cat a bag. He say, "That stuff ain't nothin'!" I say, "Look, you smoke half a j a day and you be together! Any more, you be dead!" I found so many highs—Vicks Nasal Spray, beer an' ashes, else you can mix weed with heroin. Coke is nicer. OOOHHH, looky here, i's worse den dat LSD! But got to know how much.

The real connoisseurs also know how to handle the drugs they score; they know the side effects and the limits to which they can take their high without becoming a drug casualty. They also know where to stash them so they won't readily be found. "You cop a bag and you roll a few joints. Den you put 'em in your hat linin', else put 'em in d' cigarette pack or in your hair. Someplace you kin hide 'em or dump 'em fast."

At the same time that a regular user may boast about how high he can get, there is, as mentioned, a great deal of disdain for those who abuse drugs or let drugs abuse them. Among those I talked with, the heavy users were the most critical of lame behavior. "Some people they don't know how to take drugs. Take 'em, just take 'em. But you just take enough to get you feelin' good. You don't hafta take 'em so you be all—aaaaaagggggghhhh! Just be stumblin', feet cain't even keep straight, jus' be staggerin'. People don't respect drugs, drug ain' gonna respect them."

This almost moralistic tone pervades much of the conversation about use. The contempt for those who overuse drugs is particularly apparent among those who claim to deal. "I'm dealin' now. Been dealin' fo' two, three years. I dealin' weed, pills, some coke when I can. Mos' of 'em get busted for dealin', 'cause dey run around high all d' time. Make mistakes, act d' fool. Tha's not cool right off. Cain't deal and do like dat. Fools ain't ought to be messin' with no drugs."

Ideally, then, the mark of the seasoned user is not only drug knowledge and experience, but the ability to know when, where, and in what quantity to use drugs.

MALE VERSUS FEMALE USERS

There is a double standard at work when it comes to how people respond to the female as user when compared with the male. Certainly the female who overindulges in drugs or marijuana falls victim to the same effects as the male, but attitudes toward her are qualitatively different. Whereas a male who can't maintain his high is seen, by turns, as foolish, a drag to be with, dangerous to himself and others, he is seldom seen as immoral or not nice. And in many cases, it is other young women who are the most critical of the female user. "One my friends just got out d' 9th grade, she dropped out. She not doin' nothin'. She's just a little ol' pillhead. I as' her why she do it. She said she don't know. And pills make you skinny. She's no bigger 'n my thumb. And she is so small. Ever'time I see her, staggerin' down d' street. An' tha's not ladylike. Okay for young men, but young lady don' be actin' like dat. Disgraceful."

Men, on the other hand, sometimes see the woman who is "loaded" as potential game for conquest. It is important to note that sexual aggression is often the fate for the young woman who, on her own or through persuasion, takes too much dope. "Like a lotta dudes rip off one girl. Dude start talkin' to her, ask she wanna get high. I's same thing as creepin', but i's more than one person. Like when she loaded. One dude go in there, come out. Another go in there, come out. Another go. Jus' righteously run a train on her! *Dog* nigger."

But as one young woman put it, "We smoke, and we drop a few pills, but we do it mostly where we be knowin' the people or in our house. Don't look good for a young lady to get loaded at a party. Some nigger take advantage of her." Some young women deal and are as knowledgeable as men when it comes to knowing the drug scene. But, for the most part, drug use is not as frequent or as conspicuous.

## PRESSURES TO USE

There is ready access to a variety of drugs—on the streets, at social functions, around the schools, in jail. At probation camps it is an easy matter to smuggle contraband. One youth who went AWOL and was returned to a forestry camp told how he did it. "I was jus' slick. I was bringin' narcotics back—stick 'em in my natural. I was throwin' it in d' bushes. Go to work, get what I need. Sell some, leave d' rest."

Another teenager who was incarcerated in a California Youth Authority facility got his by speaking out to visitors as they came past his work site. "Dey had me workin' out in front. I had all dat, you know, visitors. I work over by d' visitin' hall, people hadda pass me to go on through. Hit on them. Say, 'Hey man, what is it?' Dude drop some and I work my way over, pick it up, put it in my suit, take it in dere. Dey pat you down, but don' never look in yo' shoes. Dey know I'm in jail and cain't get it."

Sometimes friends or relatives are asked to bring drugs for an inmate, and teenagers went to great ends to keep their requests secret. In discussing euphemisms for pills—ju jus, jellybeans, candy—one young man told how he got his drug requests past the institution censors. "Like if I'm writing a letter to you, and I want you to send me some dope. I say, 'Send me some ju jus and wham whams,' which s'pose' mean candy. And, like if I was in jail and you were comin' to see me and I wanted you to bring me somethin', I write out a sentence and I put down 'Bring me some candy,' scratch the candy out, so you could see I scratched it out an' I don't want no candy."

On the streets there is not the same need for deviousness in the acquisition of drugs. Pills and pot are not only easy to come by, but the pressure to buy and use is great. The drug traffic is active around the schools. The following descriptions of drug activity around schools in South Central are not isolated incidents. It goes on around many public schools—grammar, junior, and high schools—in all sections of Los Angeles.

> For two months, it'll be cool. The security guards lighten up. They don' say nothin' to you. May even let one, two cats slide on by when they kinda loaded. Around 6th period, you can see some cats and just *know* they don't go to school and they walk around campus and they say, "You wanna buy some red devils, red devils for sale here." It happen on and off. Just like the fevers—sometime you don't see nobody and then all a sudden cats gettin' loaded.

> You kin go by Fremont any time of d' day and somebody's out dere dealin' by d' hamburger stand. But mos' dealin' after school. Like when school first turn out at 3:10, you could see everything. You can look at 'em and tell—clothes, the attitudes. They get *mad* if you don't wanna buy pills. They push 'em *hard*. "Aw, come on, drop some stoms. Ain't gonna hurt you, gonna help you. Take one free." Dat just what they be sayin' to you. It's hard! You might find one day thirty dudes askin' you wanna cop a roll. Wanna get a bag. They get angry. You walk by, people look at you kin'a funny. Like if they ask you, "You wanna buy some?" And you say, "No, I don' mess with 'em." They say, "What *do* you mess with!" "I stick to liquor."

The scene inside many schools is often no different. "After school, soon as that bell rings, you'll find more people in bathrooms wif roll red devils, sellin'. Security guards cain't bust 'em. I be goin' to class and I see people comin' down d' stairs and they all smokin' weed. Sellin' up and down d' hall. I's 'bout mostly the same every school—I been to mos' of 'em."

For a number of the teenagers I met, pills and marijuana were a way of life, a way to get through the day. One young man, who had more or less given up pills, explained his life and the drugs he used in the following way:

'Fore I lef' home, I used to blow some gauge, maybe. Den in school
dem teachers wadn't teachin' nothin' just old stuff I already knowed.
Git high to learn somethin'. Only time I learn when I'm high. 'Cause if I
wadn't high, I had go find a high. After school—DURIN' SCHOOL!
They be standin' in the hall waitin' fo' you. "Hey, you wanna cop?"
Dey be a lotta fightin', ditchin' everyday. Get loaded everyday. Da's
why I'm not there anymore. Got kicked out fo' ditchin'.

See, ain't nothin' happ'nin' in school. Ain' learnin' nothin'.
Teacher jus' collectin' they paycheck. Ain' no place to go 'cept to get
high. Just standin' 'round. So da's what a lotta people do. But it don't
do you no good. I cut it loose, try to better myself. I's hard.

So drugs are ubiquitous and can offer an escape: "From whatever ails
you. World ain't so bad behind some reds. Da's what you say to
yo'self. For awhile, it ain't—till you get into some kinda trouble."

But trouble is often the price to pay for using and staying loaded,
and trouble comes in many forms. It can be a near fatal overdose. It
can be ingesting unknown substances that are not what you expected
or are poisonous: "Shit! People put thangs off in them pills and you
don't know what you takin'. All you know is the color! So I can *not*
fool wid dose pills, no mo' den when I go to the doctor. Could be gittin' some donkey duck baby shit. And you come up with—they ain't
invented a disease! My cousin got burned like dat. Arsenic. He died
behind it."

Trouble can be a confused mind that leaves you no memory and
easy prey: "You drop too many 40s, you jus' be wasted. You don't
know your left foot from your right! Some dude jus' jack you up, take
you money and you stash! I use drop pills, but no mo'. Never in life!
Like it was jus' a hangup. Drop pills one night, wake up d' next
mornin' you still be loaded. Cain't get thangs together an' your mind
is all gone. Cain't recall what happen' d' night befo'. When you
smoke weed, you jus' feel good all over."

Trouble can mean addiction: "Getting righteously strung out behind anything! Bennies, reds, heraron, yellows. You just have a steady
hunger and you never git filled up. Like with smack. Geeze. Da's a
hope-to-die habit. An' you don't have d' money to do it. You rob, do
ever'thing. Do what you can to keep yo' habit. I knew women dat
went dat way. Git 'em strung out—turn 'em out on drugs—put 'em on
the block."

Trouble can also mean fights or "bad-mouthing" some teacher,
getting kicked out of school, passing out in school or on the street,
cutting out school altogether or being busted for possession, disturbing the peace, or a score of other mishaps. One young man's story
speaks for a number of teenagers who have backed away from heavy
drug use.

In the A10, I got busted, went back and got busted again for sales. I'z
at Locke [high school] three weeks, got busted again. Suppose' go to
Washington [high school] but ain' never went. Knew I'd git in trouble
wid drugs an' sellin', so I cut school loose. Finally froze on pills, 'cause
they too tough. 'Cause I always wind up in trouble, in jail or somebody's house, fightin'. Don' associate with too many of my partners no
mo'. You know, this is my last straw, so I just gotta make it dis time. So
I don't get too much involved. I jus' go to school and take care o' bidness.

## ADVANTAGE-TAKING AND DRUG USE

For many younger people, trouble is most often synonymous
with getting burned, being taken advantage of around drugs or while
under their influence. Among teenagers who value the one-up position
in their interactions with others, "getting loaded" potentially puts you
in a one-down position. You are vulnerable to others. "Seconal, red
devils, dem pills gits you H-I-G-H as a kite! You take too many (kin I
say the term?) git fucked. You lose yo' strength. You like Samson and
Delilah. You ain't got no fire power. Somebody kin burn you den."

A person can be burned in any number of ways when it comes to
drugs in general. In the transaction: "You cheat 'em. If you buy a bag
of weed from me and I burn you, that mean you only got a dime bag.
Or say if you sellin' me some weed, and I tell you, 'Don' half step on
me, man. Don' be cuttin' dat weed with no catnip. You half steppin'.
Straighten it out!' " People can have their cache of drugs stolen:
"Like when you see 'em when dey stash and you go back 'n git it, and
burn 'em for they stash. Or like you gonna get a bag together and you
d' only one's s'pose' be rollin'. Den somebody pinch d' bag!" You
can get even for a past burn by planting drugs on another and calling
in the police.

But being exploited while under the influence of drugs is another
matter. Because you are out of control and literally cannot stand up
for yourself, you are easy game: "Dude get all fucked up. He deserve
what he git!" One of the burns that was most often related to me was
a situation in which a young man—less often a young woman—would
get loaded on pills or marijuana, pass out, and somebody would rip
him off: "Like when he get all fucked up. Have a pocketful o' money,
you jus' take it all. Creep on his bag o' weed. When dey flake, you
take half. Somebody be on flake, like people gonna creep on dem. If
you in an environment where you might be out, i's not cool because
you get ripped off. But if you at home wi'cho' man, lady, you can
flake."

Probably the most manipulative burn is to get someone high,
then beat him up, and steal what he has. Few street-wise teenagers

allow themselves to get into that kind of situation. "I only gits high with my partners. Cain't be trustin' niggers you don't know."

How you burn a young man and how you burn a young woman is quite often a different matter. A man might get his money or his stash ripped off; a woman is likely to get her body ripped off. As already pointed out, sexual exploitation is sometimes the name of the game, in regard to women. Not only is the female fair game, but the explanations given to rationalize such aggressive behavior often fall back on a cliche: "You give her some red devils. Git her loaded. Den dey be fightin' for it. I guess i's her fault. She want it done. She askin' fo' it."

Women may be more critical of other women—but they are also more concerned about what happens to other females. They often express strong feelings of anger at men for their actions. Harsh epithets like *dog, dog nigger*, and *dirty, dirty dog* were used to vent their feelings toward sexual aggression. One young woman's response is typical:

> These niggers dey fill dese girls wid dese pills and they take d' money and let some dude go in dere and screw all he want to. Dog nigger do dat. It's a doggy, doggy world out there. I hit some shit I ain't *never* heard before. Boy, some o' dese niggers they's *dogs!*
>
> Like dis li'l ol' joint up near 46th, i's s'pose' be a dance hall. It ain't nothin' but a pill joint! It's for these rowdy kids and shit like dat. You 'pose' be over twenty-one, but shit, when you live that hard life what *dey* have, you look forty—and dey fourteen! Nice-lookin' girls too. They steady feed 'em them reds—and they be steady eatin' them. Don' know what they doin' after while. Den, one dude dat stand by hisself, he'll take her over to his house, throw in on d' bed an' he stand outside the door and say, "I got a broad in dere! You want some, gimme $3." Shit! Next, she wakin' up, "Nigger you done screwed me!" "Aw bitch, what you talkin' 'bout? Done screwed you, git yo' ass out my house!" Fonky nigger done ripped 'er off. I hates dat.

Many men are opposed to such exploitation, though not as publicly vocal in their condemnation as women are, since it may tarnish the macho front. As one young man told it, "Ain't decent. No way to treat *any* young lady—even chickenhead. I just shine it on. Like dude say, 'Me an' you, we gonna share some pussy.' Like if you get a young lady to speed, get her loaded, den he say, 'Me an' you, man!' Happen las' week. Told dude ain't cool. Turn it down. Just can't see doin' dat kinda shit."

## DRUGS AND ALCOHOL

Pills and pot are not the only ways to get high. They tend to be the most talked about. But liquor, which has the advantage of being legal and readily available, is probably just as popular. The liquor store, still a popular hangout for oldtimers and young people alike, has a number of vernacular names—*LIQ, juice house, rescue station, filling station, brew house, leeky store.* It is easy enough to ask someone to buy you a bottle or a six-pack. And in stores where you are personally known, the sale is made with no questions asked.

Taken alone or in combination with, say, marijuana or pills, liquor is still the standard high. And among the available liquors, wine is probably the one most commonly consumed by teenagers. There are many vernacular terms for wine—*the grapes, the berries, the vine, pluck, smash,* to name a few. All of these terms characterize wine in its natural state. Usually these terms are identified with the "cheapie" wines—Santa Fe Tokay, Ripple, Silver Satin (with a twist of lemon), Eden Roc. Certain wines have their own longtime vernacular designations, attesting to their widespread popularity and inexpensiveness. Santa Fe Tokay was wryly referred to as *railroad whiskey*: "Santa Fe Tokay, all d' way. It don't taste too swift, but it do d' job." Silver Satin with lemon juice was called *Satin, shake-em-up,* and *WPLJ* (white port and lemon juice). And since many wines could be had in pint bottles, they too had their special names—*short dog, puppy, mickey* (little mouse).

Many teenagers saw cheap wine as unacceptable (*dog juice*) or juvenile, kid's stuff. In fact wine itself was disparagingly referred to as *schoolboy scotch, sixteen-year-old shaving lotion,* and *sixteen-year-old after shave.* Some claimed more sophisticated tastes in liquor and wanted nothing to do with the *real* cheapies: "Sometime, I drink Akadama or brandy. I don' like to drink no off d' wall stuff. I jus' drink brandy." Hard liquor also had its own vernacular labels—*oil, ignite oil, do-it fluid, jump steady, swag*; and *panther piss* and *white lightnin'* for home brew.

One step up in class and taste are the specialty wines, such as plum wine and sparkling burgundy. During the early 70s, Andre's Cold Duck and Akadama were all the rage. Later, Spanada joined the ranks. "Get me some Cold Duck—like champagne. I's okay. That use' be my serenadin' drink. Go buy one of dem before I go over little girl's house." I asked one young man why he felt that pills and marijuana came up so often in conversation, but liquor much less frequently. His explanation was echoed by others:

See juice been 'round *long* time. Great-great granddaddy time. Ain't nothin' special. Oldtime high. Take it for granted. Oldtime slangs for it too—like "short dog."

My father uses that—short dog. Like he has this ol' wino friend he's been knowin' for years that sit on the corner. So, everytime it's his birthday, he go buy 'im a short dog—a little bottle of wine.

Kids now got weed, hash, reds and all that stuff. So we don' be
talkin' too much 'bout pluck—but we still be drinkin' it!

Other teenager tastes ran to scotch: "I can't drink no wine, jus'
scotch—Johnny Walker Red. I was at dis party d' other weekend. Dey
had two 'frigerator full of whiskey 'n beer. I jus' lay back an' drank
all d' scotch." Certainly scotch and some bourbons are very popular,
especially the "right" brands: Johnny Walker Red, Black and White,
Chivas Regal, I. W. Harper. But, in fact, expensive name brands are
out of the reach of most ghetto teenagers, and the talk about those
tastes is mostly just that.

In South Central, drugs and liquor have long been available for
those who had the resources, financial or otherwise. Pills are a relatively new occurrence. They are particularly attractive as a high because they are relatively cheap. Also pills are thought by many teenagers to be less dangerous and addictive than heroin (though, in fact,
they may not be) and easier to come by. In combination or alone, they
create a buffer zone between reality and oneself. One teenager put it
this way: "See, down here in the ghet-to not too many people goin' to
Hawaii—dig? Ain' got the bucks. Ain' never gonna. But looky here!
Gimme some bennies! Gimme some reds! Gimme that weed! Gimme
pluck! I righteously be trippin'—and won't need no ticket on no airplane. You be in another world. All by yo'self. Take you own trip!
Dig?"

For many young people who seldom get beyond the boundaries
of the ghetto, drugs provide emotional release and psychological
escape into other worlds, other levels of consciousness and other ways
of being in this world. Whether or not these ways are ultimately self-
destructive or self-defeating is another matter. "When you high, you
ain't thinkin' 'bout trouble, you jus' kickin' back and feelin' good."

Throughout history, people have discovered ways of relaxing for
a while, of escaping or transforming reality. China had opium; Vic-
torian England, laudanum; the United States, alcohol and, in more
recent times, pills. Even though alcohol is still this country's public
(acceptable) high, barbiturates and amphetamines are the "closet"
high. Mainstream Americans are often appalled by the drug problem
among the young, but we have the dubious distinction of consuming
more tranquilizers, more sleeping pills, more diet pills, and more pain-
killers than any other nation in the world. "Marijuana" has become a
middle-class household word—times change, and so do morals. And
language will continue to chronicle those changes and the expressions
that characterize drug use, for grown-ups as well as young people.

# 6. talkin' my talk

## the dynamics of vocabulary use

ANYONE WHO HAS heard black teenage dialog cannot help being struck by the richness and vividness of the vernacular vocabulary. No written record can convey the intricate play between the word, the body, and the voice—the lyrical qualities of the oral form. The rich performative aspect of a black teenager "runnin' down some lines" is diminished when set down in linear form. Yet perhaps some of the rhythm and intonations of the words and phrases can still be appreciated, even in print.

The metaphoric and lyrical quality of the lexicon is heard in such ritualized rhymed couplets as "Take it slow/And go for what you know"; "Ain't nothin' to it!/ A baby could do it"; "I'm Jack/ You better step back"; "Santa Fe Tokay/ All the way!"; "If it ain't cuz/ It's fuzz." In addition to the lyricism of such couplets, there are numerous combinations of assonance, alliteration, and consonance in other kinds of vernacular phrases—*ace boon coon*; *ace coon poon*; *fried, dyed, and combed* (*swooped*) *to the side*; *bust some booty*; *jawin' at the jibs*; *chili chokers*; *cock pluck*; *chump change*.

Metaphors, of course, abound in the lexicon. Vernacular vocabulary by its very nature is figurative. Many of the metaphors are not only vivid, but strongly laced with irony, wit, and humor—*African grape* for watermelon or *the extra car* for public transportation or *rescue station* for liquor store or *four sisters on thumb street* for masturbation.

Though similes are less apparent in the vernacular, they stand out in contest-oriented situations, such as shooting the dozens. There you get improvised and ritualized similes that compare mothers, fathers, and other relatives to a variety of unlikely or purposefully demeaning things: "Your momma's like a doorknob, everybody gets a turn" or "Your momma's like a diesel, big, broad and full of gas." Again, the dozens reflect another figurative dimension of the lexicon, hyperbole. The more outrageous the statement, the better and funnier it is:

190

"Man, you so ugly, King Kong thought you was his baby!" or "You so black, they made you paint Day Glo on yo' ass so you be seen at night!" Much contest-oriented banter is peppered with hyperbole. Dramatically, it makes for a better performance.

The intention of this chapter, however, is not a literary analysis of teenage vernacular vocabulary. These brief remarks about the vernacular are to remind the reader of the expressive, lyrical, aesthetic qualities of the form. The real business of this chapter is to look at some of the dynamics around teenage usage. What are some of the major factors that affect usage? How does a person go about learning the lexicon? How is it passed on? Who uses the lexicon and under what circumstances? What are considered to be appropriate and inappropriate lexical contexts? What are some of the teenage attitudes and opinions about using vernacular vocabulary?

## FACTORS AFFECTING USE

There are a whole variety of factors that directly or indirectly affect usage. The ones that proved to be the most influential among the teenagers I encountered were (1) age, (2) gender, (3) peer associations, (4) levels and kinds of shared experiences, (5) socioeconomic background, and (6) geography.[1]

### AGE

Introduction to the vernacular lexicon comes early in a young person's life. From the time children are able to talk—even before the stage of real comprehension—small children mimic older brothers and sisters, parents, relatives, and friends of the family. And in a culture marked by a strong oral tradition and a rich vernacular form, the vernacular lexicon gets passed on from generation to generation early on. One young woman explained it this way: "I's handed down just like the English language. I's like you teach yo' baby to talk. Sometime, I do it accidently—jus' come natural. Like be tellin' my sister's baby, 'Man, put that shit down, let that shit go.' Den he go downstair' and tell the lady, 'Put that shit down.' Shit, he ain't but fo' year old!''

I have heard children of six, seven, eight—male and female—running down lines that would make even older youths envious. Indeed, several teenagers admitted that their younger brothers and sisters had taught them new words. "My little brother hip me to 'bhani ghani' and he ain't but seven. Dey hear dey friends talkin'—else brothers and sisters talkin' 'bout dat stuff. 'Oh, punk, you cain't do nothin' '—stuff like dat.''

One exchange is worth sharing because it gives the reader some sense of the ease and facility with which youngsters pick up the vernacular. The following could easily be an adult exchange, but the two involved were eight and ten years old respectively.

> A: Hey, man, what 'tis?
> B: What it was.
> A: What it gonna be?
> B: Wanna fall by my brother pad? He got some new sounds—d' Pips 'n Stevie—get down!
> A: Aw-right! Le's do it!

Both speakers already demonstrate a great facility not only with the vernacular, but with the paralanguage and body language appropriate to its use. Of course, not all children become so skillful with the lexicon at such an early age or, for that matter, even later on. The point is that many children are consciously or unconsciously exposed to the vernacular vocabulary from infancy on. In many cases, vernacular vocabulary usage is implicitly or expressly allowed and encouraged among small children, because it is "cute" or "funny" and demonstrates quickness of wit and an independent and assertive nature. More important, it is the language of many young ghetto residents. Though later on parents may come to look at their children's use of the vocabulary in a different—and more critical—light, when a four-year-old says something like "Oh, punk, you cain't do nothin'!" it is very arresting.

As Paul Lerman (1967) has pointed out, the age at which youngsters become the most ardent users of vernacular vocabulary is approximately between ten and thirteen. Lerman further claims that the period between sixteen to nineteen is the time for expanding one's knowledge of the vocabulary. However, older adolescents, and those moving into their twenties, claim to use less of the vernacular and in a more limited number of contexts. As one twenty-year-old said, ''I don't use it no more. Da's in my gang days. In, you know, junior flip days. I ain' no junior flip no mo'. I *could* be one—jus' don't be one.''

My own interactions and experiences tend to reinforce this claim—at least among those who seem to be turning their attention to "getting over," making it in the mainstream white world. When attitudes toward vernacular vocabulary use are discussed, it will be seen that many adolescents and those in their young twenties want to move away from the vernacular vocabulary because they see it as "not proper English" and a detriment to getting across in the Man's world.

However, old habits and old involvements die hard, and few of those I talked with had actually given up their vernacular ways. What was apparent in teenage talk was that the older users seemed more selective about when they used the vernacular. When we turn to appropriate and inappropriate contexts for use, we will see that vernacular vocabulary may be less frequently used in a person's overall conversation, but, finally, circumstance will determine just when (and in what quantity) it gets used.

Many young adults who continue to identify with or participate in street life continue their adolescent patterns of heavy vernacular vocabulary use. As one ex-gang member put it, "Some dudes ain' never come out with anything but slangs. They stuck in they ways. Always be runnin' d' streets. 'Specially, gang bangers, gangsters, low riders. People dat's been hardheads all they life, sometimes they never put it down."

Indeed, one of the important sources of vernacular word knowledge for children and adolescents *is* the older street man (and sometimes street woman) who have never "put the vernacular down" and, therefore, become resource people by the very nature of their conversation. One eighteen-year-old remembered back to his childhood mentor: "An older brother use'a run it down to me and my cousins. He set up dere wid his little ol' Ripple and cigarette—out front d' liquor store. He a righteous dude—knew all kinds slangs. He hip to what's happ'nin' in d' here and now too. Learned a lot from him."

A youth's age, then, may affect his or her usage, particularly in terms of exposure to the vocabulary, its acquisition, and periods of active participation in its use. Though the quantity of vocabulary use can be age-graded, there are many other factors—such as continued identification with street life, the desire to get over—that figure in the pattern of age and usage.

### GENDER

Most accounts of black expressive behavior have not only focused on males but have made the assumption—implicitly or expressly—that vernacular expressive forms, such as shooting the dozens or toasts, are the male's exclusive domain.[2] This is not especially surprising, given the fact that most contemporary studies of black expressive behavior have been done by males, from a male perspective. Urban anthropologists like Ulf Hannerz, Roger Abrahams, and Elliot Liebow have admitted that they know little about black female behavior because they have had little, if any, close or ongoing contact with women informants. Female resistance, suspicion, shyness, and a variety of other factors have appeared to stand in the way of open dialog between male and female. As one young woman, Clara, bluntly saw it, "Dey out fo' one thang—pus-sy. Men jus' cain't be trusted. Dey all dogs to me. Don't be tellin' ever'thin' to my ol' man, so ain't no way I'ma tell some off d' wall honky—even a brother—'bout my life. Uh uh! May talk to a sister. Like I consider you like a sister. We got a whole lotta things together. Hear what I'm sayin'?"

Clara's feelings were not particularly unusual. Many young women I talked with had varying degrees of resistance to talking to men about their personal lives. Though the fact that I was a woman certainly did not assure open dialog, it proved to be an important factor. If and when I got to know a young woman, it allowed the potential for sharing of common female experiences, even across differences in background. As Clara said, "We got a whole lotta things together"—and we did.

Whether lack of accessibility, lack of interest, or other factors have intervened, the fact is that the black female's expressive behavior has generally gone undocumented and is assumed by some to be limited in scope. (See, however, Claudia Mitchell-Kernan, 1971, for a discussion of the black female's "signifying" behavior.) At least among the young women I interviewed, familiarity with and use of the vernacular vocabulary was not only evident but sometimes equivalent or even superior to the men's. At the same time, it cannot be said that overall male and female knowledge and use of the vocabulary was equivalent—that is, in the number and kind of terms known and used or in the specificity of usage. Here, too, a variety of factors affect knowledge and use.

As already noted, ghetto children are exposed to the vernacular vocabulary of their parents, older brothers and sisters and others in their environment. Most teenagers I encountered seemed to feel that little distinction was made between what vernacular vocabulary got used in front of small girls as opposed to small boys. And, in turn, whether it was a little girl or boy, it was seen as cute or clever or quick-witted to parrot grown-up usage.

However, as youths move from childhood to adolescence, different standards begin to operate.[3] Where the parents and relatives of many adolescents were certainly seen to be critical of boys' use of vernacular vocabulary—in the home in particular—these same parents or relatives were much more adamantly opposed to adolescent girls' usage. Almost without exception, the young women I talked with indicated that they had been sharply reprimanded at one time or another by a parent or other relative for use of the vernacular. For girls, it was considered coarse or vulgar (cussing) and "young ladies should use proper English."

It is a matter of respectability and decorum in the home. As Roger Abrahams (1976) has pointed out in regard to young women's language use, "Respectibility is expressed . . . in the strategies and styles of communication insisted upon as appropriate in the house . . . In general, women are expected to be more restrained than men in their talk, less loud, less public, and much less abandoned . . . Girls are lectured by both Daddy and Momma on never talking loudly or cursing, not even when involved in street encounters" (p. 69).

Nevertheless, many young women use the vocabulary outside the earshot of critical parents and other adults. The kinds of words and phrases that males and females use are often different. Not only do adults exert varying degrees of pressure on young women to limit their vernacular output, but peers do also. Ostensibly, young ladies should not use cuss words or fight words or sex words or low-rider words or junkie words or hooker words or getting-on-your-case words—"else they ain't actin' like nice young ladies. When a woman out on d' streets, they use it worse den d' men. I don' like no young lady be talkin' like no man—'gon' whup yo' ass'—shit like dat. Ain't ladylike."

And ostensibly young women acknowledge what is appropriate and inappropriate usage for a female—at least in male company. "I don't hardly use it with dem [males]. I use it when I'm talkin' to my friends and [female] cousins, but when I'm out wid a young man, I don't like to hear a young lady use slang. Jus' when we be jivin' around by ourselves. I don't hardly use it at all wid men. I jus' like to know what it mean in case somebody basin' on me. Got to know what they sayin'!"

But, in fact, young women who considered themselves—and were considered to be—quite respectable use a wide range of vernacular terms, including those that relate to sex, fighting, drugs, verbal confrontation, swearing, and other so-called taboo topics. The constraint many seem to experience is more the constraint of context rather than content.

And that constraint was experienced much more strongly and under many more circumstances for females than for males. Jessie speaks for a number of young women:

> Shit, me an' my friends be usin' slangs all d' time. Young men dey
> thank we ain't down wid d' slangs. Girl, you should hear d' sisters
> blow!

One time, me an' Joyce we at dis party. Dude runnin' his li'l ol' mack down. Brother jammin' her [Joyce]—an' she ain't bitin.' Dude get sorta belligerent. Man, she blowed on d' sucker hard, fast an' heavy. Dude eyes open real wide. Put his stuff down for days!

But, see like young lady ain't s'pose' be shootin' like dat. Get on yo' case—"Girl, you got a foul mouth! Yo' momma done taught you some evil ways." Shit like dat. So, young lady don't be talkin' too much like dat. Leastways, not just ever'where. Sometimes you gots to fire.

"If a woman places herself in a public situation, she is in jeopardy of having to contend with men and their *jive* . . . If a woman's sense of respectability is challenged in such a situation, she may fight fire with fire, becoming as verbally open and aggressive as her contenders, resorting to a very tendentious sort of *smart talking*" (Abrahams, 1976, p. 75). What a number of young women related, and what I myself experienced, was that females might tone down their vernacular use in front of males—unless "push came to shove"—but with other young women, in an all-female context, the constraint was often more what you didn't know than what you ought to say or not to say. When I was privy to all-female conversations, I found that the quantity of talk, joking, boasting, argument, cursing, and even shooting the dozens rivaled male expressive behavior. One of my female acquaintances, who had just finished a very lively exchange with her cousin, paused in the conversation to reflect on her verbal behavior:

Like me, myself, I shoots wid' d' best o' 'em. Me an' my sister we gets to shootin' on each other. It starts slow. "Hey bitch, how come you smell so fonky, ain' you heared 'bout soap?" "Girl, if I looked like you, I stick my face in my ass and *sit* on it." We shoots hard on each other. Call each other "a sack o' mothafuckas"—it jus' get vulgar! An' my brother jus' say, "Oooh, I never knowed how nasty young ladies get! Boy I got some nasty sisters!" We tell 'im, "Punk, who you tryin' to play dumb with?" Man, we get on him!

Indeed, some of the most original and graphic dozens I've heard were shot back and forth between females. The following brief exchange gives some sense of this adeptness:

A: Hey, girl, wha' chu got on yo' hair? You smell like a skunk in a shit house! Cain't get no funkier.
B: Well, bitch, leas' I got hair. You hair so short cooties on yo' haid be starvin' to death.[4]

It is especially apparent in all-female environments the extent to which the merest lip service gets paid to acting like a lady. But, among those females I talked with, it can be said that on the whole young women did use less vernacular vocabulary than did males—particularly in male company—though they knew many more taboo expressions than their male companions often thought they did.

There is another way in which context—or more appropriately accessibility or familiarity with context—limits female knowledge and use of the vernacular vocabulary. Many young women are not especially familiar with, interested in, or privy to certain "male" activities —such as low riding, gambling, gang banging, sports, or certain specific street hustles or activities. What this means in terms of the vernacular is that the female's definitions for or application of, say, car-related or fight-related terminology is often less specific, less concrete, and less elaborated than in the case of male usage. The exception to this are females who "ran the streets" and were in contact with the male domain and its activities. But, by and large, young women demonstrate a less specific and comprehensive knowledge of vernacular expressions than males do. This was apparent in the number and kind of primary and secondary definitions the respective groups could offer for a given expression.

Actually, there were three sets of vernacular expressions elicited from the teenagers I met. There were those words and phrases used primarily or exclusively by males—low rider, fight and gang expressions, and the like; those used jointly by males and females—vernacular that related to common activities such as dancing, partying, some forms of manipulation, male-female relations, some drug activities, sexual encounters of certain kinds; and those terms used primarily or exclusively by females. Males may not necessarily have a "superior" knowledge of the vernacular vocabulary per se, but they demonstrate a superior knowledge of certain classes of terms related to drinking, fighting, gang activity, or low riding. Females, on the other hand, may have a superior knowledge of terms related to other activities, such as giving birth, childrearing, children and children's behavior, menstruation, female hygiene and appearance, female talk and feelings about men.

In fact, there are a number of expressions that come from young women—some of which have been noted—which center on female activities and concern. For example, there are expressions related to pregnancy, menstruation, birth control, and female hygiene: *preg* (for pregnant); *sling shot, diaper* (sanitary napkin); *diaper the baby* (put on one's sanitary napkin); *red Mary* (menstrual period); *rack, roll* (month's supply of birth control pills); *washing powder* (douche powder); *washer-dryer* (douche bag and towel). Another group of expressions address female appearance: *crinkle top* (black woman with an Afro or natural); *raspy, rugy* (unattractive, unkempt); *hully* (obese person); *duck's butt* (unkempt hair); *Ruth Buzzy* (woman whose appearance never changes, no matter what she wears or does); *welfare mother* (woman who dresses badly or inappropriately). There were also terms related to men and sex: *puppy* (young or inexperienced male, small penis); *butter, little pretty, sweet* (attractive male); *get some sweet, get some brown sugar* (engage in sex, kiss); *sweet potato pie* (attractive male, male genitalia); *high waters* (erection); *muddy waters* (loss of an erection); *frick and frack* (testicles). There were terms related to gossip and those who gossiped: *set mouth, snipe, deal/do dirt* (gossip, talk badly about someone); *dirt farm* (source or place of gossip). And there were abbreviations for women's penal institutions: *C.I.W.* (California Institute for Women); *S.B., S.B.I.* (Sybil Brand Institute).

I administered a select number of female-generated expressions to thirty young men. They demonstrated roughly the same degree and specificity of knowledge for these female-linked terms as did women when exposed to so-called male-linked expressions. These findings are not especially surprising given the fact that Abrahams, for one (1972, 1976), differentiates the kind and content of talk that goes on away from home (on the streets) and within the home (the household and related environments, such as church).

Though the findings are merely suggestive, they do point up the potential bias in assuming that vernacular vocabulary—its knowledge, use, and innovation—is preeminently a male activity. Rather, there may exist an independent female domain—a sphere of interest and interaction—where the frequency and intensity of expression parallel the male sphere and generate a discrete female lexicon. The terminology found in this book was elicited primarily from males, as I have said. What needs to be done is to elicit terms from a large black female population and then test male comprehension.

Gender does affect the access to vernacular vocabulary, as well as the scope, depth, and sureness of knowledge and use. In summary, males tended to use more vernacular expressions and knew half again as much terminology as females. They were privy to a wider range of activities that generated the vernacular expressions found in this book and, therefore, were often more specific and elaborate in their definition of such expressions. Though females demonstrated knowledge of and skill with this vernacular lexicon, especially out of earshot of critical others, they used less vernacular vocabulary in their conversations (by word count) than males did—especially in the company of adults. However, questions of superior or inferior knowledge and usage need to be examined in light of activities being detailed and the domains being explored. Limited data suggest that females may have their own lexicon and demonstrate a command of it that is comparable to that of males in relation to a male-related lexicon.

PEER ASSOCIATION AND SHARED LIFE EXPERIENCE

Who you "hang out with" is also a significant determinant of the kind of vernacular vocabulary you are likely to know and the extent to which you use it. As we have seen in the chapters on name terms and forms of manipulation, one important distinction between the lame or homeboy/homegirl and the together brother/sister is that the latter terms are often associated with the skilled talker, one who has a rich command of the vernacular lexicon. Implicit in the concept of the homeboy or homegirl is not only that they have little experience of the streets, but that watchful parents or relatives don't want them to learn bad ways. Therefore they are kept close to home. It is no accident that those teenagers who knew the fewest vernacular expressions were the ones who, by their own admission, stuck pretty close to home, school, church, family, and a small, like-minded circle of friends.

By its very nature, much vernacular vocabulary is going to be used more and heard more in street-life situations—among car "freaks," street-corner habitués, hustlers, users, dealers, fighters— than in the church or the home. However, few who live in the ghetto are immune to the vernacular. It is an integral part of daily conversation. "I was brought up in the ghetto. Everyday, you learn something different—even when you're not tryin', you gonna learn it. The slang is just there, where people be talkin'. Just what people pick up—the everyday words of black people in the ghetto. Can't help but pick it up."

But it is one thing to pick up words and phrases by accident or by osmosis and another to be in daily situations where vernacular word usage is the rule, not the exception—where it is the lexical coin of the realm. Though a variety of older people contribute a fair share to the vernacular repertory of the adolescent user, most vernacular is picked up from peers and peer role models who share activities, interests, attitudes, and experiences, and the terminology to detail them. Most teenagers who were conversant with the lexicon claimed that their knowledge came from older and same-age adolescents. Furthermore, depending on one's front or scene or bag, a teenager demonstrated the greatest in-depth knowledge of, say, terms related to fighting, low riding, hustling, or whatever special area(s) of experience or expertise each claimed. Of course, the greater the range of life experiences, the greater the command over the full scope of the lexicon.

The two kinds of life experiences (and peer associations) that were most often cited as the source of vernacular knowledge were jail and the streets. Many youths who had been incarcerated claimed that they first heard many of the terms they knew from fellow inmates. But the streets are finally seen as the great vernacular marketplace—and for most of those who run the streets, the vernacular is a tool for survival, as well as a mode of creative expression. "Slang is just common everyday language over there on the block [neighborhood]. Jus' bein' dere when it used. Just pick it up. I think street life is part of every black person's life—'cept maybe d' lame who stays all the time in d' house. Because if you're not hip to street life, you can't make it. Like somebody's tryin' to blow on you, y' know, you better know what to do, how to talk. You have to know how to rap. That's the way you gonna survive."

Some teenagers do not have direct, firsthand involvement in aspects of street life and the activities surrounding it but are, nevertheless, members of what might be termed the street-life network. Therefore they are indirectly privy to both general and special interest terminology. For example, young women and younger male members of a network may learn from their male friends what types of accessories adorn a low ride. Here it becomes not so much a matter of shared interest or personal experience, but of intimacy with those in the know.

Peer associations and shared life experience, then, affect the kind of vernacular one will know and use. Since the streets in particular are seen as primary sources for the acquisition and dissemination of terms, the more direct one's involvement there, the more one is likely to know and use. Contact with street life and activities may be direct or indirect, since even those who stay clear of street activities are invariably exposed to some vernacular just because they share in the experience of living within its sphere of influence.

### SOCIOECONOMIC BACKGROUND

Most of the black teenagers I met over the years came from South Central Los Angeles, the major low-income black community in Los Angeles County. As I have noted, not everyone living in the ghetto uses vernacular vocabulary. Some do not understand very much of it, although virtually everyone is familiar with it and uses certain words and phrases in their daily dealings. Others understand it but choose not to use it. It depends on your life style. The point is that being *in* the ghetto does not necessarily mean being *of* the ghetto, as the dichotomy between the lame and the cool person suggests.

By the same token, young middle-class blacks may demonstrate as much knowledge of and proficiency with the vernacular lexicon as their ghetto counterparts. Knowledge and use of the vernacular vocabulary is seen as an identification with one's heritage rather than a denial of it. Middle-class blacks who have physically moved away from their beginnings or have never known life in the ghetto do not automatically reject their roots in order to make it in the white world. The young, in particular, see their identity and vitality rooted in ghetto culture. It is not surprising, therefore, to hear affluent young blacks, running down some lines with much of the same style and force as their ghetto brothers and sisters. So being of the ghetto can be as much a state of mind as well as a matter of economics or geography.

My involvement with teenagers who lived in the ghetto and on the Hill suggests that being black in white America is probably the basic connection among blacks across geographic, economic, and linguistic boundaries. There is a well-formed black vernacular lexicon which is known and used by middle-class and ghetto teenagers alike. However, the day-to-day life experiences of the affluent black and the ghetto black are not the same—and even the most politically active or cultur-ally identified young black is not going to know those words and phrases that are "ghetto-specific" unless he or she lives there. For ex-ample, few middle-class teenagers I met had comparable knowledge of fight terms, low-rider terms, or even drug terms when compared with their ghetto counterparts, unless they were specifically involved in one or another of those activities.

There are ghetto realities that most middle-class teenagers simply have no contact with. As one politically active middle-class youth put it, "Sure, I know a lot of the words [in the lexicon], but I'm not livin' down there. It's different. Can't pretend it isn't. Some of those terms just not part of my life." His ghetto peer agrees: "Dig. The brothers up dere in dem Hollywood Hills, out dere at UCLA and all dem li'l ol' colleges, they okay—hear what I'm sayin'? They hip to some o' d' happ'nin's, they blood. But when dude come down here, better take it slow, 'cause gon' be lot shit he ain' got together. Some blood blow his mind, send 'im on a hombug. Run down some lines he done *never* heard!"[5]

Though my research indicates that much teenage black vernacu-lar vocabulary is known and shared across economic or geographic boundaries, there is still a disparity between knowledgeable ghetto teenagers and knowledgeable middle-class teenagers based on the degree and kind of exposure to certain environment-bound life experi-ences and the type of vernacular that gets generated and used. In fact, a number of my Educational Opportunities Program students have noted that even if you're from the ghetto, you "lose it"—some of the nonverbal and verbal ways of being in that world—when you go to the Man's college. A black colleague once commented to me that young black men tone down their cock-of-the-walk style of walking, for example, when they are in a predominantly white college setting. Still other young adults who come from the ghetto to college try to return to work in their own communities—and meet with varying degrees of wariness and suspicion. "It's like I ain't one of the people no more. I've got to prove myself. First day I was there [at a Watts recreational facility], dude come up to me and asked me what I was doin' there. Shit! I was born three blocks away! Said to me, 'How come you act funny?' Now ain't that somethin'!"

Though much black vernacular vocabulary crosses economic lines and potentially binds blacks together through a common pool of experiences, there are other social and economic factors that finally determine the kind of vernacular one knows, the frequency of usage, and the familiarity with certain aspects of the lexicon. Finally, there is a real and psychological outsider-insider dichotomy that affects what gets put out and received intraracially—not only in terms of vernacular usage but in terms of the degree of self-disclosure. One needs to prove oneself at the outset to establish or reestablish trust and identification.

The reverse can also be seen in terms of the Black Power experience and its relationship to knowledge and use of certain vernacular expressions. That is, a variety of vernacular terms that deal with black consciousness or are pejorative labels for Establishment blacks or ironic labels for stereotypic aspects of black life—such as food identifications—are more often known and used among young middle-class blacks than among ghetto teenagers. For the most part, the middle-class blacks I met were more closely identified with black awareness and political consciousness than were those from South Central.[6] And the knowledge and use of certain terms reflected this identification.

But matters of racial identification and allegiance across socio-economic lines and the impact of class on one's ethnic orientation or social aspirations are very complex issues. And they have only been touched upon in this discussion of lexical usage.

GEOGRAPHY

Just as gender, peer association, and socioeconomic status affect use and knowledge of the vernacular lexicon, so regional considerations most certainly affect the degree and kind of shared terminology, but in a somewhat different way. So far we have been talking about teenagers who live generally within the greater Los Angeles area—with most living in a rather circumscribed geographical area, South Central and Central Los Angeles. Certainly there are many "regional" words and phrases within even the Los Angeles area as a comparison between, say, Venice and South Central black usage indicates (Edith Folb, 1972). There is also "intraregional" variation, as suggested by male versus female and ghetto versus middle-class usage. But, for the most part, there is a large network of vernacular vocabulary that crosses these groups.

Regional, in this instance, refers to differences between North, West, and South, between urban and rural. Since the lexicon in this book was primarily elicited in Los Angeles, with some terms coming from teenagers in San Diego and San Francisco, it is essentially an urban California glossary. However, through the years, I have had the opportunity to share a sizable portion of the lexicon with teenagers from both the industrial Midwest and the East, as well as those from the rural and urban South. A significant percentage of the words and phrases in the lexicon were known and shared across regional boundaries, *especially* among urban dwellers. I have also had the chance to look at black vernacular lexicons compiled in New York City, Louisville, Chicago, Washington, D.C., Philadelphia, and San Diego.[7] Again, the overlap with the lexicon in this book is considerable. Not only does this comparative information suggest a common pool of urban black vernacular expressions (and life experiences), but it indicates the existence of a stable core lexicon that has prevailed through time.

I have not found the same shared knowledge and use between teenagers from Los Angeles and those from the South, especially the rural South. Though my sample of newly arrived rural southerners is quite small (25 teenagers), still less than 25 percent of the Los Angeles expressions were known to those who came from small towns in Texas, Georgia, Alabama, and South Carolina.

In addition, teenagers from Los Angeles consistently remarked about how much more difficult it was to "get an understanding" with a new arrival from, say, Alabama than one from Detroit. "Seem like we just use different slangs or somethin'. Like this one dude from Florida he act geechie, you know, square. He talk funny, didn't know no slangs. We didn't beat him up or nothin', but he wadn't in on the rest of the clan." Though the data are only suggestive, it seems that there is more shared usage among urban youths from different regional ghettos than among southern and northern or western teenagers, particularly if the southern youth is from a rural town rather than an urban center. Additional comparative data, however, are necessary to determine the validity of this claim.

What seems less questionable are the attitudes manifested toward "out-of-towners." Most newcomers are tested and evaluated by teenagers before they become part of the "in" group. And, at least among some of those I talked with, language use is particularly scrutinized and evaluated. "I had to have a fight in order to get in with the 'in' crowd. I'z from Chicago and they wouldn't accept me because I was someone foreign in my language and my slangs were different. Like they call 'cafeteria' out here, we called it 'lunch room'—go in an' have you lunch! Where dey call places 'clubs,' we call 'tavernette,' this bar.''

Even nonverbal vernacular gestures get the once-over—and sometimes become the source for great amusement. Here is the story one young woman told about "giving someone the finger":

> Jus' like I hadda come in and learn about how dey do the finger. Dey do it like dat [demonstration], we used to do it like dat [a different demonstration]. One girl name Pat—she a stepper now—she knew me when I first come here. She remember. She falls out ever'time. She say, "Chicago! Do your finger!" I do it and she jus' *cracks* up. Dey used to sit down and practice. In school, you learn. But here, you just stick it on up and get on it—lay down for it. You don't be doin' all dem extra curvin' and things—so it look like the thing and the balls. Different way, you know. I learned dat quick!

The reaction to southerners is even more pronounced. Until southern teenagers can prove themselves to the satisfaction of the group, they are often teased and put down because of their "country ways" and "geechie" speech. "It took me long time to git in with d' group. Use'a call me geechie, homeboy, Georgia boy. Say I got a funny accent. We don't use much slangs in Georgia. We taught to respect our elders.'' As indicated, the label geechie is generally a putdown term for anyone who talks or acts differently from the speaker. Teenager perception of geechie talk or Gullah talk is that it is weird, funny, and basically unintelligible.

Regional differences, then, also affect what someone will know of the local vernacular lexicon, what expressions will be shared across regions vis-à-vis shared life experiences, as well as how teenagers will respond to outsiders' speech and the "alien" words they bring with them. There seems to be a greater pool of commonly shared vernacular among urban dwellers—whether ghetto or middle-class, male or female—than between this group and southern youths.

## THE LEXICAL PROCESS:
## ACQUISITION AND TRANSMISSION

### CONTEXT AND MEANING

Most vernacular vocabulary is learned in context. That is, no one goes to a dictionary to look up soul or crumbsnatcher or booty. In fact, many of the teenagers I met felt uncomfortable even asking a friend what a term meant. "You be kinda ashamed in a group, 'specially if you with a group that's not one of your own—dudes shootin' different words. Mostly, be cool an' wait 'til d' conversation develops, so d' cat don't think you lame. Honestly, most people don't wanna act like they don't know somethin'. Might ask my partner, but not all the time, 'cause makes *me* look lame."

The comment is typical of many: to ask what a word means is to be seen as lame. Peer pressure to be cool often prevents asking even a friend. Such a show of ignorance can provide others with an opportunity to "shoot on you." "Can't actually let them know you don't know. Say, 'Man, I cain't dig wha' chu talkin' 'bout.' Gonna look at you funny, make you look like a clown. 'Cause friends you have to watch out fo'. You friends have d' mos' access of hurtin' you."

Teenagers sometimes use bluff or bravado to find out the meaning of terms they don't know. "If a dude was to come up to me, I say, 'Hey man, why don' you be cool?' An' he say, 'Hey man, wha' chu talkin' 'bout?' But *I* say, 'You usin' all dis off d' wall jive, nobody heard of befo'.' Even though whole L.A. area might know it but me, I tell 'im nobody else know it. I'd psych him out. 'What dat shit mean!' I do it in a sneaky way. Den, right den, they explain it." For the most part, then, the lexicon is learned by listening to the words and figuring out their meanings from the contexts in which they are used.

The notion of context operates on several levels. There is the syntactic environment and the semantic field that surround the unknown vernacular terms and give them meaning: "Usually, you can tell 'bout what they mean in the way they use the word in a sentence. Like you know some o' d' words. Put 'em together. Like, 'Hey man, I burned this cat for his old lady'—somethin' like that. I kin jus' 'bout tell by d' other words he say." There are paralinguistic features—intonation, stress, rate, and the like—that provide cues to how a term is being used in a particular context: "Like 'do your thing.' It can be a lotta ways—dancin', lovin', smokin', catchin', really gettin' down. All depend how person say it—like d' voice he be usin', way he emphasize d' words, you be knowin' which way." There is the kinetic context— body movements, gestures, facial expressions—that accompanies paralanguage: "Like 'funky'—it kin be really *good* or really *bad*. All depends. You kin tell by d' way dude say it—watch his face, move his body certain way. Like, 'He's funky, man!' Move way from d' dude —he stink! 'Hey, dude's funky!' Nigger be smilin', make d' fist— dude's okay."

Context also operates on the level of the immediate social setting and the emotional-psychological factors that affect it. "Like 'me an' you.' All depends. 'Me an' you gonna get high, me an' you gonna go over dis young lady's house, me an' you mostly gonna fight.' You kin figure out wha's happ'nin' by checkin' out d' scene. Dude ain't gonna share no smoke when he angry, got his piece out."

Context preeminently means the vast deposits of shared experiences that come from common life conditions. It is this subtle mosaic that allows each person to figure out "what's goin' down." "Jus bein' in d' ghetto, livin' where it's used, you learn. Jus' pick up on it. If somethin' come out—it'll be somewhere, party, somewhere it'll spread. Mostly people be usin' the same slangs in Frisco, Chicago, Detroit. Same thangs happ'nin'. People live in d' ghetto, they gonna know what you sayin'. Life d' same in all dem cities. Like I'z from Detroit. Soon I come out here, I picks up what they be sayin'. Same action goin' down." Context—in its various senses—provides the literal and figurative frame of reference that allows a young person to decipher the ordinary language meanings for a variety of vernacular terms that he or she may have heard since childhood.

Of course, terms are learned out of context as well. Some claim they have no problem directly asking someone a term's meaning. In fact, to play cool in some situations is not only dumb but dangerous. "I *definitely* stop 'em right then. Even if I don't know 'em, because I feel like dis, why you goin' on fakin'? He might be sayin' something —'We're gon' blow your brains out!' And you up dere—'Umm hm, uh huh.' 'Well, she goin' fo' it—BANG!' You dead. I say, 'Wait a minute, explain yo'self, brother.' " However, implicit in the act of asking is often an attempt to manipulate the situation so as to come out on top—making the other feel she is doing you a favor or getting someone to think he is actually ignorant or inarticulate. "Like you say, 'Man, what kinda shit you talkin'? Ain't never heard dat shit 'round here.' Jus' blow hard an' dude think you be knowin' somethin' he don't." As already suggested, bluff and bravado are always available if you ultimately can't figure out what's happening.

Reliance on contextual meaning certainly leaves room for possible misinterpretation of words and phrases. And, in fact, the misreading of expressions does occur. "I'z in jail once. See couple dudes. We all get to rappin'. Get out, see 'em on d' street. I say, 'Y'all didn't tell me you stay in Venice!' When we was up in jail, they be callin' it Ghost Town. I thought they talkin' 'bout Watts. See, I never knowed 'bout dat. I calls it Quiet Village. Dey look at me like, well, where y' think we is? I didn't know till I hit d' streets."

Indeed, errors in hearing, understanding, using, or pronouncing a vernacular expression provide the basis for the creation of new expressions or the assignment of new definitions to old terms. As one teenager pointed out, "Anything that comes out yo' mouf and it be funny, else you hear somethin' different, becomes a slang. Like if you can't pronounce somethin'—one person can't—and it sounds funny, nex' person they go for it, 'cause it something different."

Despite the potential for misunderstanding, most expressions are deciphered correctly—that is, the meanings assigned to the expression fall within the range of appropriate contextual readings. This was substantiated in the course of my work and suggests the overall accuracy of learning vernacular vocabulary through a variety of indirect means.

### TRANSMISSION AND USE OF THE LEXICON

The lexicon is seen by most ghetto teenagers as a natural part of conversation, the way you talk. However, all words and phrases are not equally attractive or potent or expressive in their appeal to these young people. Again, a variety of factors affect not only how terms are learned but what terms are learned, which ones are retained and which ones get passed on to others.

One of the most potent factors influencing what gets learned, retained, and passed on is the degree to which the expression characterizes the day-to-day experiences, needs, interests, problems and activities of those using it. Contrary to what many writers say about slang and argot, there is strong evidence in my research to suggest that a great many vernacular expressions have withstood social, economic, political, and generational shifts because they are still expressive of black life in this country.

One of the important advantages of engaging in field research of the black vernacular vocabulary over time is that one can see the degree to which the lexicon has remained the same. Of the over 2500 terms I have collected in almost nine years, fully 75 percent of the expressions represented in the lexicon are known to black teenagers, and approximately 50 percent of those terms are claimed as active words and phrases in teenage vocabularies. That information is significant. For one, it suggests the degree to which there is continuity of experience—both good and bad, painful and poignant—from generation to generation which continues to be aptly characterized by long-standing vernacular terminology. It also suggests that vernacular vocabulary is more conservative than innovative in its development—that is, one relies on the perennials to do one's work, as long as they accurately mirror one's life and times. And even those terms that have been dropped (at least for the time being) are still retained in the collective lexicon of a given group.

Various life histories are connected with vernacular expressions. There are terms I have identified as perennials which persist through time and across various boundaries because they consistently reflect the life experiences of the group. There are also what I call the recycled expressions. These terms are ones that pass beyond the group—through cultural intermediaries—into other subcultures or into mainstream culture, take on new or different meanings, and finally return to the "parent" group, where now the new meaning predominates or becomes one of the multiple meanings attached to the expression.

In my experience, "uptight" exhibits such a life history. When the term was first defined for me back in the late 60s, it meant emotionally self-possessed, together. Though the term also meant tense, nervous, or upset, it was the positive emotional association that was most often cited.

The expression found its way into the white drug culture of the 60s as well, and the meaning got extended to the negative effects associated with drug experiences. The term's negative meaning was emphasized in white usage. As the term found its way into white mainstream use, it came to mean being nervous, restless, or upset. The expression finally became so conventional that the media coopted it and it became a household word—even before Spiro Agnew did. In the early 70s, when I checked on the word's status among some of my informants, I found that the negative mainstream reading had overtaken the positive dimension that had earlier been assigned to it, and was often associated with a bad drug experience.

There are also reclaimed vernacular expressions, as well as those that are recycled. These are terms that pass out of use and are discarded. They lay dormant, but not forgotten, in the vernacular pool and are reclaimed when the expressive force of the word is again desired. Sometimes new meanings are assigned to them.[8]

There are also expressions that can be considered fad words, seasonals. They are usually short-lived, literally flash on the scene for a brief period of time, and are quickly dropped or used only by a limited number of people. They may be associated with some television celebrity, sports figure, or local or national hero, but they never catch on in a big way. For a long time, teenagers in South Central were using Muhammed Ali's claim—"I'm the greatest"—in response to any triumph or challenge. Though Ali remains a great hero for many, the expression seems to have died off. I recently heard a young man proclaim, "I'm the greatest," after he won a pool game. The retort from his companions: "Hey man, that shit is dead!"

Reclaimed words themselves can exhibit fadlike characteristics. Some stay for awhile; others go out of style or revert to more restricted application. "Terms go in and out after a few months—like 'dealing.' Dealin' everything for awhile—pussy, dope. Now it back to just plain dealin'."

There are newly coined terms that, like fad words, may pass quickly from the scene or be retained in the lexicon. Jimmy Carter's reign has produced a spate of new expressions that may or may not outlast his presidency—*Mr. Peanut*, *Mr. Cracker*, for both Carter or any white male; *I've been born again* to euphemistically refer to the positive effects of getting high or engaging in good sex. *Miss Lillian* and *Amy* have taken their place alongside *Miss Ann* as expressions for a white female.

One kind of newly coined word comes from the idiolects (personal dialect) of individual speakers. "Like call a car a 'cootch' [coach]. My friends use dat. Don't think the whole world know about 'em. They find out what I'm talkin' 'bout, they start usin' it too." If a person is prominent or powerful and provides a peer or adult role model for teenagers, his (and sometimes her) vernacular will be picked up, at least by the immediate "set." Whether or not these words are disseminated beyond the circle depends on factors like the inherent potency of the expression, the "rep" of the role model, and the other circles and sets in which the original hearers move.

Two terms that had intense, if limited, use sprang from the creative mind of a local pool sharp in Watts. I happened to be present when H.B. introduced one of the terms to some friends. The term was "vasculated" and it meant the same as being high on drugs. Another term H.B. coined, out of my presence, was "histophonic." This became an intensifier much like "stone" or "righteous." When H.B. would see a good-looking woman walk by the pool hall, he would say, "Now that is one his-to-phonic woman!" The expression got picked up and used by his group. Whether or not it traveled beyond H.B.'s circle, I don't know, but it does suggest the way in which words can be individually coined and find their way into the larger group lexicon.

These are some of the life histories of words and word use. Implicit in the foregoing discussion is the impact of role models and other lexical emissaries on not only the innovation and retention of words in the vernacular pool but on their transmission beyond the group.

As is apparent by now, role models—whether they be famous celebrities or folk heros or local leaders—exert an important influence on what expression gets heard, literally and figuratively, and which one is deemed expressive or important enough to pass on. Emulation of significant others operates not only on the level of assuming the person's front but in terms of imitating the other's turns of phrases, whether they are new, recycled, or reclaimed. "Like you be listenin' to dude, he real together, people turn round, den dey be sayin' it. Like, 'lighten up blood.' Hear dat from J.R.—he a big dealer. Everybody say 'blood' now. Dude come into pool hall. He play pool *real* good. He say, 'I shoot my stick, take my licks—play anybody in d' house!' Nex' day, dudes be sayin' the *same thang*."

Of course a person need not be that much respected or famous to introduce a new phrase that sticks. But there seems to be a feeling that the stronger the rep, the more likely an expression is to be incorporated into the vocabulary of others. And slips of the tongue, misheard words, or mispronounced words all are grist for the vernacular mill. "I'm from the ghetto and sometime you take words that can get over and you use that—anythin' that sound slick like den dat, becomes a slang. It sounds good, next person they go for it, start it around."

The lexical emissary may not only be a respected black; he or she may be from another racial or ethnic group. A number of Chicano terms are used by teenage blacks. I asked about such terms as "ese vato" ("cool" male), "chingazo" (act of intercourse), "puta" (prostitute), and "penocha" (vagina). Many said the terms were picked up from Chicanos who were well-liked and respected. "Yeh, he a cool dude. He taught me some o' dat Mexican slang. I's okay."

A number of teenagers who regularly used drugs or smoked marijuana noted that they had picked up (and exchanged) many drug-related terms from white hippies they had encountered "on the street" (Hollywood and the Sunset Strip) or "in the joint." At least during the late 60s, the hippy symbolized for many young blacks some of the more positive aspects of the white person. The sharing of some of the vernacular paralleled the sharing of one important aspect of youthful culture, the use of drugs. So, at the same time that there was an attitude of amusement or contempt for the white hippy—particularly among ghetto teenagers—there was also a connection and a kind of respect for what was seen as an antisocial (read antiwhite) life style. "Yeh, hippy they okay. Smoke weed, get down, got some righteous dos. I likes 'em."

Another, somewhat different, source of teenage knowledge of the vernacular is the media. Here the effect is not so much a matter of introducing new terms into the lexicon, but more a case of recycling or reclaiming—terms take on new or extended meanings and old terms come back into use. Most of the expressions used by the mass media—especially television—are not new to vernacular-savvy teenagers; rather they remind them that they are still around and potentially usable. But for the young person who has less direct contact with the vernacular and the contexts in which it is used, the media become more potent educational resources.

Two related sources of vernacular vocabulary are the black disc jockey, with his patter or advertising "riff," and the black singer. Together, musician and disc jockey provide a steady stream of vernacular terminology for those who listen—and many, many do. Though possessions are not easy to come by among ghetto teenagers, one that is frequently seen and regularly heard is the portable radio. One of the more common sights on the streets is to see a young black (often a male) striding along, transitor radio to his ear, "diggin' on the sounds."

Billboards in South Central Los Angeles and in other black communities reflect back terms and expressions that are part of the vernacular—and those products that will appeal to a black audience. So you get pictorials with such copy as "Make it with Harper's," or "Cool it baby, have a Club in the tub," or "Country Club Malt Liquor —the bad dude's brew." A few youths admitted that they learned new expressions from such advertisements, as they also did from so-called black exploitation movies such as "Sweet Sweetback" or "Coffee" and the black magazines *Jet*, *Ebony*, and *Essence*. But the most powerful medium was still television. It provided regular vernacular users with a reflection of their lexicon—at least superficially; it informed the lame who was often too embarrassed to ask what terms meant; and in some cases it introduced new terms into the lexicons of both the regular user and the neophyte alike.

Some of the favorite vernacular sources were "Baretta," "Kojak," "Police Story," "Streets of San Francisco," "The Rookies"— all police shows, all violent. "Like we be layin' up watchin' TV. Baretta come on. It's a trip! We get to playin' with some slangs he be usin'. Nex' day, you take it out on d' street."

In some way, it can be said that television characters like Baretta and Kojak also become role models for some of those who watch them. Even though they are cops, they are tough—even brutal—and they often buck the system. They are also resourceful and use their wits—qualities of great appeal to young blacks. Again and again, they were mentioned as cool dudes, together, heavy. Indeed, much more was said about these cop characters than any of the lead characters in the constellation of black sitcoms that perpetuate black stereotypes.

So words have their own life, death, and rebirth cycles, and much of their life history depends on the nature and conditions of the times —that is, their attractiveness in fulfilling expressive, psychological, cultural, or social needs. Though vernacular vocabulary is seen by most teenagers as an integral part of their expressive behavior, there are constraints on usage. Not all contexts are "appropriate" for vernacular usage. Part of the process of acquiring and transmitting vernacular is learning when you should and should not use it.

## APPROPRIATE AND INAPPROPRIATE
## CONTEXTS FOR USAGE

In the simplest terms, it can be said that vernacular vocabulary is generally appropriate on the streets, in the jail or probation camp setting, and at certain social events (shooting pool, playing cards, sports). What most of these contexts have in common is their decidedly male flavor. The vernacular is generally not appropriate in the home or in church (the world of the black female) or on the job (the world of the white). However, this breakdown hardly tells the tale, for it is the people who populate these contexts and the situations their presence generates that finally determine how much and what kind of vernacular gets used.

When teenagers were asked where they learned the vernacular and where they most often used it, their responses were virtually unanimous: the streets. For most, the streets are predominantly seen as male territory and the vocabulary is the natural lexical fare. "Da's jus' the way I talk with the brothers. I jus' be talkin'—they know me. I'm not gonna try an' front off. I jus' gonna be myself out dere [on the streets]."

However, the situation changes when females enter the scene—for example, at parties, dances, or other mixed social gatherings. Most males acknowledge the fact that they tone down their vernacular usage around young women. That is, they do not use the full range of terms in their lexical arsenal. To do so is to show disrespect—and to risk their chances of getting over. The following statement speaks for a number of the males I talked with.

> With a young lady, it all depends. I say, "What's happ'nin'?" Little stuff like dat. Like I wouldn't say, "Lemme have some cock!" Wouldn't use no sex slangs. It's not respectful. Maybe with a chickenhead, I might. It all depends. If I liked her and I wanna try and get over, go wid her, ain't gonna be usin' most slangs. If I have a lotta respect for her and she has a lotta respect for me, I won't hardly use it. Don't be cussin' with a young lady. They tries to have manners—and I respects that.

So terms that are considered crude or vulgar or are seen as cuss words are often consciously eliminated from the male's vocabulary—except perhaps with a young woman who is perceived to be a "chickenhead." As already pointed out, women are well aware of the price they may pay for using "coarse" words in mixed company. Whether they play the game or not, most are aware of the rules—and the risks involved in breaking them.

If males (and females) tone down their respective vernacular usage in mixed company, both groups are even more restrained in the quantity and type of words they use in the home—particularly with their mother, older female relatives, and their mother's female friends.[9] Again, the majority of those I encountered notably curtailed their vernacular usage around their mother. "Mom, no lawd! I don't even curse in front of her. I don't tell her nothin' like dat. My brother do when he get mad. She git on his case hard! I think she hear me say 'damn you' and 'shit' about twice. I use some old slang like 'poontang' or 'pussy,' I be wakin' up in d' hospital. A lotta slangs moms wouldn't know what it mean anyway—but I ain't takin' no chances. I learn to venerate my elders.''

Of course, some terms are permissible in the home. And in fact, teenagers may teach their elders some of these. "I got moms to use 'swoop' and a few other slangs. I's righteous.'' Many young blacks claim that most of the vernacular vocabulary is unknown to their mother anyway, at least to older mothers and older adult females.[10] It seems that the younger the mother (that is, the closer in age to the youth), the easier it becomes to use more vernacular in her presence. And the younger she is, the more likely she is to understand a good portion of it and to use it herself. "Moms she still look young. She *is* young. She don't look like she should be our mother. She looks more like our sister. Most slangs I kin use and she understand them. I use a lotta slangs in front of her. She's young, hip to what's happ'nin'.'' So the relative age of the parent figures prominently in the degree and kind of terms used. Less of a lexical gap seems to be experienced when ages are close. (Whether, in fact, this true—that older women know less vocabulary—is another matter.)

Another context in which vernacular vocabulary is closely monitored is on the job. For many, the white man's world is alienating and intimidating, a place to be on guard. Many young blacks recognize the need to "play whitey's game to get over.'' This can mean adopting the linguistic behavior of the white world (and hiding one's own). As one teenager put it, "When you get a job, you got to have good language. I try to make a good impression.'' Another amended the statement when he said, "I don't be usin' no slangs on the job. No. Not from what I see. Like you suppose' be on your best behavior. You suppose' act real straight—be as straight as possible.''

Many teenagers are very adept at lexical code switching and are quite able to adopt a more "standard'' (white) lexicon when at work. Most take a wait-and-see attitude toward vernacular usage at work. "I keep it cool, stay down low, till I see what's happenin'. Depends how dey [white coworkers and supervisors] act. See where dey comin' from.'' If whites prove themselves—are seen to be cool—a teenager may begin to loosen up and use more of his or her lexicon. "Like if he [the boss] cool, he use it himself, we get along. We have an understandin', it would be okay to use slangs. But if he too old, it might scare 'im off. Might lose d' job.''

Again, the age of the boss or coworkers seems important. The younger the associate, the more likely he or she will be viewed as potentially cool or hip. Interestingly, age seems to make more of a difference than race in determining whether or not a teenager will eventually open up in a job situation. That is, a black person is not automatically viewed as okay—though there is an initial feeling of identification that gets reinforced or not by the person's subsequent behavior. In all cases, age seems suspect. An older person who acts young (dresses or behaves like the younger generation) is viewed with suspicion—whether black or white. In fact, such a person causes more restrained behavior, vernacular and otherwise, than the less hip counterpart. As one teenager saw it, "Jus' because dis dude think he's together, don't mean he *is* together. He still from d' older generation. Don't matter how slick he dress, don't make him young. He frontin' off."

Finally, a place where vernacular usage is often curtailed is in the classroom. Depending on the teacher's personality, educational philosophy (or lack of it), feelings about "standard" versus "nonstandard" usage, a young person might be made to feel that his or her grammar is inadequate, incorrect, or inappropriate in the classroom setting. Stories about teachers correcting "bad" grammar or "meager" vocabulary use abound. Most stories tell of an intense struggle between student and teacher for control and power, as much as a consideration of what constitutes good grammar. One young man's story speaks for a sizable number of black teenagers:

> I think I lost 'bout 1000 points for talkin' shit [vernacular]. I walk off by her and say, "Ain't that somethin'!" She [his English teacher] say, "Good mornin', Jerry." I say, "What it is!" She say, "Tha's no way to answer me." I say, "Why not?" Well, da's a 100 points right dere. I said, "What it is" and two "ain'ts." My teacher she taught me all dem fundamentals, don't want to hear no slang. She don't *know* no slang. An' everybody be runnin' it down every day. But not dere.

The one place in which vernacular usage abounds is the penal institution—the jail, the probation camp, and quasi-institutional settings like the work camp, the Job Corps, or the training center. For those who have served time, the jail runs a close second to the streets as not only an arena for vernacular usage but a source of much terminology.

Vernacular usage is often curtailed, then, around "nice" girls, parents—particularly mothers—older women, older coworkers and bosses (regardless of racial or ethnic background), and "square" teachers. The lexicon that is most often censored relates to sex, drugs, fighting, gambling, and drinking. It is most often heard, used, and promulgated on the streets—out of the earshot of establishment powers and parental ears—and in penal institutions where it operates as a secret vocabulary among inmates and as a tool against the authorities. "Appropriate" often means a teenage black male context marked by solidarity. "Inappropriate" gets associated with the presence of women, whites, establishment authorities, and other "outsiders"—where the sense of someone else's norms and standards are present.

## ATTITUDES TOWARD USAGE

How do teenagers feel about using the vernacular lexicon? There were a range of attitudes and feelings expressed by those I met. Some opinions were quite explicitly voiced; others were embedded in dialogs.

Most young blacks are keenly aware of the differences between so-called standard usage and the vernacular. And most teenagers make a distinction between standard and nonstandard usage in normative terms. That is, standard word use is labeled proper, good English, the way to get over, school talk, proper grammar, and the like. Nonstandard use is seen as street talk, not too cool, low class, kid's stuff, and, sometimes, bad English. Many are cognizant of the power of standard usage in the white man's world. "You cain't come on the job usin' slang words and think you gonna get bidness. Need to keep it cool, stay down low. I'ma try an' get dis job, I'ma try an' be a clean-cut young man. I try to make a good impression." As already noted, vernacular usage is seen as not too cool in the context of the job, at home, with people you respect (or fear), and at school.

Yet despite pressures to steer away from vernacular usage, there are many countervailing factors that encourage and reinforce continued practice. For one, most teenagers feel that vernacular terminology is the more natural, more comfortable way to express oneself:

> People feel more comfortable usin' it. It's easier to come out with than bein' more conventional. Slang is sayin' what you really wanna say. Makes you feel easy—talkin' the way you wanna talk. I's subconscious. You don't really be thinkin' 'bout it. Like some Mexican I know want to learn d' raps. They so nervous, they wanna get black's philosophy so *quick!* Don't happen dat way. All you hafta do is jus' blend in and let yo'self go. Don't try to talk proper, really think out what you gonna say. It jus' come natural. I mean, that jus' how we have a conversation.

Vernacular usage is seen not only as a natural mode of expression but as one that is often more expressive, more direct, and more creative than standard forms:

> You feel more easy with it. Like if we was to set up here and we didn't use no slang, we'd use a long, dictionary book conversation. Conversation dead. It's more expressive. People can identify with it easier den big, formal words. People understan' slang more an' dey get they point across. Like I kin walk right out here on the street and run up to a pa'tner of mine, run it down, everythin's cool. Say, "Le's slide over to d' set and dig on the young ladies try an' catch." I's different an' better

way. Mo' fun way. Communicate with somebody and dey can understand exactly what you talkin'. And, besides, it don't give you away.

As the last line above suggests, secrecy is also one of the advantages of vernacular usage. And secrecy is integral to still another
factor that reinforces teenage use: peer identification and group pressure to use the lexicon.[11] One young man summed up much teenage
feeling when he said,

> People use slangs to be part of d' in-crowd. If you just say plain gram-
> mar and have all your pronunciation right, they call you studious and
> square. Tha's how you kin tell a square mos' d' time. You see a dude,
> he say, "Hey man, got any weed?" I's the way he say it, word he use.
> You can tell he police or he a square wants get high, be cool, be with the
> in-crowd. He tryin' sound cool—but he ain't.
>     Me an' my partner meet and wants to get high, say, "Hey, what's
> happenin'?" "Wha's happen', man?" Say, "Wha's good." I say,
> "You got?" He say, "No, I'm lookin' for Herb." I say, "Le's find
> 'im!" Somethin' like dat. But some dude come up an' say, "You got
> some joints?" He could be the police. It jus' don't sound right.

So, even though most teenagers are aware of standard usage, recognize its selling points in many marketplaces, even identify it as the
proper way to talk, still many choose not to (or sometimes, cannot)
use standard terminology within their primary groups or in contexts
where peer-group pressures prevail.

Implicit in much dialog—especially that of black-identified middle-class teenagers—is a kind of inverse snobbism connected with vernacular vocabulary use, a disdain for blacks who discard the lexicon
when they leave the ghetto in their move up the social and economic
ladder. As one middle class teenager saw it, "Parents who have es-
caped the ghetto don't want to hear them [vernacular terms] now. I
never accepted that as my class. A lotta black people are phonies. For-
get where it's at. Where they come from." Another ghetto youth put it
more graphically—and in the vernacular: "Diddyboppers shine on d'
slangs. But dey niggers all d' same. Blood to d' bone! Oreo cain't
change d' outside—no matter *how* white he git inside!"

Yet the dismissal of those who cannot or will not use vernacular
vocabulary is not unmixed with some real feelings of envy, inade-
quacy, and even outright resentment. Many recognize a hard fact of
life: the way you talk and the words you use greatly influence your
ability to manage in a white-dominated society. And moving outside
the ghetto and the safety (and pressure) of the peer group often gets
linked with giving up—or at least toning down—the vernacular output. Ghetto teenagers who have moved into the white work world or
to white colleges and universities are the most acutely aware of this

linguistic conflict. As one of my students put it, "Speakin' proper English wadn't my thing. Long as I got my point across, I didn't care. Come here [San Francisco State University], I've taken it upon myself to learn to speak the white man's language. You got to—to survive." Another student said it somewhat differently. For him, it was important to retain his vernacular (and his ghetto connections) and also learn the white code. The ability to code-switch was, for him, the ultimate ability to communicate and survive:

> I came from d' ghetto and I am part of d' ghetto—and tha's for real. But, I hate to see a brother that kin righteously shoot you down wid all sorts of slangs, and den you be talkin' about economics or history and he don' know how to express himself any other way. You say, "Well, brother, you hip to d' slang, but you got a language barrier which ain't gonna get over." When you can speak standard, you kin be half and half. Da's not bein' a phony, it just means you know how to get over to *any* group. You need to know both to communicate. Hear what I'm sayin'?

So a variety of factors influence attitudes toward vernacular vocabulary use: habit, ease of usage, expressive power, survival, peer pressure and group identification, a sense of roots, and the desire to "make it" in disparate, often conflicting worlds. The attitudes voiced by black teenagers are complex and often contradictory. It could not be otherwise, given the complex and contradictory messages white America continues to communicate to its black population.

The discussion in this chapter of the dynamics of vernacular vocabulary use is, at best, limited in scope and detail. Many complicated conditions and constraints are at work in the whole process. What I have attempted to do is to highlight some of the more apparent factors that influence usage and user. Finally, however, it is the voices that have spoken throughout this book that tell the most about the nature, function, form, and focus of black teenage vernacular.

# bibliography

ABRAHAMS, ROGER D. 1963. *Deep Down in the Jungle*. Chicago: Aldine.

—— 1970a. *Positively Black*. Englewood Cliffs, N.J.: Prentice-Hall.

—— 1970b. "The White Community and Black Culture." Paper prepared for the workshop Issues of Community and Research Group Relationships. The National Institute of Child Health and Human Development. New Orleans, March 8-10.

—— 1972. "The Training of the Man of Words in Talking Sweet." *Language in Society*, 1.1 (April).

—— 1976. *Talking Black*. Rowley, Mass.: Newbury House Publishers.

ARDREY, ROBERT. 1966. *Territorial Imperative: A Personal Inquiry into the Animal Origins of Property and Nations*. New York: Atheneum.

BROWN, H. RAP. 1969. *Die Nigger Die!* New York: Dial Press.

DALBY, DAVID. 1973. "The African Element in American English." In Thomas Kochman, ed. *Rappin' and Stylin' Out*. Urbana: University of Illinois Press.

DAY, BETH. 1972. *Sexual Life Between Blacks and Whites*. New York: World.

DILLARD, J. L. 1977. *Lexicon of Black English*. New York: The Seabury Press.

DUNDES, ALAN. 1978. "Into the Endzone for a Touchdown: A Psychoanalytic Consideration of American Football." *West. Folklore*, 37.

FOLB, EDITH A. 1972. "A Comparative Study of Urban Black Argot." *Occasional Papers in Linguistics*, 1 (March). Los Angeles: UCLA.

—— 1973. "Rappin' in the Black Vernacular." *Human Behavior*, 2.8 (August).

—— 1976. "Vernacular Vocabulary: A View of Interracial Perceptions and Experiences." In Larry Samovar and Richard Porter, eds. *Intercultural Communication: A Reader*, 2nd ed. Belmont, Calif.: Wadsworth.

FRAZIER, E. FRANKLIN. 1957. *The Black Bourgeoisie*. New York: Macmillan.

GRIER, WILLIAM H. and PRICE M. COBBS. 1968. *Black Rage*. New York: Bantam Books.

HALL, EDWARD T. 1969. *The Hidden Dimension*. New York: Doubleday.

HANNERZ, ULF. 1969. *Soulside: Inquiries into Ghetto Culture and Community*. New York: Columbia University Press.

HEISE, DAVID. 1966. "Social Status, Attitudes and Word Connotations." *Sociological Inquiry*, 36.2 (Spring).

HOLT, GRACE SIMS. 1972. " 'Inversion' in Black Communication." In Thomas Kochman, ed. *Rappin' and Stylin' Out*. Urbana: University of Illinois Press.

JOHNSON, KEN. 1972. "The Vocabulary of Race." In Thomas Kochman, ed. *Rappin' and Stylin' Out*. Urbana: University of Illinois Press.

JOHNSON, KENNETH R. 1973. "Words Used for Skin Color in the Black Culture." The Florida *FL Reporter*, Spring/Fall.

KANTROWITZ, NATHAN. 1969. "The Vocabulary of Race Relations in a Prison." *PADS*, 51 (April).

―――― and JOANNE KANTROWITZ. 1973. "Meet 'Mr. Franklin': An Example of Usage." In Alan Dundes, ed. *Mother Wit from the Laughing Barrel*. Englewood Cliffs, N.J.: Prentice-Hall.

KING, WOODIE, JR. 1972. "The Game." In Thomas Kochman, ed. *Rappin' and Stylin' Out*. Urbana: University of Illinois Press.

KOCHMAN, THOMAS. 1971. "Cross-Cultural Communication: Contrasting Perspectives, Conflicting Sensibilities." The Florida *FL Reporter*, Spring/Fall.

―――― 1972. "The Kinetic Element in Black Idiom." In Thomas Kochman, ed. *Rappin' and Stylin' Out*. Urbana: University of Illinois Press.

―――― 1974. "Orality and Literacy as Factors of 'Black' and 'White' Communicative Behavior." *International Journal of the Sociology of Language*, 3. The Hague: Mouton.

―――― 1976. "Perceptions Along the Power Axis: A Cognitive Residue of Inter-Racial Encounters." *Anthropological Linguistics*, September.

LABOV, WILLIAM, PAUL COHEN, CLARENCE ROBINS, and JOHN LEWIS. 1968. "A Study of the Non-Standard English of Negro and Puerto Rican Speakers in New York City." 2 vols. *Cooperative Research Project No. 3288*. New York: Columbia University.

―――― 1973. "The Linguistic Consequences of Being a Lame." *Language in Society*, 2.1 (April).

LANDY, EUGENE E. 1971. *The Underground Dictionary*. New York: Simon and Schuster.

LERMAN, PAUL. 1967. "Argot, Symbolic Deviance and Subcultural Delinquency." *American Sociological Review*, 32.2 (April).

LEWIS, DIANE K. 1975. "The Black Family: Socialization and Sex Roles." *Phylon*, 36.3 (Fall).

LIEBOW, ELLIOT. 1967. *Tally's Corner*. Boston: Little, Brown.

LORENZ, KONRAD. 1966. *On Aggression*. New York: Bantam Books.

MILNER, CHRISTINA, and RICHARD MILNER. 1972. *Black Players: The Secret World of Black Pimps*. Boston: Little, Brown.

MITCHELL-KERNAN, CLAUDIA. 1971. "Language Behavior in a Black Urban Community." *Monographs of the Language-Behavior Research Laboratory*, 2 (February). Berkeley: University of California.

MOYNIHAN, DANIEL P. 1965. *The Negro Family: The Case for National Action*. Washington, D.C.: Department of Labor.

PACKARD, VANCE. 1957. *The Hidden Persuaders*. New York: D. McKay.

PORTER, HERMAN. 1973. "Introduction." In Malachi Andrews and Paul T. Owens. *Black Language*. Los Angeles: Seymour-Smith.

STACK, CAROL B. 1974. *All Our Kin: Strategies for Survival in a Black Community*. New York: Harper and Row.

TENHOUTEN, WARREN D. 1970. "The Black Family: Myth and Reality." *Psychiatry*, 33.2 (May).

VALENTINE, CHARLES A. 1968. *Culture and Poverty: Critique and Counterproposals*. Chicago: University of Chicago Press.

# notes

## 1. SETTING THE SCENE

1. The very fact, for example, that so pervasive a force as the Black Power movement should generate a negligible set of terms is provocative—especially since many of the militant organizations of the day, such as the Black Panthers and the Muslims, were housed in South Central Los Angeles.

2. In the early years of my field work, I used a reel-to-reel portable tape recorder that was quite conspicuous.

3. Only those expressions found in the text of this book are included in the glossary. The full lexicon will appear in a separate publication.

## 2. NAME TERMS

1. For different perspectives on black family life and culture, see Valentine, 1968; Abrahams, 1976; TenHouten, 1970; Day, 1972; Stack, 1974; Lewis, 1975.

2. Indeed, TenHouten, 1970, found that "the most common family structure among blacks is one in which there are both a husband and a wife present in the home. In urban areas, where the black family is alleged to be rapidly deteriorating, the percentage of such families is 65" (p. 153).

3. See Kochman, 1976; Johnson, 1972; and Kantrowitz, 1969, for different perspectives on the dimensions of intra/interracial naming terms.

4. See Johnson, 1973, for a discussion of the sociocultural aspects of skin color.

5. As Johnson, 1973, points out, "One indication that skin color is important in Black culture is that skin color—to be specific, a particular descriptive term or label identifying an individual's skin color—is one of the first adjectives used when describing a Black person" (p. 15).

6. For another more formal but equally fascinating description of the term "motherfucker," see Kantrowitz and Kantrowitz, in Dundes, 1973.

7. See Labov, 1973, for a grammatical analysis of the lame.

8. Most of the expressions in this section characterize the white man rather than the white woman, since the white male was the focus of most discussion and vernacular description.

9. Though there are black as well as white police on South Central streets, teenagers tended to equate the police with the white man. The vernacular reflected this line of vision.

## 3. FORMS OF MANIPULATION

1. However, the concept of slumming implies the recognition of space as territory, albeit alien territory, such as trespassing on forbidden ground or crossing forbidden streets. It also implies a condescending attitude toward the territory being invaded.

2. It is not uncommon to see girls and women wearing bedroom slippers on the streets (men too) as well as housecoats and dusters. On hot evenings, meals are also brought out onto porches and steps.

3. For other discussions of kinds of talk, see Kernan, 1971; Kochman, 1972; Abrahams, 1972.

4. See also Holt's discussion of inversion in black language use, 1972.

## 4. MALE-FEMALE INTERACTION

1. The welfare system makes it impossible for husbands to reside with their wives if they are receiving aid. Therefore, the system undermines conjugal living and encourages people to live apart (if the men can't get a job) or to sneak around to be together.

2. See King, "The Game," 1972, for a prime example of two males trying to outwait each other in their attempts to get over to the same woman.

3. As Kochman has pointed out to me, "Samuel Charter's *Poetry of the Blues* has a blues lyric that highlights the 'fo' day creep.' Literally, the *before day creep*, which refers to spouses sneaking home before their wife/husband wakes up. Thus, if you need to creep, you were probably cheating on your spouse. In this way, creeping has come to mean simply cheating."

4. Abrahams, 1970, has suggested that such attitudes (especially on the part of males themselves) stem from "residual guilt feelings concerning infidelity, both to mother and to other women, feelings which themselves must be rationalized. This [in black folk tales] is done commonly by picturing men as supersexed animals who cannot control themselves when they see another woman" (p. 112).

5. Unless otherwise indicated, oral sex refers here to cunnilingus. Most male and female dialog focused on cunnilingus rather than fellatio, in part because reaction to it was so strong, opinionated, and vocal.

6. This aversion to cunnilingus is hardly limited to teenage men. As Liebow, 1967, points out, older black men also share this view (p. 141).

7. See Dundes, 1978, for a discussion of sexuality and the macho game of football.

## 5. THE VOCABULARY OF DRUGS

1. Selected portions of the discussion and narrative material in this chapter were taken from an earlier work on teenage drug use. See Folb, 1976.

2. The power and mystique of psychedelics gave birth to a whole generation of middle-class white rebels who—along with Timothy Leary, the guru of mind expansion—"tuned in, turned on and dropped out." However, blacks did not tune in to the white drug prophets, nor did they turn on to psychedelics. As far as dropping out, many of them had been forced or chose to

reject mainstream white values long before any of the psychedelic savants appeared on the scene. If anything, blacks during the 60s were marching to the tune of a different set of drummers—Huey Newton, Rap Brown, Stokely Carmichael, and Malcolm X.

## 6. THE DYNAMICS OF VOCABULARY USE

1. These factors are not rank-ordered in terms of their relative impact on informant usage. Taken together, they represent different spheres of influence rather than a hierarchy of influence.

2. I also operated on this assumption for the first years of my field work. It was only with increased exposure to female usage that I began to seek out more women informants. They still constitute only a small percentage (one sixth) of those interviewed, though many more were informally met. However, the lexical data I collected from young women are rich and, I believe, the findings are suggestive of the potential range of female expressive behavior.

3. See Lewis, 1975, for an interesting view of the differential socialization of black adolescents as the result of pressures exerted by the mainstream macrostructure on black life styles.

4. As Rap Brown said in his autobiography, 1969, "Some of the best Dozens players were girls" (p. 27).

5. Whether or not middle-class black teenagers know and use their own specific vernacular vocabulary is beyond the scope of this book. However, data I collected suggest that such a discrete set of terms does exist. And the lexicon seems to reflect the influence of college, sports, black studies, political concerns, and the like.

6. As already suggested, the Black Power movement generated little in the way of vernacular vocabulary—especially among ghetto teenagers—particularly when compared with other areas of youthful concern. The most visible linguistic impact can be seen in the smattering of Arabic, Moslem, and Swahili words and phrases that appeared in exchanges, a legacy of cultural and political groups like Ron Karenga's Los Angeles-based group US and the Muslims.

Some young people took "African names," though few actually gave up their "slave names" completely. Expressions like *blow black*, *blow change*, *blow revolution*, *heavy knowledge*—and the new context for terms like *brother* and *sister*—signaled a new sense of black consciousness.

Expressions like *Afro bag* characterized the taking on of a new social costume, if not always a new way of being politically or socially. The Afro bag referred not only to a new style of dress—dashiki, caftan, djellabah, African beads, bracelets, earrings, necklaces, sandals—but a new hair style. The *process* (which emulated the white's hair texture and style) gave way to the *Afro* and *natural* hair style. In the wake of the then "new Afro look," a whole industry grew up to care for it. Vernacular terms like *natural pick*, *fork*, *rake pick*, *rake* all identified the large-toothed comb used to style one's Afro, while other expressions, such as to *get your hair blowed out*, to *have your hair pulled out*, to *get your wig yanked*, referred to having the Afro professionally coiffed. In the last years, the Afro has moved over to share space with another hair style—the *corn roll*, *corn row*, or *French roll*—an intricately and decoratively braided and plaited hair style associated with Africa.

But form is not necessarily substance. And for many ghetto teenagers the new Afro look was more a new style of costuming than a new kind of social identity. But the issues of Black Power and youthful identification with it is a very complex issue.

7. Thomas Kochman (Chicago), "Glossary of Slang Terms"; Hermese E. Roberts (multiple sources), "The Third Ear: A Black Glossary"; David W. Maurer (Louisville), "Glossary of Inner City Black Terminology"; Hy Lit (Philadelphia), "Dictionary of Hip Words"; Nathan Kantrowitz (Illinois), "Statesville Names: A Prison Vocabulary"; New York Department of Corrections (New York City), "Glossary of Black Slang"; Samuel Gompers Junior High School students (San Diego), "Slang Words and Expressions and Their Meanings."

8. See Dalby's discussion of Africanisms in black English-language use in support of the notion of reclaiming words (1973). Indeed, he relies on the concept of reclaiming words to account for the African origins of some of the terms that are in contemporary usage.

9. Again, matters of respectibility and what is permissible within the house influence usage. "The house as locus of a woman's sense of respectability causes Momma to monitor constantly her own as well as others' talk" (Abrahams, 1976, p. 70).

10. Whether or not the vernacular vocabulary is actually unknown—or just generally not used—by the older female in the household and in front of her children is another issue. Children perceive older females as not using vernacular as much as their younger counterparts. In fact, older females have been shown to exhibit a command of the vernacular lexicon. As John Baugh has pointed out to me, "Some of my best informants were unwed mothers in their mid 40's. Their command of both slang and vernacular dialect was far superior to that of any of their children."

11. See Labov's classic study, 1968, of language use among black and Puerto Rican youths and the impact of peer pressure on usage.

# glossary

THE GLOSSARY THAT FOLLOWS is a concise guide for the reader's reference. It is limited to the vernacular expressions found in this book. Also, it is limited in the scope and subtlety of the definitions offered for a given entry. That is, expressions are defined as briefly as possible and only in relation to how they are used contextually in the descriptive and narrative passages of the book. In many cases, the words and phrases have other meanings as well. The standardized definition for a number of expressions is, at best, a rough approximation. In any "translation," something of the original subtlety and vitality of meaning is lost. Words in general circulation have been omitted.

Generally, the entry is listed alphabetically in the glossary just as it is found in the text rather than under the key word in the phrase. However, some expressions like to *roll/run/throw some sets* are listed under the key word, *sets, roll/run/throw some* for purposes of brevity. It is hoped that the rest of the glossary is self-explanatory.

**a.b.c.**   Abbreviation for *ace boon coon.*

**Acapulco gold**   Potent form of marijuana grown in and around Acapulco, Mexico (so called because of its high quality and its golden-brown color).

**ace**   n. 1. Best friend, close companion (one who can be trusted). 2. A single barbiturate or amphetamine-filled capsule or pill.

**ace**   adj. 1. Best. 2. Finest. 3. First, primary.

**ace boom boom, ace boon coon, ace coon, ace coon poon**   See *ace* n., **1.**

**ace-deuce to the side**   1. At an angle. 2. To the side.

**acid**   Lysergic acid diethylamide (a synthetic hallucinogenic chemical).

**act funny/the fool/the nigger**   Display childish, disruptive, or otherwise inappropriate behavior; call attention to oneself.

**action, the**   1. Exchange or interaction (especially between males and females engaged in seductive overtures). 2. Important or noteworthy events or activities of the day. 3. Whatever is occurring at the moment.

**African golf ball, African grape**   Ironic reference to watermelon.

**Afro**   Black hair style in which the hair is allowed to grow full and *nappy*.

**ain't holding no air**   1. Be unimpressive. 2. Lack credibility. 3. Possess little or no knowledge of *the streets.*

**ain't long enough**   Be insufficient (reference to money).

**ain't shit**  1. Be worthless. 2. Be untrustworthy, unreliable.

**Al Capone ride**  1. Old-model car (especially 30s and 40s models). 2. Any older-model car, with or without the latest car accessories.

**alligator**  n. 1. Any male out to *catch*. 2. Sexually active male.

**alligator**  adj. Alligator-skin.

**apple**  1. Seconal (secobarbital), barbiturate. 2. Any barbiturate compound encased in a red capsule. 3. Vagina.

**apple, apple hat**  Large-brimmed, oversized cap like those worn in the 30s and 40s.

**apples**  Breasts.

**ask for the ring**  Engage in anal intercourse.

————— **ass/assed**  Suffix used to intensify a variety of adjectival phrases: smart-ass, bad-ass, funk-ass, jive-ass, trick-ass, strong-ass, etc.

**associate**  1. Acquaintance. 2. Sometime companion.

**Astros, astro supremes**  One of several decorative wheels or wheel covers.

**Aunt Jemima**  Female counterpart of *Uncle Tom* (see *Tom*).


**B.**  Abbreviation for the Cadillac Brougham.

**B.B. head**  1. Unattractive female. 2. Unkempt female. 3. Female with short, *nappy* hair.

**baby**  1. Form of address among black males who are friends. 2. Sexually desirable member of the opposite sex.

**back-to-back**  1. Together. 2. Side-by-side.

**bad**  1. Outstanding. 2. Satisfying. 3. Formidable. 4. Stylish.

**bad-ass(ed)**  1. Mean. 2. Belligerent. 3. Worthless. 4. Shiftless (negative intensifier).

**bad-ass(ed) nigger**  1. Troublemaker. 2. Fighter. 3. Hot-tempered person. 4. General reference to a male who mistreats or demeans another, especially a female.

**bad-boy**  1. Fine. 2. Good-looking. 3. Sharp.

**bad in the head**  1. Out of control. 2. Emotionally hurt, troubled, or disoriented.

**bad man**  See *bad-ass nigger*, **1-3.**

**bad mouth**  One who talks in a provocative, belligerent, or argumentative manner. 2. One who talks badly about others.

**bad news**  Undesirable, unattractive person.

**baddest**  Very best.

**bag**  n. 1. A quantity of marijuana (so called because the marijuana is packaged in plastic food bags). 2. Life style. 3. Preference.

**bag**  v. To swallow semen or vaginal fluid during oral sex.

**baggies**  Plastic food bags used to package marijuana.

**bahama mamma**  Reference to an obese, unattractive female.

**bait**  Bad-smelling female.

**base (on one)**  Disparage, ridicule, or confront another.

**bat**  1. Unattractive female. 2. Unkempt female. 3. General reference to any female the speaker finds undesirable.

**bato, vato**  1. Chicano. 2. Any Latino.

**bato/vato loco**   Crazy-acting male (usually refers to a Latino in general and a Chicano in particular).

**bean**   1. See *bato*. 2. Benzedrine (amphetamine sulfate), stimulant produced in white, double-scored tablet form.

**bean choker**   See *bato*.

**bear, booga bear**   1. Especially unattractive female. 2. Especially unkempt female. 3. General reference to any female the speaker finds especially undesirable.

**beast**   1. See *bear*. 2. White person.

**beat the dummy**   Masturbate.

**bebopper, bopper**   1. Socially naive, inexperienced, or inept person. 2. Young or immature person. 3. General pejorative for one who is disliked by or different from the speaker.

**beef**   Penis.

**behind**   1. Because of. 2. Involved with, in sympathy with.

**benny**   1. See **bean, 2.** 2. Coat.

**Benz**   Abbreviation for Mercedes Benz automobile.

**berries, the**   Wine.

**bhani ghani**   Expression of greeting, "What's happening" (probably from the Swahili "abari gani"—"What news?").

**big John**   Police.

**billy**   1. Police. 2. Police riot stick.

**bird**   Female.

**bitch**   1. Designation for a female (positive or negative). 2. Designation for a male who is forced to engage in homosexual relations.

**black and white**   1. Police. 2. Squad car.

**black ball, black bird**   Especially dark-complected black person.

**black gungeon**   Potent form of marijuana, usually gummy in consistency (grown in Jamaica and Africa).

**black mo', black moat**   Potent form of marijuana, distinguished by its unusually dark color.

**black on black**   Car that has an all-black interior and a black paint job.

**blade**   1. Cadillac, often associated with a Coupe de Ville or Fleetwood. 2. Knife.

**blanket party**   Initiation rite in prison whereby a new inmate has a blanket thrown over him after lights out and is beaten up by others.

**blaze on (one)**   1. Hit one quickly or unexpectedly. 2. Knock one down.

**bleed**   Black person.

**blinker**   Police helicopter.

**blood**   Black person.

**blow**   1. Talk forcefully and energetically. 2. Talk seductively to a member of the opposite sex.

**blow ass**   1. Move quickly. 2. Walk fast.

**blow black/change/revolution**   Talk, write about, initiate action regarding revolutionary activity, social change, or black pride and consciousness.

**blow fire**   Perform something with particular skill and relish, such as dancing, playing an instrument, etc.

**blow gauge**   Smoke marijuana.

**blow heavy**   Convey important information (often associated with black awareness).

**blow (one) away**   1. Kill. 2. Verbally devastate. 3. Talk aggressively.

**blow (one's) mind**   1. Manipulate the behavior or feelings of another. 2. Destroy equanimity. 3. Impress. 4. Overwhelm (used in both positive and negative senses).

**blow (one's) pipes**   Race a car motor to produce loud sound through the exhaust pipes.

**blow (one's) stuff away**   1. See *base*. 2. Talk forcefully to another.

**blow some tunes**   Engage in cunnilingus.

**blowed out**   1. Coiffed. 2. Fluffed out.

**blue**   1. Amytal (amobarbital sodium), barbiturate, white powder encased in a blue capsule. 2. Police.

**blue and white**   1. Police. 2. Squad car.

**blue angel**   See *blue*, 1.

**blue boy(s)**   Police.

**blue coat(s)**   Police.

**blue-eyed soul brother/sister**   1. Designation for a white person who is in sympathy with things black. 2. White person who is accepted as a friend by blacks.

**blue gum**   See *black ball*.

**blue heaven**   See *blue*, 1.

**blunt**   1. Diluted secobarbital (barbiturate) compound encased in a blunt-ended capsule. 2. Any black-market barbiturate compound encased in blunt-ended capsules. 3. Hypodermic syringe.

**bogard/bogart**   1. Take advantage of. 2. Forcibly interfere with. 3. Take more than one's share of (especially puffs of a marijuana cigarette).

**bomb, bomber**   Very large marijuana cigarette.

**bone**   Penis.

**bone, clean/fonky/mod/ragged/sharp/silked/tabbed to the**   Exceptionally well-dressed.

**boo**   Marijuana.

**boobus**   Small or flat breasts.

**boogers**   Nasal discharge.

**boogie**   Engage in sexual intercourse.

**boojie, bojie, boochie**   1. Bourgeois black person. 2. Upwardly mobile black person.

**boot**   Black person (derogatory).

**booty**   1. Female body. 2. Vagina.

**bop**   Thoughtless or foolish talk.

**borders, border reds**   Noncommercially compounded capsules of secobarbital or other barbiturate compounds encased in red capsules.

**bounce**   Set the body of a car in motion so that it bounces up and down.

**bounce (on one's) lifts**   Outdo or show off by rapidly and dramatically moving the body of a car up and down through the use of hydraulic lifts.

**boy**   Heroin.

**brand X**   Marijuana.

**cock-of-the-walk stride** Style of walking where the person bobs up and down and moves from side to side.

**cock pluck** Manually stimulate a female's genitalia.

**coke stare** 1. Evil look. 2. See *evil eye*.

**cold** 1. Unnecessary, uncalled for. 2. Belligerent. 3. Nasty. 4. Difficult. 5. Fine, exceptional.

**cold case** 1. Bad situation. 2. Particularly strong rebuke.

**cold shot** Uncalled for or belligerent behavior.

**color bar** Electronic color band that connects to a car radio or tape deck and creates different patterns and colors in response to the different frequencies emitted from the electronic source.

**color guard** See *caution sign*.

**come down** Physiologically or emotionally lose the effects of a *high*.

**come down fonky; come down hard (on one)** Confront or assault.

**come up** Grow up (place of residence).

**cook** See *blow fire*.

**cool** 1. Fine, outstanding. 2. Under control. 3. Aware, knowledgeable.

**cop** 1. Secure. 2. Steal. 3. Negotiate.

**cop a block** Come around a street quickly or abruptly, especially with the intention of *catching*.

**cop out** 1. Desert. 2. Inform the police.

**corn rolls/rows** Black hair style in which the hair is intricately braided and plaited with ribbons, baubles, etc.

**corroded** Unattractive, unappealing.

**cotton** Female pubic hair.

**Coupe** Reference to Cadillac Coupe de Ville.

**cow** 1. Female (derogatory). 2. Obese female.

**cowboy** n. and v. See *bad-ass nigger*, **1-3**.

**crack (jokes) on (one)** See *cap*, **2-3**.

**cracker** White person (derogatory).

**Cragers, Crager mags** Reference to a wide variety of decorative wheels and wheel covers produced by the Crager company.

**creep** 1. Be someplace one doesn't belong, especially with another's mate or lover. 2. Cheat on one's mate. 3. Engage in any kind of illicit, suspicious behavior. 4. Drive slowly, often with only parking lights on. 5. Sneak up on someone, often with assault or robbery in mind. 6. Steal away.

**crib** Place of residence (apartment, house, etc.).

**crinkle top** Black female with an *Afro* or *natural* hair style.

**cripple** 1. Poor athlete. 2. Any physically uncoordinated person.

**crowd (one)** 1. Physically assault. 2. Overwhelm or pressure. 3. Gang up on.

**crumbsnatcher** Baby.

**crutch** Some implement for holding the butt end of a marijuana cigarette.

**cubes** Morphine, natural alkaloid of opium.

**cuff** Hit, fight.

**culture fruit** See *African grape*.

**cum freak** See *cock hound*.

**cut** 1. Reduce the potency of, dilute (as in drugs). 2. Stab. 3. Verbally disparage or harass.

**cut a side**   Engage in sexual intercourse.

**cut (one) loose**   1. End a relationship with. 2. Let go of, release (literally and psychologically).

**cut (something) loose**   1. Give up something. 2. Free oneself.

**cutthroat**   See *bad-ass nigger*, **1-3.**

**cutty, cutting man**   See *ace*, n., **1.**

**cuz**   1. Friend or acquaintance. 2. Form of address, especially among black males (abbreviation for cousin).

**D.V.**   Abbreviation for Cadillac Coupe de Ville.

**dad**   Form of address among black males.

**daddy**   Form of address for a male mate, lover, etc.

**daddy one**   1. Male who provides for a female. 2. Female's lover or mate.

**dagger**   Lesbian.

**dairies**   Breasts.

**dance, dance on (one's) lifts**   See *bounce on (one's) lifts*.

**dance on (one's) lips**   1. Hit about the face and mouth. 2. Kick in the face.

**dap daddy**   Well-dressed male.

**dap(ped) down**   Well-dressed.

**dap(ped) to a tee**   Exceptionally well-dressed.

**dead**   1. Uninteresting, unexciting. 2. Devoid of heart or vitality.

**deal**   Sell drugs or marijuana.

**deal in dirt, do dirt**   1. Gossip. 2. Talk badly (about another).

**decked out**   1. Well-dressed. 2. Decorated. 3. Equipped.

**decked to death, decked to kill**   Exceptionally well-dressed.

**deputy do-right**   Police.

**destroyed**   Excessively *high*.

**deuce**   Two barbiturate or amphetamine pills or capsules.

**deuce 25, deuce and a quarter**   1. Buick 225. 2. Any car with a 225-horse-power engine.

**devil, the**   White person (especially derogatory).

**diamonds**   Diamond-shaped car window design.

**diaper**   Sanitary napkin.

**diaper the baby**   Put on a sanitary napkin.

**diddybopper**   1. One who is pretentious or pompous (often refers to up-wardly mobile black person who identifies with white mainstream culture). 2. Black person who lives in a middle-class neighborhood. 3. Immature or socially inexperienced person.

**didn't catch shit**   Didn't impress anyone.

**dig (on one); dig (one's) action**   1. Like, appreciate one's style, behavior, etc. 2. Be attracted to. 3. Enjoy. 4. Stare at, pay close attention to. 5. Look intently, especially at one of the opposite sex.

**dike**   Lesbian.

**Dillinger front**   Style of dress associated with the gangster look of the 30s.

**dime bag**   Ten-dollar plastic bag's worth of marijuana.

**dinosaur**   Penis.

**dip the fly**   Engage in sexual intercourse.

**dirt farm**   1. Source of gossip. 2. Place where gossip occurs.

**dirty dozens**   Ritualized or spontaneous insults directed at another's mother or sometimes other relatives.

**divine right**   Police.

**do**   Hair-do.

**do-it fluid**   Liquor.

**do (one)**   1. Disparage or harass. 2. Physically assault. 3. Take advantage of.

**do (one's) thing**   Do whatever gives one pleasure or satisfaction, regardless of its acceptability to others.

**do the finger**   Hold up the middle finger at the same time one bends down the other fingers in a gesture that means "fuck you."

**do the do/nasty/natural thing/pussy/thing**   Engage in sexual intercourse.

**Dodge City**   Reference to the black community in Venice, California (so-called because many consider it to be a tough part of town).

**dog, (dirty)**   1. Any male who mistreats or demeans another (often used by females in reference to males). 2. Bad or evil-tempered male. 3. Male who aggressively pursues sexual relations with a number of women (implies infidelity).

**dog food**   Heroin.

**dog fuck**   Engage in anal intercourse.

**dog juice**   Cheap liquor, especially wine.

**doggy**   1. Hard. 2. Mean. 3. Unfeeling.

**don't hold no air**   1. Doesn't carry weight or impact. 2. Doesn't talk or act sensibly.

**don't give no slack**   Doesn't allow for any chance or consideration.

**Don't let your mouth overload your ass; don't let your mouth write a check your ass can't cash**   Don't talk too much, in such a belligerent manner, or there's going to be a fight.

**doogie daddy**   Well-dressed male.

**double clutch**   General reference to taking more than one's share of a marijuana cigarette in a group situation.

**double punch**   Severely beat.

**doughnut (wheel)**   Small, car steering wheel, approximately seven inches in diameter.

**down, downer**   1. Any barbiturate. 2. Any pill or capsule that produces a narcotic state.

**down**   1. Prepared, ready. 2. Very well. 3. Knowledgeable.

**down in (one's) silks**   Dressed in silk clothes.

**down (one's) shit**   Knock one down or out cold.

**down with**   1. Knowledgeable about. 2. Involved with.

**dozens, the**   Ritualized or spontaneous insults directed most often at another's mother (the *dirty dozens*) or an opponent (the *clean dozens*; see also *cap*).

**Dr. Thomas**   1. Bourgeois black person. 2. Black person who has taken on white middle-class values.

**drapes**   Clothes.

**dress(ed) down/tight**   Very well-dressed.

**dribble**   See *bounce*.

**drink at the fuzzy cup**   Engage in cunnilingus.

**drive on (one)**  Hit one quickly or unexpectedly.

**drive to the bridge**  Move quickly and aggressively to score points in a basketball game.

**drop**  1. Take. 2. Ingest (usually refers to drugs).

**drop a dime**  1. Inform the police. 2. Set up for a police arrest.

**drop a rack/roll**  Ingest three to five pills or capsules, containing any variety of drugs.

**drop lugs on (one)**  See *cap*, **2-3**.

**drop (one)**  See *down (one's) shit*.

**drop, drop (one's) ride**  Outdo or show off by dramatically or suddenly dropping the body of a car to the ground with hydraulic lifts.

**dubee**  Marijuana cigarette.

**duck's butt**  Female with unkempt hair.

**duckhead**  See *B. B. head*.

**dude**  Term of address for a male—like "guy" in general slang.

**dump on**  Disparage or ridicule with particular force.

**dust (one)**  See *down (one's) shit*.


**El D.**  Abbreviation for Cadillac El Dorado.

**easy ride**  Sexually promiscuous female.

**eat a fur burger**  Engage in cunnilingus.

**eat out**  Engage in cunnilingus.

**eat pie**  Engage in cunnilingus.

**Elvis (Presley), the**  Hair style that emulates Elvis Presley's (slicked straight back from the forehead).

**ese**  See *bato*.

**ese bato, ese vacho, ese vato**  Reference to a Latino the speaker considers *cool*.

**evil**  1. Mean. 2. Violent. 3. Worthless.

**evil eye**  Look capable of jinxing another.

**evil ways**  1. Bad habits. 2. Inappropriate behaviors.

**eyeball**  See *dig on (one)*, **4**.


**F-40(s), 40(s)**  Seconal, 1.5 grain secobarbital (so called because of the pharmaceutical letter and number stamped on the capsule for identification).

**F-60(s)**  Histadyl, three-quarter grain.

**F-66(s)**  Tuinal, 1.5 grain amo- with secobarbital.

**fake on (one)**  Ignore.

**fall by**  Drop by.

**fall on (one)**  See *drop (one's) ride*.

**fall out**  Laugh uncontrollably.

**fall out in**  Be dressed in.

**fast-talking Charlie**  1. Jew. 2. Anyone perceived to be Jewish.

**fat mouth**  n. See *bad mouth*.

**fat mouth**  v. Argue, talk back.

**feel froggy**  Feel like fighting.

**Felipe**  See *bato*.

**fender bender(s)**   See *down, downer*, **2**.

**fiend (on one)**   1. See *drop (one's) ride*. 2. Outdo or best another in any variety of ways. 3. Show off what you have and who you are.

**fiendish**   See *bad*.

**fiendishly**   Especially (often used as positive intensifier).

**fifty-cent bag**   Fifty-dollar plastic bag's worth of marijuana.

**filling station**   Liquor store.

**fine**   1. Outstanding, exceptional. 2. Stylish. 3. Especially good-looking.

**fine as wine**   Response to a good-looking, sexually appealing male or female.

**fire**   Attempt a basketball shot.

**fire (on one)**   1. See *blaze on (one)*. 2. Disparage, ridicule or confront. 3. Shoot.

**fire power**   Physical or mental strength and ability.

**fire up**   Light up a marijuana cigarette.

**fish**   1. Female. 2. See *bebopper*. 3. One who is easily duped or confounded.

**fist junction**   Point at which a fight begins.

**fittin', fixin'**   1. About to, ready to. 2. Intend to.

**five-and-dime**   1. Small-time. 2. Not classy.

**fix**   Inject (a drug).

**flairs**   Flair-legged pants.

**flake (out)**   1. Pass out. 2. Fall asleep, sometimes for an extended period of time (drug-related).

**flash**   1. Conspicuously display a large amount of money. 2. Show off whatever one has.

**flat head**   See *blunt*, **1-2**.

**flesh hound**   See *cock hound*.

**flick**   1. Small knife. 2. Razor blade with one side heavily taped (used as a weapon).

**Flip**   Filipino person.

**flood**   Have an erection.

**fluff**   Vagina.

**fly, fly high in the sky**   Be especially *high*.

**folks**   1. Black people. 2. Kin.

**fonked out heavy**   Exceptionally well-dressed.

**fonky, funky**   1. Positive or negative intensifier, depending on what it modifies (widely used in conversation). 2. Unusually fine, good. 3. Bad-smelling. 4. Good-smelling.

**fool**   See *fish*, **2-3**.

**for days**   1. Indicates extended period of time or great degree ("That dude was loaded for days!"). 2. Indicates a sense of the ultimate ("That chick is foxy for days!").

**fork**   Wide-toothed comb designed for combing and styling an *Afro* or *natural* hair-do.

**foul**   1. Unnecessary. 2. Belligerent. 3. Ruthless.

**foul mouth**   See *bad mouth*.

**four sisters on thumb street**   Masturbation.

**fox**   Very attractive, sexually appealing female.

**foxy** Sexy, attractive.

**freak** n. 1. Male or female homosexual. 2. Enthusiast.

**freak** v. 1. Outdo in a variety of ways. 2. Show off whatever you have.

**freak fuck** 1. Engage in anal intercourse with a female. 2. Engage in cunnulingus.

**freak off** 1. Engage in unconventional sex. 2. Masturbate. 3. Engage in homosexual relations.

**freak off (something)** Decorate or fix up something in a lavish manner.

**freak out** 1. Lose control. 2. Engage in wild or bizarre behavior. 3. Have a particularly fine time.

**freeway Freddy** 1. California Highway Patrol. 2. Any police in a patrol car.

**freeze on (something)** Discontinue use of, avoid.

**freeze, the** The "cold shoulder."

**French rolls/rows** See *corn rolls*.

**fresh hide** New sexual partner.

**frick and frack** Testicles.

**fried** Excessively *high*.

**fried, dyed, combed/swooped to the side** Reference to straightened hair which emulates white hair texture, styling, and sometimes color.

**'fro** Abbreviation for *Afro*.

**froggy** 1. Belligerent. 2. Out-of-line.

**front** 1. Personal image presented to others. 2. Facade.

**front off** Outdo, show off what one has or what one is.

**fronts** Clothes, especially a suit or sports jacket.

**frozen** Excessively *high*.

**fruit** Male homosexual.

**fuck up (one's) pussy** See *cock block*.

**fucked up** Excessively *high*.

**fuck with (one's) mind** See *blow (one's) mind*, 1-2.

**funny** Homosexual.

**funny money** Limited amount of money.

**funny style, a** 1. Anyone who is unusual or somehow different from the speaker. 2. Male homosexual.

**fuzz** Police.

**fuzz, fuzz head** See *B.B. head*.

**g** 1. Abbreviation for "goodies," sexually desirable parts of a female's body. 2. Vagina.

**GFC** Abbreviation for Godfather Crips (a gang in Los Angeles).

**game (on one)** 1. Manipulate the behavior or feelings of another. 2. Outdo.

**game, the** 1. A *hustle* to reap financial, material, or psychological benefits. 2. Survival. 3. Act of seducing/winning the favor of another.

**gang-bang** Fight.

**gang-banger** 1. Fighter. 2. Troublemaker.

**gangster** 1. Marijuana. 2. Troublemaker. 3. Physically aggressive or abusive person. 4. Any person associated with gangsterlike behavior.

**gangster doors** Four-door sedan.

**gangster fronts**  Style of dress associated with the gangster.

**gangster ride**  1. Old-model car. 2. Any big car, especially one painted black.

**gangster stick**  Marijuana cigarette.

**gangster walls**  Wide white-walled tires.

**gas**  Enjoy, have a good time.

**gash**  Vagina.

**gauge**  Marijuana.

**geechie, geech**  n. 1. See *buckwheat*. 2. Black person who speaks in the Gullah dialect (associated with the Sea Islands off the coast of South Carolina and Georgia). 3. Any black person whose speech is peculiar or unintelligible to the hearer.

**geechie**  adj. 1. Unusual. 2. Unintelligible.

**geek**  1. Weird, unusual, or different person. 2. Studious person.

**geeze**  Inject drugs (usually refers to heroin).

**gestaps, gestapo(s)**  Police.

**get a shot of leg**  Engage in sexual intercourse.

**get across**  1. Succeed in life. 2. Acquire status. 3. Talk seductively and persuasively to a member of the opposite sex. 4. Get one to agree to sexual relations.

**get an understanding**  Establish a close, trusting relationship.

**get beautiful**  Get *high*.

**get behind**  1. Get involved with. 2. Get interested in.

**get business**  Succeed in life.

**get deep in (one's) ass**  1. Fight. 2. Beat severely.

**get down, get down to the ground**  1. Do something exceptionally well. 2. Engage in something with great zest. 3. Initiate some activity. 4. Conduct serious business.

**get down dirty/fonky/foul/shitty**  1. Become particularly abusive. 2. Cause trouble.

**get down from the Y**  Fight.

**get down to the natural thing**  Engage in sexual intercourse.

**get down with**  1. Enjoy. 2. Get involved with.

**get funny**  1. Engage in unpredictable or disruptive behavior. 2. Start something dangerous or threatening.

**get high**  Experience the physiological and psychological effects of drugs, alcohol, marijuana, etc.

**get in (one's) eye**  1. Fight. 2. Beat severely.

**get it on**  Initiate some activity.

**get low**  Drive or ride in a car so that only the tops of the occupants' heads are visible from the outside (*low riding*).

**get off**  Begin to feel the impact of a particular drug or substance.

**get on (one's) case**  See *base*.

**get on (one's) job/j.o.b.**  Attend to *business*.

**get (one's) act/game/self together**  Assert control over one's life (financial, emotional, situational, etc.).

**get (one's) nose cold**  Get *high* from cocaine.

**get over**  See *get across*.

**get some big leg/cock/leg/pussy/soft leg/tail**   Engage in sexual intercourse.

**get some booty**   1. Engage in sexual intercourse. 2. Engage a male in anal intercourse.

**get some brown/tight eye**   Engage in anal intercourse with another male.

**get some brown sugar/sweet**   Engage in sexual intercourse with a male.

**get some duke**   1. Engage in anal intercourse with another male. 2. Engage in sexual intercourse.

**get with**   1. Get in step with. 2. Find out about.

**ghost town**   Reference to the black community in Venice, California.

**gigolo**   1. Steal away another's mate or lover. 2. Cheat on one's mate.

**girl**   1. Form of emphatic address used when conversing with a female (used to focus attention on what a speaker is saying, often used in a playful manner). 2. Cocaine. 3. Male homosexual.

**git-go, get-go**   Beginning.

**Give me five (on the sly); give me five (on the soul side)!**   Signal for the slapping of palms—usually between two black men—as a way of greeting or congratulating each other.

**give head**   Engage in oral sex.

**give her the jam pot**   Engage in sexual intercourse.

**give it up**   Agree to have sexual intercourse.

**give the Man the play**   Inform the police about another's activities or moves.

**go down**   Happen.

**go down (with)**   1. Help out a friend in trouble, especially when a fight is imminent. 2. Fight.

**go down wrong**   Turn out badly.

**go from the fists/shoulders/Y**   Fight.

**go head up**   Engage in any kind of activity with another.

**go through (some) changes**   Undergo intense or difficult emotional experiences, life situations, etc.

**go to fist junction**   Fight.

**go upside (one's) head**   1. Hit in the face and head. 2. Beat up.

**Goldberg, Goldstein**   See *fast-talking Charlie.*

**golden girl**   1. High-grade cocaine. 2. Attractive female.

**gone**   1. Unconscious. 2. Incoherent. 3. Physically or psychologically dysfunctional.

**good hair**   1. Straight hair. 2. Soft, loosely curled hair.

**goodies**   1. See *g.* 2. Vagina.

**goon squad**   Police.

**gorilla**   n. 1. See *bad-ass nigger*, **1-3**. 2. Incorrigible.

**gorilla**   v. 1. Severely beat. 2. Rape.

**gorilla in the washing machine, a**   Cunnilingus.

**grapes, the**   1. Breasts. 2. Wine.

**gray**   White person.

**gray boy(s)**   White male.

**gray dog**   Police.

**green**   Money.

**greens, collard greens**   1. Marijuana. 2. Money.

**grind**   Engage in sexual intercourse.

**groove**   n. Life style, interest, way of thinking or acting.

**groove**   v. Get involved with.

**gumdrop**   1. Seconal (secobarbital), barbiturate. 2. Any kind of drug in tablet or capsule form.

**gun**   1. Look for trouble. 2. Look for an enemy. 3. Shoot a basketball an unnecessary number of times during a game (suggests missing shots).

**gunny**   Marijuana.

**guns**   Breasts.

**gunzel**   Fight.

**hair, conk/fry/gas/press (one's)**   Straighten one's hair.

**half moons**   Small wheel covers that do not cover the entire wheel surface.

**half step**   Display inappropriate, ineffectual or uninformed behavior.

**hammers**   Female thighs.

**ham hocks, hocks**   Female legs and ankles.

**handkerchief head**   Female equivalent of a *Tom*.

**happenings, the**   1. Important, interesting, or vital daily activities, experiences, or situations (often linked to one's ability to survive in the world). 2. The *action*.

**happy grass**   Marijuana.

**hard (fast) and heavy**   With considerable force and effect (used as an intensifier).

**hardhead**   See *bad-ass nigger*, **1-3.**

**hardmouth**   See *bad mouth.*

**have a good/natural feeling**   Engage in satisfying sexual relations.

**have a ring through (one's) nose**   Be emotionally or sexually obsessed with another.

**have a sack lunch**   Engage in cunnilingus.

**have a thing/something going; have an understanding**   Be involved in a close, trusting relationship.

**have it covered/together**   1. Be in control. 2. Have it taken care of.

**have (one's) act/game/program/shit together; have (one's) game uptight**   Have control over one's life (financial, emotional, situational, etc.).

**have (one's) nose; have (one's) nose wide open**   Have another blindly in love or infatuated.

**have papers**   Be married.

**have the slows**   Be excessively *high.*

**head**   1. Any black male. 2. See *bad-ass nigger*, **1-3.**

**head got bad**   1. Got out of line. 2. Lost control.

**head hunt**   Look for trouble.

**head not right**   1. Disoriented, upset, vulnerable. 2. Excessively *high.*

**head up**   See *back-to-back.*

**headlights**   Breasts.

**heat, the**   Police.

**heat the springs**   Heat the springs in a car so that the body of the car is permanently lowered.

**heavy**   1. Profound. 2. Important. 3. Knowledgeable. 4. Steady.

**heavy into**   Deeply involved with.

**heavy knowledge**   Important or wise information (reference to survival, street life, black identity, etc.).

**heavyweight**   1. Person whose ideas or observations have depth and meaning. 2. Person who has succeeded in life.

**heifer**   See *cow*.

**hen**   See *B.B. head*.

**herb(s)**   Marijuana.

**high, a**   State of being exhilarated, peaceful, etc. (with or without drugs, alcohol, or other substances).

**high**   Experiencing the effects (physiological, psychological, spiritual) of drugs, alcohol, or other substances.

**high-and-goodbye**   Unreliable, untrustworthy.

**high sign**   n. Special colors, sign, or greeting that designate group or gang affiliation.

**high sign**   v. See *front off*.

**high water(s)**   Erection.

**high yellow**   See *casper*.

**hincty**   1. Pretentious. 2. Aloof, "stuck-up" (often refers to blacks who identify with white values).

**hip**   1. Knowledgeable. 2. Street-wise. 3. Self-possessed. 4. Articulate.

**hip (one)**   See *break it down*.

**hit, a**   Puff of a marijuana cigarette.

**hit on**   Approach, usually with a request for something.

**hit some shit**   Encounter some difficult situations or people.

**'ho**   General designation (and pronunciation) for a whore.

**hog**   1. Cadillac. 2. Obese female.

**hog(s), the**   Police.

**hold no weight**   1. Be unimpressive. 2. Lack credibility. 3. Possess little or no knowledge of *the streets*.

**hold (one's) high**   Maintain physical and emotional control when under the influence of drugs, alcohol, etc.

**hole**   Vagina.

**holler**   Disparage, ridicule, or confront with particular force.

**Hollywood swoop**   Car maneuver in which one car cuts abruptly in front of others across several lanes of traffic.

**hombug, humbug**   n. 1. False arrest. 2. Bad situation. 3. Fight.

**hombug, humbug**   v. 1. Deceive. 2. Manipulate. 3. Fight.

**home squeeze**   Lover or mate.

**homeboy/homegirl**   1. One who spends much time at home. 2. One who is under the domination and control of the mother. 3. Local inhabitant, neighborhood person. 4. Friend. 5. Black male/female.

**honky, honky beast**   White person (especially derogatory).

**hood, hoodlum**   See *bad-ass nigger*, **1-3**.

**hook (nose), hook (face)**   See *fast-talking Charlie*.

**hoopdie swoop**   Execute a fast pick up of a female or male.

**hope-to-die**   1. Closest. 2. Best.

**hors d'oeuvre(s)**   Seconal or other barbiturates or amphetamines encased in capsules.

**horse**  Heroin.

**hound**  See *bear*.

**hully**  Obese person.

**hump, hump ass**  Engage in sexual intercourse.

**hung out**  1. Addicted to. 2. Obsessed with.

**hung up**  Involved with.

**hurt**  1. Ugly. 2. Excessively *high*.

**hurtin' for certain**  Ugly.

**hustle**  1. Any one of several activities—legal or otherwise—where one uses wits, skills, or personality to gain financial and psychological rewards. 2. Sexual overture toward a member of the opposite sex. (Also used as a verb.)

**ice**  Kill.

**ignite oil**  Whiskey or any liquor.

**irvine, irv**  Police.

**it**  Quintessence of things black; the indefinable spirit, vitality, heart of a person or thing or event.

**j**  Abbreviation for *joint*, marijuana cigarette.

**J. Edgar (Hoover)**  Police.

**Jack**  Form of address among black males (used emphatically or as verbal punctuation).

**jack up (one)**  1. Physically assault. 2. Surprise with a sudden approach or attack. 3. Overpower. 4. Engage in sexual intercourse.

**jam**  n. 1. Female's genitalia. 2. Attractive female.

**jam**  v. 1. Play a musical instrument with great vitality and feeling (often refers to a spontaneous exchange with other musicians). 2. Engage in sexual intercourse.

**jam (one up)**  1. Beat severely. 2. Talk forcefully. 3. Overpower. 4. Rape.

**Jamaica red**  Type of marijuana said to be grown in Jamaica (so called because of its reddish-brown color).

**jar**  Quantity of pills or capsules, usually 500 to 1000.

**jasper**  Lesbian.

**jazz**  Engage in sexual intercourse.

**jelly, jellyroll**  1. Female's genitalia. 2. Attractive female.

**jelly sandwich**  Sanitary napkin.

**jellybean**  See *candy*, **2**.

**jib**  Talk.

**jiblet**  See *apple*, **1**.

**jibs, jaw at the/run off at the**  1. Talk too much. 2. Engage in foolish or irrelevant talk.

**jitterbug**  1. See *bebopper*. 2. One who talks too much or talks nonsense.

**jitterbug (one's ride)**  1. Rapidly move the body of a car up and down with hydraulic lifts. 2. See *bounce*.

**jive**  1. Nonsense. 2. Thoughtless or foolish talk. 3. Improper behavior.

**jive (around)**  1. Talk nonsense. 2. Deceive, confound. 3. Fool around. 4. Act improperly or foolishly.

**jive (ass)**  1. Phony. 2. Deceitful. 3. Foolish. 4. Untrustworthy. 5. Boastful.

*243*

6. Insignificant (general negative intensifier).

**jive nigger, jive turkey**   One who *jives*.

**john**   Male who is easily duped or exploited, especially by females.

**Johnny-be-good**   Police.

**joint**   1. Marijuana cigarette. 2. Penis.

**joker**   See *fish*, **2-3**.

**jones**   1. Drug habit. 2. Marijuana cigarette.

**joy**   Marijuana.

**ju-ju(s)**   See *gum drop*.

**juana**   Marijuana.

**Judy with the big booty**   An obese female.

**juice house**   Liquor store.

**jump steady**   Liquor.

**jump up and down**   Engage in sexual intercourse.

**junior flip**   See *bebopper*.

**Junior Walker and the All-Stars**   Police.

**Juvie**   Abbreviation for Juvenile Hall.

**keep on top of the game**   1. Maintain control. 2. Survive in the world.

**keep (one's) head cool/right**   Maintain physical and emotional control over self.

**Kennedy swoop**   Hair style emulating that of the Kennedys, straightened and combed to the side.

**key**   Abbreviation for kilo, quantity of marijuana (c. 2.2 pounds).

**kick back**   Relax, enjoy.

**Kick me down/out with . . .**   "Let me have . . ."

**kicks**   Shoes.

**killing floor**   Any place used to engage in sexual intercourse.

**kitty, kitty-cat**   1. Cadillac. 2. Female.

**knobs**   Breasts.

**knock it out**   Engage in sexual intercourse.

**knuckles**   Brass knuckles.

**L.I.Q.**   Abbreviation for liquor store, liquor.

**laid to the natural bone**   Naked.

**lame, lame brain**   1. Socially inexperienced person. 2. One who has little or no knowledge of *the streets*. 3. One who commands little or no respect from others. 4. Immature or young person. 5. One who is uncoordinated. 6. General reference to anyone who is disliked by or different from the speaker.

**Later (on) for it**   "I can't be bothered."

**lay back/low/up**   1. Relax. 2. Do nothing in particular. 3. Engage in sexual intercourse.

**lay dead**   1. Do nothing. 2. Stop everything.

**lay down**   Acquiesce.

**lay down some sparks**   Depart abruptly in a car so that some portion of the car frame or body comes in contact with the street surface and gives off a series of sparks.

**lay it on**   See *break it down*.

**Lay me down with . . .** "Let me have . . ."

**lay (some) pipe** Engage in sexual intercourse.

**lay (some) rubber/wheels** Drive off abruptly so that tires spin, rubber is burned off, or tire tracks are left in the wake.

**lean** 1. Style of driving a car in which the driver leans toward the right-hand side of the car as if resting on a console or arm rest while maneuvering the car with the left hand. 2. Style of riding in a car wherein the occupant leans toward the driver as if resting the left elbow on a console.

**lean on (one)** Disparage or ridicule.

**Leap and you will receive** Challenge to a fight: "Come and get it."

**leather, leather piece** Leather or leatherlike jacket.

**leeky store** Liquor store.

**Let me hold some change** Request for money.

**let (one's) game slip** Lose control.

**lid** Quantity of marijuana (c. one ounce).

**lifted** Raised (body of a car).

**lifts** Hydraulic lifts installed in a car so that the body can be raised and lowered by an interior electrical switching system.

**lighten up** 1. Stop. 2. Calm down.

**lightfoot, lightweight** 1. One who lacks prominence or credibility. 2. One with little or no knowledge of *the streets*.

**like to** Almost.

**Lilly, Lilly F-40** Seconal, 1.5 grain secobarbital (so called because of the company and its capsule numbering).

**lily** White person.

**lines** 1. Words. 2. Smooth conversation. 3. Seductive or persuasive talk aimed at winning over a member of the opposite sex.

**little boy blue** Police.

**little pretty** Attractive male.

**lizards** Lizard-skin shoes.

**loaded** Extremely *high*.

**long bread/green/money** Lots of money.

**lose (one's) cool** Lose control.

**low-life** 1. Mean. 2. Belligerent.

**low ride** n. 1. Car whose body has been permanently lowered. 2. Car whose body can be raised and lowered through the use of lifts.

**low-ride** v. 1. Drive or ride in a car in a highly stylized manner where the occupants sit low in their seats so that only the tops of their heads are visible from the outside. 2. Drive a car equipped with hydraulic lifts or whose back or front end has been lowered (see also *lean*).

**lug** See *cap*, **2-3**.

**M and M(s)** See *gumdrop*.

**mack, the** Seductive, manipulative talk aimed at winning favor with a member of the opposite sex.

**mack man** Equivalent to *pimp*.

**mack on/to (one)** 1. Make verbal advances toward a member of the opposite sex. 2. Talk seductively to a member of the opposite sex.

**mad dog**  See *gorilla*, n.

**maharishee**  Marijuana.

**main bitch/'ho/stuff**  1. Male's favorite or most frequent sexual partner. 2. Male's mate, lover, girlfriend.

**main man**  1. See *ace*, n. **1.** 2. Female's lover, mate, boyfriend.

**main squeeze**  1. See *main man*. 2. Male's favorite or most frequent sexual partner. 3. Male's mate, lover, girlfriend.

**maintain (one's cool)**  See *keep (one's) head cool/right*.

**make a sandwich**  Two males engage in simultaneous sex (vaginal and anal) with the same female.

**make (one) right**  Feel good (especially from getting *high*).

**make the fist**  Raise a clenched fist in the Black Power salute.

**mallet**  Police.

**man, my**  See *ace*, n. **1.** (form of address between black males that connotes positive feelings between the two).

**Man, the**  Any white who is seen to be in a position of power or authority over blacks.

**man with a paper ass**  1. One whose ideas possess little import. 2. One who talks too much or foolishly.

**Man with the fuzzy balls**  Any white man (claim is that the term *fuzz* derived from this expression).

**mariweegee**  Marijuana.

**marks**  Needle marks left on the body from repeated use of a hypodermic syringe.

**maryanne**  Marijuana.

**maryjane**  Marijuana.

**mash the fat**  Engage in sexual intercourse.

**match**  Abbreviation for matchbox, a quantity of marijuana (c. one half ounce).

**mean**  See *bad*.

**meat**  1. Penis. 2. Vagina. 3. Female.

**mellow**  n. 1. Good friend. 2. Favorite lover, girl/boyfriend.

**mellow**  adj. 1. Contented. 2. Feeling good.

**mellow yellow**  See *casper*.

**melted butter**  1. Attractive female. 2. See *casper*.

**member**  Another black person.

**Mercedes**  Reference to a female body type—elegant, well-constructed, medium-size.

**mess up (one)**  1. Disparage or ridicule. 2. Physically assault. 3. Beat severely.

**mess up (one's) action/game/play/style**  See *cock block*.

**mess with**  1. Interfere with. 2. Get involved with. 3. Bother. 4. Play around with.

**mess up (one's) mind**  See *blow (one's) mind*, **1-2.**

**mess with nature**  1. Interfere with the ability to have sex. 2. Render oneself temporarily impotent.

**messed up**  1. Extremely *high*. 2. Confused. 3. Diverted from what is good or appropriate.

**metal flake**  Special paint applied to a car to give it an iridescent effect.

**Metro(s)**   Metropolitan police.

**Mex**   See *bato*.

**Mexican green**   Type of marijuana (not known for great potency, identifiable by its light green color).

**mickey, a**   Small bottle of wine.

**midnight the cat**   See *black ball*.

**mind-fuck**   See *blow (one's) mind*, **1-2**.

**Miss Amy**   Young white female.

**Miss Lillian**   White female.

**mod**   1. stylish/stylishly. 2. Up-to-date (in dress). 3. Comfortably (dressed).

**mod bag**   Modish or contemporary costuming, the latest style of dress.

**mod squad**   Young undercover police, either on the streets or on school campuses.

**momma**   1. Term of address for any female. 2. A lover, mate, girlfriend. 3. Mother.

**momma's game, the**   See *dirty dozens*.

**moms**   Mother.

**money ain't long enough; money gets/got funny**   1. Money isn't sufficient. 2. Short on funds.

**moons**   Wheel covers for car tires that are smooth and moonshaped.

**morph**   Abbreviation for morphine (see *cubes*).

**mother nature, mother nature's own (tobacco)**   Marijuana.

**motherfucker, muthafucka, mother, motha, ma'fa', ma, m.f., fucker**   Ubiquitous label used for dramatic, emotional, emphatic effect in conversation (can be positive, neutral, or negative).

**mount**   n. Sexually promiscuous female.

**mount**   v. Engage in sexual intercourse.

**move on (one)**   See *fire (on one)*, **1-2**.

**Mr. Cracker**   1. White male (derogatory). 2. Jimmy Carter.

**Mr. Do-you-wrong**   Any man who mistreats or demeans a female.

**Mr. Hombug**   1. School security officer. 2. Security police in general.

**Mr. Money**   See *fast-talking Charlie*.

**Mr. Peanut**   1. White male. 2. Jimmy Carter.

**Mr. Sin**   Vice squad officer.

**Mr. Thomas**   1. Bourgeois black person. 2. Black person who has taken on white middle-class values (see also *Tom*).

**muddy waters**   Loss of erection.

**mulat**   See *casper*.

**musty**   1. Bad-smelling. 2. Dirty.

**nail-em-and-jail-em**   Police.

**nail head**   See *B.B. head*.

**Nam black/shit/weed**   Particularly potent form of marijuana grown in Viet Nam and other parts of Southeast Asia, distinguished by its dark color.

**nappy**   Kinky or wooly head hair.

**narc(s), narco(s)**   Narcotics officer.

**nasty, the**   Sexual intercourse.

**natch**   Abbreviation for *natural*.

**natural** 1. Modified *Afro*. 2. Any natural, unstraightened hair.

**natural (born)** 1. Earthy. 2. Real.

**natural-born man** 1. Heterosexual male. 2. Good lover. 3. Down-to-earth, vital male.

**natural pick** See *fork*.

**natural woman** 1. Heterosexual female. 2. Good lover.

**negro** Ironic or sarcastic reference to a *Tom* (usually pejorative).

**nickle-dime** 1. Small-time. 2. Low-class. 3. Insignificant.

**nigger** Form of address and identification among blacks (can connote affection, playful derision, genuine anger, or mere identification of another black person; often used emphatically in conversation).

**nigger, bad-ass(ed)/dog/no-account/nickle-dime** Various references to the male who mistreats or demeans another (often used by females in describing certain males). See *dog*, (*dirty*).

**nigger flicker** 1. Small knife. 2. Razor blade with one side heavily taped (used as a weapon).

**nigger fronts** Quintessence of black stylishness in dress.

**nigger's bankroll** See *California bankroll*.

**Nip** 1. Japanese person. 2. Any person perceived to be Japanese.

**no-account** 1. Shiftless. 2. Mean. 3. Manipulative.

**no-brand cigarette, no name brand** Marijuana cigarette.

**nod out** See *flake* (*out*).

**non** See *cripple*.

**not ready for people** See *act funny*.

**number, a** Marijuana cigarette.

**number one** n. First-degree murder.

**number-one** adj. 1. Best. 2. Closest.

**octaroon** Offspring of a white and a *quadroon*.

**off brand** n. 1. Strange or different-acting person. 2. Unknown person.

**off-brand** adj. 1. Weird, strange. 2. Inferior (in quality). 3. Different.

**off-brand cigarette** Marijuana cigarette.

**off (one)** 1. See *blaze on* (*one*). 2. Kill.

**off-the-wall** 1. Irrelevant. 2. Nonsensical. 3. Inappropriate. 4. Childish.

**oil** Liquor, wine.

**old lady** Designation for a male's lover, mate, girlfriend.

**old man** Designation for a female's lover, mate, boyfriend.

**on a tight leash** 1. Deeply infatuated or in love. 2. Addicted to, obsessed with.

**on flake** 1. Unconscious. 2. Asleep (drug-related).

**on (one's) job/j.o.b.** 1. In control. 2. Successful.

**on the rag** Menstruating.

**on the _____ side** Elaboration or explanation of something ("He got busted on the hombug side," for doing nothing).

**oreo** Black person who emulates white values, attitudes, and behaviors (black on the outside white on the inside, like the cookie).

**ossified** Excessively *high*.

**out of it** Excessively *high*.

**p.t.a.** 1. Abbreviation for "pussy, titties, and armpits." 2. Any bad-smelling female.

**pack peanut butter** Engage in anal intercourse.

**paddy, paddywood** White person.

**Panama red** Type of marijuana said to grow in and around Panama.

**pancake** Drop the body of a car—first the back end, then the front end, then a reversal of the process.

**panther piss** 1. Bootleg liquor. 2. Home-brewed liquor. 3. Cheap liquor.

**papers** 1. Cigarette rolling papers. 2. Marriage certificate.

**partner** 1. Good friend. 2. Street companion. 3. Acquaintance (takes it meaning and force from context).

**pattin' leather** Ironic response to a query; reference to being out of work.

**pay no mind** Ignore.

**pay dues** 1. Suffer. 2. Go through hard times.

**peck, pecker, peckerwood** White person (derogatory).

**penocha** Vagina.

**pep-em-up(s)** Amphetamine.

**pepper-kissing** Negative intensifier—"no good."

**pet up (one)** 1. Comfort. 2. Fondle. 3. Coddle (usually refers to a child).

**Peter Jay** Police.

**piece** 1. Gun. 2. Any weapon.

**pieces** Clothes.

**pig** 1. Police. 2. Any white person. 3. Obese female.

**pig brother** Black who betrays or informs the police about other blacks (highly derogatory).

**pig heaven** Police station.

**pig-mouth, pigger** Extremely obese female.

**pile** Engage in sexual intercourse.

**pimp** n. 1. Male who makes his money from prostitution. 2. Any male who lives off a female (used in both positive and negative senses). 3. Male who can control and manipulate females for his own needs. 4. Pejorative to identify one who is a phony at whatever he does.

**pimp** v. 1. Live off the money earned by prostitutes. 2. Procure clients for a prostitute. 3. Live off a female. 4. Show off what one has or what one is.

**pimp** adj. 1. Stylish. 2. Expensive.

**pimp dust** Cocaine.

**pimp fronts** Styles of clothing associated with the pimp.

**pimp post, pimp rest** Car console or armrest between the driver and the passenger.

**pimp ride** Expensive car.

**pimp shades/tints** Sunglasses associated with the pimp.

**pimp stride** Style of walking associated with the pimp in which the walker bobs up and down and side to side.

**pin (one)** See *dig on (one)*, **4-5**.

**pinch** Quantity of marijuana equivalent to one or two cigarettes.

**pink(s), pink boy** White male.

**pink, pink lady** Darvon (propoxyphene), supposed narcotic.

**pipe** Penis.

**play chicken**   Intrude on another's sexual overtures.

**play brother/cousin/mother/sister**   Designation for friends who are like real relatives.

**play, the**   1. See *action, the.* 2. Plan of action.

**play the dozens**   See *dozens.*

**play the fool**   See *act funny.*

**play the Tom**   Act like a *Tom.*

**player**   1. Equivalent to *pimp.* 2. One who successfully manipulates or charms others for financial, social, and psychological gain. 3. Male who has a number of relationships with females going at the same time.

**pluck**   n. 1. Wine. 2. Attractive female.

**pluck**   v. Engage in sexual intercourse.

**plucked**   Sexually well-satisfied.

**plumber**   Male who frequently engages in sexual intercourse.

**point**   Hypodermic syringe.

**poke**   Engage in sexual intercourse.

**pole**   Penis.

**pole hole**   Vagina.

**poontang**   Vagina.

**pootbutt**   See *lame* (with emphasis on one who is immature or young in age).

**pop a roll**   Ingest three to five pills.

**popcorn pimp**   1. Small-time pimp. 2. Would-be pimp. 3. Phony or fraud. 4. Small-time hustler.

**pops**   Father.

**Porsche**   Reference to a female's body type—small, round, compact.

**preg**   Abbreviation for pregnant.

**prescription red(s)**   See *apple,* **1-2.**

**prescriptions**   Any commercially compounded barbiturate, amphetamine, tranquilizer, etc.

**pressed**   Well-dressed.

**process**   Straightened hair-do.

**psychedelic to the bone**   1. Extremely *high.* 2. Very colorful.

**pull**   See *catch.*

**pull a quick park**   Execute a fast pick-up of a male or female.

**pull (one's) coat**   See *break it down.*

**pull to a set**   Attend a party or other social event.

**pump**   Gun.

**punk**   n. 1. Male homosexual. 2. Pejorative to identify anyone who is disliked by or different from the speaker.

**punk**   v. Engage in anal intercourse.

**puppy, a**   1. Small bottle of wine. 2. Love-sick male. 3. Devoted lover. 4. Sexually inexperienced or young male. 5. Small penis.

**pussy**   1. Vagina. 2. Attractive female.

**pussy hole**   Vagina.

**pussy-whipped**   Subject to a female's control and manipulation.

**pussycat**   Vagina.

**put it in the wind**   Leave.

**put her on the block/corner**   Have a female working for a male as his prostitute.

**put (one's) stuff down**   See *base*.

**put (something) down**   1. Give up something. 2. Let something go.

**Put that shit down!**   "Stop acting that way!"

**put the freeze on**   Discontinue.

**puta**   Prostitute.


**quadroon**   Child of a mulatto and white.

**quarter bag**   Twenty-five dollar plastic bag's worth of marijuana.

**queen**   Male's favorite female companion, lover, girlfriend.

**quiet village**   Reference to the black community in Venice, California.


**rabbit**   White person.

**rack, a**   1. Unit of measurement for pills or capsules (usually three to five in number). 2. Month's supply of birth control pills.

**rado**   Abbreviation for Cadillac El Dorado.

**rag**   Sanitary napkin.

**ragged down heavy**   Especially well-dressed.

**raggedy**   1. Out-of-control. 2. Unkempt. 3. Unattractive. 4. Out-of-date.

**raggedy Ann**   See *bat*.

**rags**   Clothes.

**railroad whiskey**   1. Wine. 2. Any of several cheap wines, such as Santa Fe (hence railroad whiskey).

**rainbow**   See *christmas tree*.

**rack, rack pick**   See *fork*.

**rank (one)**   See *base*.

**rank (one's) action/game/play/style**   See *cock block*.

**rap**   n. 1. Talk. 2. Art of good conversation.

**rap**   v. Make conversation (word takes its meaning from the context in which it is used).

**raspy, rasty**   1. Unattractive. 2. Unkempt.

**ready**   1. Prepared (for life). 2. Knowledgeable. 3. Open to what's happening. 4. Well-dressed.

**real woman**   Heterosexual woman.

**red(s), red devil(s)**   See *apple*, 1-2.

**red Mary**   Menses.

**red dog/knight is on the white horse**   Reference to a female who is having her menstrual period.

**red neck**   White person (derogatory).

**reefer**   Marijuana cigarette.

**rescue station**   Liquor store.

**ricer**   Asian person.

**ride**   Car.

**ride (one) down to the ground**   See *holler*.

**ride punk/pussy/the bitch's seat**   Sit between two other males in a car (derogatory reference to the seat in the car designated as the female's).

**ride the rag, ride the white horse**  Menstruate.

**riff**  Familiar or habitual words.

**righteous**  1. Genuine. 2. Outstanding (often-used general intensifier).

**righteously**  1. Very. 2. Most (often-used general intensifier).

**rip off/on**  1. Physically assault. 2. Beat severely. 3. Steal, rob. 4. Engage in sexual intercourse. 5. Rape. 6. Take advantage of.

**ripped**  Excessively *high*.

**Riv, Rivie**  Abbreviaton for Buick Riviera.

**Rivie hog**  See *Riv*.

**roach**  Butt end of a marijuana cigarette.

**rock out**  See *flake (out)*.

**rod**  Penis.

**rogue**  See *cock hound*.

**roll, a**  See *rack*.

**roll**  Roll a marijuana cigarette.

**roller(s)**  Detective.

**rookie**  See *pootbutt*.

**rooster**  See *alligator*, n.

**rootiepoot**  See *pootbutt*.

**roscoe**  Gun.

**round ball**  Basketball.

**round head**  See *blunt*, **1-2**.

**rowdy**  See *bad-ass nigger*, **1-3**.

**rugy**  1. Unattractive. 2. Unkempt. 3. Ill-tempered.

**ruint**  1. Excessively *high*. 2. Ugly.

**rumble**  Fight.

**rumpkin, rumpskin**  See *pootbutt*.

**run**  Associate with.

**run a double train**  See *make a sandwich*.

**run a game (on)**  1. Trick. 2. Manipulate the behavior and feelings of another. 3. Confuse or mislead. 4. Outdo.

**run down some lines**  1. Engage in conversation. 2. Talk smoothly and seductively to a member of the opposite sex with the intention of *getting over*.

**run (it) down**  See *break it down*.

**run off of (something)**  1. Get one's energy from. 2. Sustain oneself through. 3. Maintain one's *high* through.

**run the streets**  Frequent places other than home, church, school, and work.

**running partner**  Person one frequently or regularly associates with.

**rush, a**  First experience of a drug; the initial physiological and psychological reaction.

**Ruth Buzzy**  1. Female whose appearance never changes no matter what she does or what she wears. 2. Plain-looking female.

**sack, a**  See *cripple*.

**sack mouth**  1. One who talks too much. 2. A gossip.

**salt and pepper**  1. Police. 2. Police squad car.

**Sambo**  Obsequious black person (derogatory).

**Sam and Dave**  Police.

**Santa Claus**  See *caution sign.*

**Santa Fe tokay all the way!**  Ironic reference to Santa Fe wine, a cheap brand.

**sassy**  1. Spirited. 2. Independent. 3. Back-talking.

**Satin**  Abbreviation for Italian Swiss Colony Silver Satin, a cheap wine.

**scarf/scoff**  Eat.

**scab**  See *bear.*

**scat**  Vagina.

**scene**  Circumstance or event.

**scene on (one)**  See *front off.*

**scene, the**  1. The place or locale where the most important or interesting events of the day or moment are occurring. 2. Any situation or event where things are happening.

**schoolbook chump**  1. See *pootbutt.* 2. Studious person.

**schoolboy scotch**  Wine.

**school (one)**  See *break it down.*

**scope (on one)**  See *dig on (one),* 4-5.

**scrape**  Drop the body of a car to the ground so that the body scrapes the ground, causing sparks to fly.

**scream, scream on, scream cold on**  See *holler.*

**scream (down) some heavy lines**  1. Impress or outdo with conversation. 2. Engage in extremely forceful and lively talk.

**scurvy**  1. Ugly. 2. Bad. 3. Unkempt.

**seditty**  See *hincty.*

**sell a woof/wolf ticket**  1. Boast. 2. Bluff. 3. Talk nonsense. 4. Lie.

**send on a hombug (humbug)/merry-go-round/trip**  Send someone on a wild goose chase.

**set**  1. The group that includes close friends. 2. Clique. 3. Party, social event.

**set mouth**  See *bad mouth* (also used as a verb).

**set on (one's) ass**  Be excessively *high.*

**sets, roll/run/throw sets on**  Hit with a series of quick double-fisted blows.

**shake-em-up**  White port and lemon juice.

**sham on (one)**  1. Deceive. 2. Outwit.

**shank**  Knife.

**sharks**  Sharkskin suit.

**sharp as a mosquiter's peter**  Exceptionally well-dressed.

**Sherlock Holmes**  Police.

**shine on**  1. Ignore. 2. Avoid.

**shit**  1. Heroin. 2. Marijuana. 3. Idle or thoughtless talk. 4. Nonsense. 5. What one has, how one talks and acts, how one lives. 6. General word used as a suffix for a variety of expletives—jackshit, bullshit, horseshit, etc. (one of the most ubiquitous words in the vocabulary, "No shit, this word means everything!"); used for verbal emphasis.

**shit, my**  My gun.

**shoot**  Tell.

**shoot the code**  Explain the penal code.

**shoot (a) blank(s), shoot (a) dud(s)**  1. Engage in ineffectual or nonsensical conversation. 2. Receive negative or no response to one's talk.

**shoot a brick**   Make a bad shot in basketball.

**shoot a good shot**   Make an effective response to a joke, put-down, etc.

**shoot jokes (on one)**   See *cap,* **2-3.**

**shoot on (one)**   See *cap,* **2-3.** 2. Talk seductively and persuasively to a member of the opposite sex.

**shoot (one) to**   Send someone to.

**shoot (one's) best mack**   1. Talk as seductively and persuasively as possible to a member of the opposite sex. 2. Talk as effectively as one can.

**shoot the dozens**   See *dozens.*

**short, shot**   Car.

**short**   Limited.

**short dog**   Small bottle of cheap wine.

**short nail**   See *B.B. head.*

**show (one's) color**   See *act funny.*

**sides**   Records.

**signify**   1. See *sell a woof ticket.* 2. Goad.

**silk and satin**   1. Any combination of amphetamines and barbiturates. 2. Attractive female.

**silks**   Silk clothes.

**sip at the fuzzy cup**   Engage in cunnilingus.

**sissy**   Male homosexual.

**sister**   Designation for a black female (suggests identification among blacks).

**sit on a beast**   Drive/ride in a car whose front end is *lifted.*

**sit on a dago**   Drive/ride in a car whose front end is *lowered.*

**sit on her stuff**   Engage in prostitution.

**sixteen-year-old after-shave lotion**   Wine.

**skag**   1. Heroin. 2. See *bat.*

**skank, skunk**   1. Bad-smelling female. 2. See *bat.*

**skin the cat**   Engage in sexual intercourse.

**skoofer, skoofus, skroofus**   Marijuana cigarette.

**slack**   1. Opportunity. 2. Consideration.

**slant(s), slant eye(s)**   Asian person.

**slap (palms)**   See *give me five.*

**slap (one's) shit away**   Interfere with one's action (especially in sports).

**slaughter house**   See *killing floor.*

**Slauson swoop**   Serpentine pattern of driving where one drives quickly over a dip in the street.

**slicer**   Knife.

**slick, slicker, slickster**   1. One who deceives or confounds. 2. One who outwits. 3. One who takes advantage (also a verb).

**slick**   1. Deceptive. 2. Manipulative.

**slick-em-plenty**   See *fast-talking Charlie.*

**slide by/over**   1. Drop by. 2. Pass by.

**sling shot**   1. Cadillac El Dorado. 2. Sanitary napkin.

**slit**   Vagina.

**slit(s)**   Asian person.

**slow-em-up(s)**   See *down, downer.*

**smack**   Heroin.

**smart mouth**   See *bad mouth* (also a verb).

**smash**   Wine.

**smoke**   Marijuana.

**smoke (out)**   1. Impress. 2. Outdo.

**smoke stack, smokey the fire bear**   See *black ball*.

**smoked**   Reference to tinted car windows.

**snag**   Engage in sexual intercourse.

**snipe (on)**   Talk badly about another.

**snipe (one)**   Kill.

**snort**   Ingest powdered drugs into the nose.

**snow**   Cocaine.

**snuff**   Kill.

**solids**   Reference to a solid-color paint job on a car.

**sophisticated lady**   Cocaine.

**sorry**   See *cripple*.

**soul**   Quintessence of blackness—in behavior, heart, spirit, life.

**soul brother**   Designation for a black male acknowledging black identity.

**soul food**   A variety of foods associated with a black style of cooking, as well as historical circumstance and necessity.

**soul music**   Music identified with black life in the United States.

**soul shake**   See *give me five*.

**soul sister**   Female counterpart of *soul brother*.

**soul suit**   Suit (or any costume) the wearer believes to look *"soulful."*

**sounds**   1. Records. 2. Music.

**spade**   Black person.

**speck**   Black person.

**speed**   n. See *bean*, **2.**

**speed**   v. Experience the effects of a stimulant.

**spike**   Hypodermic syringe.

**split**   Leave.

**spook**   Black person.

**spoon**   Unit of measure for powdered or crystalline drugs (c. one tablespoon).

**square, square brain**   See *lame*.

**square to the wood**   Extremely inexperienced or immature.

**squeeze**   1. Close friend. 2. Favorite male or female lover or companion.

**stallion**   1. Attractive female. 2. Sexually lusty female.

**stank**   Vagina.

**stanky**   Smelly.

**star**   1. Male's favorite woman. 2. Especially attractive female.

**stash**   n. Personal cache of drugs or marijuana.

**stash**   v. Hide, put away.

**stay down low**   1. Remain inconspicious. 2. Assume mainstream appearances.

**stay on (one's) case**   Steadily disparage or harass.

**stencil**   Long, thin marijuana cigarette.

**step**   1. Engage in prostitution. 2. Move quickly.

**step fast** 1. Move quickly. 2. Do those things one must do in order to succeed in life. 3. Depart abruptly.

**step out on the green** Challenge to a fight.

**stepper** Prostitute.

**stick** 1. Marijuana cigarette. 2. Penis. 3. Preference, specialty, particular skill or talent. 4. Hard tackle (as in football).

**stingy brim** 1. Narrow-brimmed hat. 2. Pork-pie hat.

**stink finger** Manual stimulation of a female's sex organs.

**stink pot** Vagina.

**stogie** Very large marijuana cigarette.

**stomp (on)** 1. See *holler*. 2. Physically assault. 3. Severely beat.

**stone** One of the most popular superlatives; a positive intensifier of whatever it modifies.

**stood** Leaned on.

**straight** 1. Mainstream. 2. Conventional. 3. Credible.

**streets, the** 1. Any place other than home, church, school, or work that one frequents. 2. The source of practical experience and knowledge necessary for survival.

**stride** Perform with great skill.

**string bean** Skinny penis.

**stroke** Engage in sexual intercourse.

**strong mind** 1. Resistant to the manipulation of others. 2. Psychologically strong personality.

**strung out behind/over** See *on a tight leash*.

**stud** 1. See *cock hound*. 2. Virile male.

**stuff** n. 1. Heroin. 2. Attractive female. 3. General reference to a wide variety of actions, interests, possessions, information, etc., that relate to one's life (see *shit*).

**stuff** v. Dunk a basketball by getting above the rim as one jumps in the air to make the shot.

**stum/stom; stumble bumble; stumbler** See *down*, *downer*.

**stum** Get *high*.

**style** See *front off*.

**styles** Clothes.

**sucker** See *fish*, **2-3.**

**sucker weed** Inferior or bogus marijuana.

**sugar** 1. Term of endearment used by both males and females. 2. One's lover, mate, etc. 3. Attractive male.

**sugar daddy** 1. Male lover. 2. Attractive male. 3. Term of endearment. 4. Male who provides for a female.

**sugar weed** 1. See *sucker weed*. 2. Sweet-smelling or sweet-tasting marijuana.

**suited down** Well-dressed.

**swag** Liquor.

**sweet, a** Male homosexual.

**sweet daddy, sweet poppa, sweet sugar** 1. Male lover. 2. Attractive male. 3. Term of endearment.

**sweet potato pie**   1. Attractive male or female. 2. Male or female genitalia.
**sweet-talk**   See *mack on (one).*
**swift**   1. Quick-witted. 2. Alert.
**swine eater**   1. Police. 2. White person.
**swing daddy**   1. Attractive male. 2. Well-dressed male. 3. Male lover.
**swish**   Male homosexual.
**swoop**   1. Come upon abruptly, as the police do when making an arrest. 2. Execute a fast pick-up of a female or male.

**T.J.**   Abbreviation for Tijuana, Mexico.
**THC**   Reference to tetrahydrocannabinol, active chemical substance in marijuana which can be synthetically produced in either powder or pill form.
**TLC**   Abbreviation for "tender loving care."
**tabbed**   Well-dressed.
**tackhead, tackyhead**   See *B.B. head.*
**taco, taco bender**   See *bato.*
**tail**   1. Vagina. 2. Attractive female.
**take care of business**   1. Accomplish something with efficiency, style, and skill. 2. Show off with flair. 3. Attend to life affairs, pursuits, involvements, etc.
**take on some backs**   Engage in anal intercourse.
**take (one) to the bridge/hoop**   Drive to make a basket.
**talk (one's) business**   1. Talk with intelligence, force, and knowledge. 2. Talk seductively to a member of the opposite sex.
**talk (one's) talk and walk (one's) walk**   Reference to doing whatever is natural and comfortable.
**talk out of the side of (one's) neck; talk (that) shit/stuff/trash**   1. Talk nonsense. 2. Talk too much. 3. Boast. 4. Engage in idle chatter. 5. Lie.
**tea**   Marijuana.
**tear up**   1. Engage in some activity with relish. 2. Have a particularly good time.
**teenybopper**   See *bebopper.*
**ten-cent bag**   Ten-dollar plastic bag's worth of marijuana.
**terrible**   See *bad.*
**thing, one's/the**   1. Penis. 2. Life style, interest, way of thinking or acting.
**thousand eyes**   1. Florsheim-style male shoe with a number of perforations in the toe area. 2. Wing-tip shoe.
**threads**   Clothes.
**three balls**   See *fast-talking Charlie.*
**three-bullet Joey, three eyes**   Police (especially in squad cars).
**throw**   Engage in sexual intercourse.
**throw a buttonhole on (one)**   Engage in anal intercourse.
**Throw me out with . . .**   "Let me have . . ."
**thug**   1. Troublemaker. 2. Fighter.
**thump**   Fight.
**thunder chicken**   See *bat.*

**tight** n. See *ace*, n. **1.**

**tight** adj. 1. Well-dressed. 2. Good. 3. Best. 4. Close. 5. Under the influence of.

**tight, tight eye(s)** Asian person.

**tighten up (one's) game** 1. Assert control over one's life; get organized.

**tints** 1. Lightly tinted eye glasses. 2. Sunglasses. 3. Smoked car windows.

**tip** See *creep*, **1-3.**

**to the bone** Entirely.

**toast** Epiclike vernacular poem.

**toasted** Excessively *high*.

**together** 1. In control. 2. Fine. 3. Aware. 4. Knowledgeable.

**toke** Marijuana cigarette.

**Tom** Black person who has sold out to whites in any number of ways.

**tom** Act like a *Tom*.

**Tom-a-Lee** See *Tom* (sarcastic link to General Robert E. Lee).

**tom cat** See *alligator*, n.

**tom out** Inform the police about the actions of another black.

**Tom slick** 1. Police informer. 2. One who betrays other blacks.

**toothpick** 1. Skinny marijuana cigarette. 2. Pocket knife.

**tostada, tostado** See *bato*.

**tough** See *bad*.

**train, pull/run a** Participate in serial sexual intercourse with one female.

**tramp** 1. Promiscuous female. 2. See *bat*.

**trashy-looking** 1. Unkempt. 2. Dirty. 3. Unattractive.

**trick** See *fish*, **2-3.**

**trick bag** Strange or weird position, routine, pursuit, or action.

**trim** Female genitalia.

**trip** n. Unusual, exciting, enlightening, or amusing experience.

**trip** v. Leave.

**trip off of** Amuse, inform, or otherwise occupy oneself by observing people and things in one's environment.

**trip out** 1. Have a good time. 2. Experience unusual or exciting experiences. 3. Get *high*.

**trip out (one)** See *blow* (*one's*) *mind*, **1-2.**

**trout** 1. Female. 2. Vagina.

**tube, tubesteak** Penis.

**tuck 'n buck** Style of car upholstery (diamond pattern).

**tuck 'n roll** Style of car upholstery (tufted pattern).

**tuna, tuna fish** 1. Female. 2. Vagina.

**turf** 1. Neighborhood. 2. Place or locale one regularly frequents. 3. Gang's particular territory.

**turkey on a string, a** 1. One who is deeply infatuated or in love. 2. One who is obsessed with another.

**turn on** Get *high*.

**turn out** 1. Become a prostitute. 2. Make the streets one's primary environment. 3. Become street-wise.

**turn (one) out** 1. Introduce one to his/her first sexual experience. 2. Introduce to any important first experience. 3. Introduce a female to prostitution. 4. Introduce to unconventional sex.

**turn (something) out**    Permanently break up something—a party or other social function—usually through belligerent behavior.

**turn the set/the shit out**    Break up a party or other social function.

**turnip greens**    Marijuana.

**tuskee**    Very large marijuana cigarette.

**twin knit**    Abbreviation for twin knit shirt.

**twisted**    Excessively *high*.

**uncle nab(s)**    Police.

**Uncle Tom**    See *Tom*.

**uncut**    Undiluted (as in drugs or marijuana).

**understanding, an**    1. Close relationship. 2. Love relationship.

**union wage**    Police.

**up, upper**    1. Any amphetamine. 2. Any pill or capsule that produces a stimulated state.

**uppity**    See *hincty*.

**upside**    1. Alongside. 2. Up against.

**uptight**    1. Disturbed. 2. Anxious. 3. Fine. 4. Under control. 5. Intimate. 6. Satisfied.

**use**    Use drugs or marijuana.

**user**    One who habitually takes drugs, especially addictive drugs.

**vamp (one)**    Come upon one quickly, usually in an aggressive manner.

**varmint**    1. Rowdy youngster. 2. Troublemaker. 3. Fighter. 4. Young smart-aleck.

**vine, the**    Wine.

**vines**    Clothes.

**vitamins**    See *candy*, **2**.

**WPLJ**    Abbreviation for white port and lemon juice.

**wail**    See *blow fire*.

**wake-up**    See *bean*, **2**.

**wall-to-wall niggers**    Crowded social function where blacks are gathered together.

**'wana**    Marijuana.

**wanna be**    One who wants to be or pretends to be something he or she is not.

**washer-dryer**    Douche bag and towel.

**washing powder**    Douche solution or substance.

**waste**    Kill.

**wasted**    1. Excessively *high*. 2. Ugly.

**Watts rat patrol**    Local street police.

**wear the ring**    See *on a tight leash*.

**weak mind**    1. Susceptible to the manipulation of others. 2. Psychologically unstable personality. 3. Immature or childish outlook.

**weed**    Marijuana.

**welfare mother**    Female who is tastelessly or poorly dressed.

**wetback**    See *bato*.

**wethead**    See *pootbutt*.

**what's happening**  1. What it is important to know. 2. What it is important to do in order to succeed or survive. 3. What is in fashion. 4. What is appropriate to a situation (see *happenings*).

**wheel**  Drive a car.

**where (one) is coming from**  1. What one means. 2. What one needs or expects. 3. What interests one. 4. What one is like.

**whip(ped) cream**  Semen.

**whip shack**  See *killing floor.*

**whips, the**  1. White establishment. 2. Police.

**white eyes**  White person.

**white lightnin'**  See *panther piss.*

**white(s)**  See *bean*, **2.**

**whole wheat (bread)**  See *buckwheat.*

**whup**  1. Assault. 2. Hit or beat up. 3. Spank.

**whup-a-child**  Police.

**whup upside the head**  Hit in and about the face and head.

**whup the game**  1. Succeed in life. 2. Acquire status and power.

**wicked**  See *bad.*

**wired-up**  1. Energized or agitated because of stimulants. 2. *High* on any type of drug or marijuana.

**woof**  1. See *cap*. 2. Boast. 3. Bluff (see *dozens*).

**XKE**  Abbreviation for Jaguar XKE.

**yacoo**  1. Racist. 2. White person (extremely derogatory).

**yellow/yella**  See *casper.*

**yellow, yellow jack, yellow jacket**  Nembutal (pentobarbital sodium), barbiturate, white powder encased in a yellow capsule.

**young blood**  1. Young black person (especially a male). 2. Socially inexperienced person (age-related).

**young in (one's) head**  Childish.

**young lady**  Designation for a female somewhere under 35.

**young man**  Male counterpart of *young lady.*

**yum-yum(s)**  See *gumdrop.*

**Zig-Zags**  Brand name for cigarette rolling papers.

**zoom (one) out**  See *blow (one's) mind*, **1-2.**